# Get Started in Latin

Teach®
Yourself

# Get Started in Latin
G. D. A. Sharpley

For UK order enquiries: please contact Bookpoint Ltd,
130 Milton Park, Abingdon, Oxon OX14 4SB.
*Telephone:* +44 (0) 1235 827720. *Fax:* +44 (0) 1235 400454.
Lines are open 09.00–17.00, Monday to Saturday, with a 24-hour
message answering service. Details about our titles and how to order
are available at www.teachyourself.com

For USA order enquiries: please contact McGraw-Hill Customer
Services, PO Box 545, Blacklick, OH 43004-0545, USA.
*Telephone:* 1-800-722-4726. *Fax:* 1-614-755-5645.

For Canada order enquiries: please contact McGraw-Hill Ryerson Ltd,
300 Water St, Whitby, Ontario L1N 9B6, Canada.
*Telephone:* 905 430 5000. *Fax:* 905 430 5020.

Long renowned as the authoritative source for self-guided learning –
with more than 50 million copies sold worldwide – the *Teach Yourself*
series includes over 500 titles in the fields of languages, crafts, hobbies,
business, computing and education.

British Library Cataloguing in Publication Data: a catalogue record
for this title is available from the British Library.

Library of Congress Catalog Card Number: on file.

First published in UK 1997 as Teach Yourself Beginner's Latin by
Hodder Education, part of Hachette UK, 338 Euston Road, London
NW1 3BH.

First published in US 1997 by The McGraw-Hill Companies, Inc.

This edition published 2010.

Previously published as Teach Yourself Beginner's Latin

The *Teach Yourself* name is a registered trade mark of
Hodder Headline.

Typeset by MPS Limited, A Macmillan Company.

Printed in Great Britain for Hodder Education, an Hachette UK
Company, 338 Euston Road, London NW1 3BH.

The publisher has used its best endeavours to ensure that the URLs
for external websites referred to in this book are correct and active
at the time of going to press. However, the publisher and the author
have no responsibility for the websites and can make no guarantee
that a site will remain live or that the content will remain relevant,
decent or appropriate.

Hachette UK's policy is to use papers that are natural, renewable
and recyclable products and made from wood grown in sustainable
forests. The logging and manufacturing processes are expected to
conform to the environmental regulations of the country of origin.

Impression number       10 9 8 7 6 5 4
Year                     2014 2013 2012

# Contents

Meet the author      **vii**
Only got a minute?      **viii**
Only got ten minutes?      **x**
Introduction      **xv**

1   **In silva** In the wood      **1**
    • Subjects and objects • The cases: nominative,
    accusative and ablative • **est** and **sunt**
     *The classics*

2   **Umbrae in silva** Shadows in the wood      **12**
    • Singular and plural forms
     *A question of rhetoric*

3   **Mulus gemit** The mule groans      **21**
    • Masculine, feminine and neuter nouns • Prepositions
     *Speaking as the Romans did …*

4   **Figura feminae** The figure of a woman      **36**
    • Genitive case • Questions
     *'Anyone' for a cancan?*

5   **Egbertae filia** Egberta's daughter      **48**
    • Declensions: nominative and genitive • Vocative case
    • Adjectives
     *Reformation and renaissance – Life after death*

6   **In amphitheatro saevitia** Cruelty in the amphitheatre      **61**
    • More adjectives • **potest, vult, debet** • Infinitives • Dative case
     *Latin wanted – dead or alive?*

**Revision i (Units 1–6)**      **74**

7   **Puer cum diabolo ambulat** The boy walks with the devil      **78**
    • Third declension nouns
     *Di immortales*

8   **Nos fortunatos!** How lucky we are!      **91**
    • Verbs: first and second conjugations: present and future
     *Brotherly love*

9   **Quis in silva ululat?** Who is howling in the wood?      **105**
    • Third declension adjectives • Gerundives
     *Speculator amicae*

**10 Lacrimae in monasterio** *Tears in the monastery* **117**
- Third, fourth and mixed conjugations: present and future
- How to recognize a conjugation • **esse, posse, velle** • Numbers
  *Miserabile corpus*

**11 Libera nos a malo** *Deliver us from evil* **130**
- Imperfect tense • Adjectives: **-ens** • Present participles
- Adjectives as nouns
  *Yaysoos in chaylo*

**12 In manus tuas commendo spiritum meum** *Into your hands I commend my spirit* **143**
- Perfect tense • Personal pronouns • my, your, our
  *The murder in a cathedral*

**Revision ii (Units 7–12)** **156**

**13 Paulus sub aqua** *Paulus under water* **159**
- Past participles • **eo, ire**
  *A winter's night*

**14 Venatrix in silva** *A huntress in the wood* **175**
- Fourth and fifth declensions • Pluperfect tense • Compound verbs
  *A hunting moral*

**15 Audire est intellegere** *To hear is to understand* **188**
- **Ille, hic, is, ipse, se** • Passive forms
  *All's fair in philosophy, love and war*

**16 Quis in monasterio conspirat?** *Who is plotting in the monastery?* **201**
- Subjunctive • Imperative • **ut** and **ne** • **cum**
  *Friends, Romans ... and family*

**17 Peior quam diabolus** *Worse than the devil* **217**
- More passive forms • Deponent verbs • Comparative and superlative of adjectives
  *The consolation of philosophy*

**18 Versus Catulli combusti sunt!** *The verses of Catullus have been incinerated!* **230**
- 'If' clauses • Direct and reported speech
  *Love in the rain*

*Tables* **240**
*Key to the exercises* **257**
*Latin–English vocabulary* **282**
*English–Latin vocabulary* **295**
*Index of grammar support* **300**

# Meet the author

A classicist by training, George taught Latin at the University of
Bristol for over twenty years and to adults on extra-mural courses.
He is a director of the language-training organization, Lingua
(UK), where he is responsible for the development of learning
materials in several modern languages as well as Latin: in text,
eLearning and film formats. He is a keen student of the poet Virgil
among other Latin writers, and as a result of making Latin films
and other recordings (www.lingua.co.uk/latin) has immersed
himself in practical questions of Latin pronunciation. He is married
with three daughters and lives in Gloucestershire, England.

He writes ... 'Apart from its usefulness in reading historical
documents, the value of Latin will not easily squeeze into a brief
soundbite. You'll find plenty of people like me who will tell
you about its moral importance or personal relevance – even if
sometimes we seem only to underline its lifelessness. I see Latin
as an object of curiosity, a treasure, a source of enrichment, an
unravelling of the mystery of the past. Your study is a journey of
discovery into this slowly disappearing space. Make the most of it!'

# *Only got a minute?*

Latin was spoken in and around Rome as early as the sixth century BC. The language spread with the expansion of Rome's power first into Italy and then around the Mediterranean and into Europe. When the empire eventually broke up, the spoken language (Vulgar Latin) fragmented into the emerging Romance languages of Italian, French, Spanish and Portuguese.

Classical Latin was a literary language: the work of authors who lived within a few decades either side of the life of Christ. In the first century BC there was Cicero, whose skills as a public speaker were highly regarded by politicians like Caesar and Pompey. Classical Latin – and Cicero in particular – became the model for subsequent writers of the language, ancient and medieval. Over a hundred years after Cicero, the historian Tacitus wrote Latin which was still broadly classical but penned in a sharper more elliptical style that suited his theme of moral collapse under the early Roman emperors.

Among the classical poets the best known is perhaps Virgil. His story of the founding of Rome by the Trojan fugitive Aeneas was recognized immediately as a masterpiece. Horace, a friend of Virgil, wrote his Odes, four books of lyric poetry touching on love, friendship and happiness: themes as old – and young – as time itself. The love elegies of Propertius and Tibullus echo the earlier poems of Catullus and foreshadow the work of Ovid, a poet much imitated by medieval writers.

Literary (as opposed to Vulgar) Latin kept its identity long after the fall of Rome, and survived in medieval Europe for roughly a thousand years as the language of politics, law, education, story-writing, history, poetry and religion.

# 10 Only got ten minutes?

People do not learn Latin for the usual reason they learn a language, i.e. to communicate with other people. That is because no one speaks it any more, apart from one or two groups of engagingly committed oddballs dotted around the world. No, the chances of your turning to a Latin phrase book to help you choose a nice piece of cheese are exceptionally slim.

The only Latin you are likely to find is a few fragments in law, in antiquarian writings, in medicine, in lists of flowers, on commemorative inscriptions, tattoos, or adding gravitas to headed notepaper. And *'gravitas'* itself, one of a handful of Latin words to make the jump into English in their original form.

Every few weeks there appears a headline that Latin is making a comeback, but each time in the present tense. Never 'has come back'. A Finnish radio station keeps us tickled with the world news in Latin. A Vatican priest runs conversational courses inventing quaint Latin names for the latest gadgets. But it's a bit like wiring up a dead body to move its arms. There's no getting away from it: Latin is seriously discontinued, as stiff as the stones it's inscribed on.

Causes of death are not shrouded in mystery. We go back to the earliest appearance of Latin and from the mist of prehistory looms this little city-state in southern central Italy, allegedly founded by Aeneas and built by Romulus and Remus, peopled by a stubborn farming community who fought off the bigger power to the north, the Etruscans. In time these Romans took over Etruscan lands plus a lot more besides elsewhere in Italy. Some Latin inscriptions survive from the halfway point in the millennium, but authored writing doesn't appear until the third century BC, when Greek books start to be read and copied in Latin. With the fall of Carthage, Rome becomes the most powerful state in the region. Spain, north Africa, Greece, Macedonia, the near east, Egypt, Gaul – all fall to this rising empire. Their taste for the Greek experience in all artistic and literary endeavour (speech-making, poetry, history) became insatiable, and by the first century BC Latin writers were beginning to perfect the art of blending Greek models with their own times. This was the classical period of Rome: Cicero and Caesar, Virgil and Horace, Catullus and Ovid; followed in the next century (first century AD) by Martial and Juvenal, Tacitus and Pliny.

These were the writers who themselves became models for imitation. To write Latin well was to hear your teacher say how like Caesar or Cicero your work was – much as the Romans had reproduced their Greek models. This rigid standard set a conservative and durable quality to literary Latin, which managed to survive the fragmentation of the Roman empire and the onset of divided medieval Europe as the one language common to all. The church was largely responsible for this. All people routinely heard or read Latin liturgy and other religious texts, while secular writings, including manuscripts of the classics, were read and housed in the monasteries. Latin was the primary language of education as more schools and universities came to be formed towards the end of the first millennium.

In the second millennium vernacular languages in Europe, already the principal vehicle of speech, grew stronger in competition with Latin as the medium for the written word. The vernacular languages gained further ground during the Reformation, for Latin was the language of the church in Rome. Politicians who wanted to shake off papal control supported Protestant efforts to translate religious texts into their own languages.

The Renaissance too, which happened more or less at the same time, further diminished Latin as a living language. This was an irony given the Renaissance was a rekindling of interest in all things classical. Scholars sought to improve the style of the Latin in use, demanding a closer observance of the ancient classical standards. Much of the Latin in use was too imperfect to survive.

So from the seventeenth century onwards, Latin's role grew ever narrower. It was still the language of the Catholic Church, and remained the universal language of academia for some time yet as scholars and scientists wrote papers in Latin so that different nationals might understand them; and it was a fruitful source for botanists to name their plants, for ornithologists, for medics, for motto writers. To get into a university or become a doctor or join the ranks of the learned in just about any discipline, Latin remained a **sine qua non** until well into the twentieth century. By then other disciplines were emerging, in both humanities and sciences, and classics teachers, who had never had to fight their corner, started to lose students to history, English, modern languages and other arts disciplines.

Latin has been a very fruitful provider of words to English. Relics like **'sine qua non'**, **'QED'** and **'status quo'** stand out. There are at least as many Latin words that have settled in English in their original form or very close to it whose origins are not as noticeable: *area, arena, computer, exit, extra, premium, recipe, squalor, video, virus.*

And far greater in number are English words created on the model of Latin ones, an influence that has had a negative impact on people's perception of the older language. One of the spurs of the Renaissance was the development of printing presses, which enabled Greek and Latin texts (and translations) to reach a far wider readership. The translators frequently settled for the original word where there was no English equivalent or if the existing English one was not sufficiently 'splendidious'. This practice of borrowing from Latin and Greek soon became an academic obsession, and in the sixteenth and seventeenth centuries hundreds of new English words were created on the model of Latin ones. Most remain in use today; a few were modified – 'splendid'. Some are showy, others more settled. Many have a string of long syllables and pepper the language of education, politics, professional conduct and formality in general: *collaborative, communicative, diversification, functionality.* Others are not as dull, like *loquacious, truculent, indefatigable*; and most of the shorter creations have settled well: *acute, agile, fatuous, insane, lenient, trite.*

By lending English the tools of snobbery and affectation, these scholars made Latin the language you borrow from to raise the tone, the quickest way to social polish ('fatigued', 'remiss', 'condolences'). The executive who speaks of his qualitative super-remuneration scheme is only talking about how much tip he is pocketing: it's the language of people who don't have much to say or who want to disguise the message. It is inevitable, if misleading, that some of this should rub off on our perception of Latin itself.

So much for the written language. We know a lot less about the Latin spoken in the ancient world. A little can be gleaned from plays and other writings which include dialogue in their narrative, and even less from letters, which while less formal than forensic speeches still retain a literary flavour. The majority of Romans will have spoken a less cluttered Latin than the lawyer or politician, with a looser structure, inflections slipping, and briefer sentences. Inscriptions back this up (**'Illa amo'** *I love her*, which on the page would be **'illam'**). Other languages are similar. When we write we stiffen and compose more carefully what we say; when we speak, we just speak, less fussed by structure and syntax. One of the few case-inflections left in English has now all but disappeared from speech, but lingers on the page: the object 'whom'. Most of us now say 'Who did you see last night?' A few still prefer to read 'Whom did you see last night?'

Words cropped up in spoken Latin which appeared less in the written version: Latin students will know the Latin for '*horse*', **equus**, which has given English *equitation, equestrian, equerry*, etc. The word for horse in spoken Latin, perhaps reflecting a less fancy steed, was **caballus**. It is this word, not **equus**, which is the direct ancestor of the words for '*horse*' in all the different romance languages (French – *cheval*, Italian – *cavallo*, Spanish – *caballo*, Portuguese – *cavalo*). In English we can trace *cavalier, cavalry, chivalry* and even *cabbie* back to **caballus**. Derivatives from **equus** also exist in the Romance languages (French *equitation*) but these are late arrivals: the work of those scholars in the mid-second millennium.

The spoken language was the language of the wider public, of the crowd, called 'Vulgar Latin' (**vulgus** = *a crowd*; **vulgari** = *to put about, spread abroad*). St Jerome's fifth century Latin translation of the Bible is called the Vulgate because it became the standard (widely used) version – and it was written in a style accessible to all. It does not mean it used rude words or was touched by people with dirty hands.

A spoken language cannot be constrained in the same way as a literary language, except perhaps in the most conservative oral societies. Vulgar Latin made its way around the empire nestling with local influences and evolved into what we know as the Romance languages: French, Italian, Spanish and Portuguese. Romanian too is Latin-based. So too are languages and dialects such as Sardinian (Italy), Occitan (France), Catalan (Spain) and Romansh (Switzerland). All these are direct descendants of the spoken form of Latin.

The influence of Latin, in both its written and spoken forms, is immense. It remains the key to exploring many different corners of the ancient and medieval worlds, a timespan lasting well over a thousand years. As a dead language it still has great value; it is there for us to scrutinize on the cold slab, picking over the detail, analysing inflexions, shuffling words, exploring influence and heritage, reading historical texts. A rounded study of Latin will also pursue the living language, to recapture the moment, a language rising and falling, its songs and histories, the thoughts and feelings of a culture so like our own and yet so different. It will be a while before the present world language has a life as long and as fruitful.

# Introduction

### Flogging a dead course?

It may seem odd to find Latin alive and well at the beginning of the twenty-first century, and yet here it is, one of nature's survivors. And why? Because beyond this course there is a literature teeming with good things, with high life, with low life and, most of all, with life. All we have to do, of course, is read it ...

### Paulus and Lucia
The story is a foil for the grammar and exercises. It is set at a monastery in northern Europe around the ninth century AD. An English translation of the Latin story is available at the LATIN QVARTER (www.lingua.co.uk).

### Living Latin
Assembling all the information about words and endings is a necessary but sometimes slow process. This section offers the chance to hear some excerpts of authentic Latin. You do not have to study these in detail to make progress. They are included to give you an idea of what there is to enjoy once you have mastered the language.

### Recording
A recording of the story and 'Living Latin' sections of the book is available. This is not an essential aid to learning the language, but will enhance your enjoyment of the poetry, and give you an idea of what Latin sounded like.

## Pronunciation guide to Classical Latin

As in English (standard southern British), except:

| | |
|---|---|
| **a** | 'c<u>u</u>p' (short vowel) or 'f<u>a</u>ther' (long vowel) |
| **ae** | '<u>eye</u>' |
| **au** | 'h<u>ou</u>se' |
| **c** | 'c<u>a</u>t' (always hard; *never* as in '<u>ch</u>alice') |
| **ch** | 'k' with a sharper expulsion of breath (as in '<u>c</u>urses!') |
| **e** | 'p<u>e</u>t' (short vowel) or 'p<u>a</u>y' (long vowel) |
| **ei** | 'r<u>ei</u>gn' |
| **eu** | two sounds run together: 'e-oo' |
| **g** | '<u>g</u>ag' (almost always hard, not as in '<u>G</u>eorge') |
| **gn** | at the beginning of a word 'n', and in the middle of a word 'ngn' |
| **i** | 'l<u>i</u>p' (short vowel) or 'l<u>ea</u>p' (long vowel) |
| **i (j)** | consonant: as English 'y' |
| **ng** | as in 'a<u>ng</u>er' (not 'ha<u>ng</u>ar') |
| **o** | 'n<u>o</u>t' (short vowel) or (long vowel) 'n<u>o</u>te' (as the Scots would say it) |
| **oe** | '<u>oi</u>l' |
| **ph** | 'p' with a sharper expulsion of breath (as in '<u>p</u>easant!') |
| **qu** | 'kw', as in '<u>qu</u>ack' (as English 'qu', not French) |
| **r** | trilled with the tip of the tongue (again, think Scots...) |
| **s** | as in hi<u>ss</u> (not hi<u>s</u>) |
| **th** | as 't' with a sharper expulsion of breath |
| **u** | 'p<u>u</u>ll' (short vowel) or (long vowel) '<u>poo</u>l' (not with the 'y' sound in 'pew') |
| **v** | as English 'w' |
| **y** | French 't<u>u</u>' (short vowel), French 's<u>ur</u>' (long vowel) |

### *Yoolius Kysser, Joolius Seezer, Yoolius Chaser*

The story of Lucia and Paulus, though set in a later period, is narrated according to the guidelines above. The selections in 'Living Latin' are also read in the classical manner, except post-classical ones (marked \*). You will hear one or two different sounds in the post-classical sections, such as our own 'v' sound in the v; the erosion of **ae** to **e**; and the Church/Italian 'ch' sound in ci/ce (e.g. **caelum**: classical – **kylum**, ecclesiastical – **chaylum**).

These changes should be taken as characteristic only, and not as precise, scientific reconstructions according to date, region and speaker. It's hard enough reaching any certainty about Cicero's Latin, never mind the multitude of evolving and fragmenting forms which followed.

Verse-rhythms of later Latin changed too. The rhythms of classical poetry were founded on an interplay of natural stress and quantity (i.e. the metre), but later poets came to disregard metre and used stresses alone to maintain rhythm.

Our efforts of recreation are inevitably hit and miss, no doubt betraying more than a few signs of the present day. For a further discussion of pronunciation see 'Speaking as the Romans did' (Unit 2, About Latin), and those who wish to explore this topic in more detail should look at *Vox Latina* (W. Sidney Allen, CUP, 1965).

### Essential grammar

#### Nouns
A noun is a word like *mule*, *monk* or *wood*. Something you can see or at least feel. English nouns often have *the* or *a* in front of them. Latin has no equivalent words for *the* and *a* so when you translate a noun you must decide whether or not to add them. Names are also nouns, like *Paul*, *Rome*, etc., and so are abstract ideas like *peace*, *kindness*, *fear*, which are real enough but cannot be identified in the same way as concrete objects.

#### Verbs
A verb is a 'doing' or 'being' word; it describes the action, what happens or what is done, e.g.

*The mule <u>watches</u> the wood.*
*The monk is not <u>carrying</u> the bag.*
*Paul <u>is</u> a student.*

English verbs often comprise more than one word (e.g. *is carrying*). Most Latin verbs are expressed by one word only. A verb like **spectat** has three possible versions in English: watches, *is watching* or *does (not) watch*. As with 'the' and 'a' and nouns above, a judgement has to be made from the context, from what 'sounds right'.

Verbs are listed in columns of six 'persons' (*to be* appears in Unit 4 and others start in Unit 8). There are three persons in the singular and the same three persons in the plural:

*I ...*
*you (sing.) ...*
*she/he/it ...* *
*we ...*
*you (pl.) ...*
*they ...* *

*these pronouns are used where there is no subject (e.g. 'Paul ...', 'the Danes ...').

---

## Symbols and abbreviations

◀) This indicates material that has been recorded and is available on CD.

m. masculine; f. feminine; n. neuter; pl. plural; sing. singular; nom. nominative; voc. vocative; acc. accusative; gen. genitive; dat. dative; abl. ablative; *post-classical

---

## Acknowledgements

The publishers and author thank The Finnish Broadcasting Company, Finland, for permission to include an excerpt from

**Nuntii Latini** (Vol. 3); the Latin Qvarter (<u>www.lingua.co.uk</u>) for permission to adapt the story of Lucia and Paulus for the *Teach Yourself* series.

I am grateful to my students for their valuable feedback while the course was being developed; to Niall Rudd, P.O'R. Smiley and Amanda Lee for many helpful comments and corrections; and for their input to this second edition to Linda Knox of the University of Glasgow and to Helen Conrad-O'Briain of Trinity College Dublin. And thanks to Keely Mitchell for her excellent drawings; to my editors at Hodder; and for their humour and unqualified support to my wife, Sarah, and our three daughters, Rebecca, Meg and Flora.

**George Sharpley** *2009*

# Credits

**Front cover:** Hideki Yoshihara/AFLO Royalty Free/
Photolibrary.com

**Back cover and pack:** © Jakub Semeniuk/iStockphoto.com,
© Royalty-Free/Corbis, © agencyby/iStockphoto.com, © Andy
Cook/iStockphoto.com, © Christopher Ewing/iStockphoto.com,
© zebicho – Fotolia.com, © Geoffrey Holman/iStockphoto.com,
© Photodisc/Getty Images, © James C. Pruitt/iStockphoto.com,
© Mohamed Saber – Fotolia.com

**Pack:** © Stockbyte/Getty Images

# 1

# In silva
## In the wood

In this unit you will learn about
- **Subjects and objects**
- **The cases**
- **And find out more about Latin in 'The classics'**

### Subjects and objects

Latin is an inflected language. This means that the final syllable(s) of a word can vary according to the way the word is being used in the sentence:

**Mul<u>us</u> silv<u>am</u> spectat.**    *The mule is watching the wood.*

Here the mule is doing the watching, the wood is being watched. The mule is the *subject* of the sentence, the wood the *object*, the difference being that the subject is the 'doer', the object is on the receiving end and is 'done to'. Latin makes this clear by having different endings for subject and object.

**Mu<u>lum</u> silv<u>a</u> spectat.**          *The wood is watching the mule.*

Now **silva** no longer has a final 'm', and **mulus** has been changed to **mulum**. This makes **silva** the subject and **mulum** the object. English word order is more restricted because we recognize a subject by its position in a sentence, not by its ending. Latin's word order is more flexible: in general the subject appears before the object, with the verb at the end to complete a sentence or word-group, although variations, for a particular emphasis or rhythm, often occur. The verb's place at the end may seem strange at first, but you will get used to it. Reading is a process of anticipation and completion of meaning; in English this function is often performed by the object:

*Today the milkman delivered ...* (*bottles of milk* is the anticipated object; *the post* would come as a surprise, and *twins* even more so).

Latin has us predicting the action, not the object:

*Today the milkman ... two pints of milk ...* (*delivered* **is what we are expecting, ahead of** *stole* **or** *threw at the boy on the skateboard*).

**Insight**

A subject does it, an object is the thing done to:
'the mule (subject) watches the wood (object)'.

### *Paulus in silva* Paulus in the wood

◀) **CD1, TR 2**

Paulus in silva ambulat. Mulus cum Paulo ambulat. Mulus non
Paulum sed sarcinam portat. Fessus est Paulus et mulus est lentus.
Mulus silvam non amat. Mulus silvam spectat. Silva mulum
spectat. Mulus est territus.

| | |
|---|---|
| **amat** | *likes, loves* |
| **ambulat** | *walks, is walking* |
| **cum** | *with, in the company of* |
| **est** | *is* |
| **et** | *and* |
| **fessus** | *tired* |
| **in** | *in, on* |
| **lentus** | *slow* |
| **mulus, mulum, mulo** | *mule* |
| **non** | *not* |
| **Paulus, Paulum, Paulo** | *Paul* |
| **portat** | *carries, is carrying* |
| **sarcina, sarcinam** | *bag* |
| **sed** | *but* |
| **silva, silvam** | *wood* |
| **spectat** | *watches, is watching* |
| **territus** | *scared* |

QUICK VOCAB

## Insight
The final syllable of a Latin noun tells us if it is the subject or
object:
**mul<u>us</u>** (subject) **silv<u>am</u>** (object) **spectat** = *'the mule watches
the wood'*
**silv<u>a</u>** (subject) **mul<u>um</u>** (object) **spectat** = *'the wood watches
the mule'*.

### Practice (I)

**1** There are a few English words which change their form
according to whether they are subject or object. These are
pronouns, words we use in place of nouns. Complete the table
with the missing subject or object forms:

**(a)**

| Subject | Object |
|---------|--------|
| I | ......... |
| she | ......... |
| ......... | him |
| we | ......... |

**(b)**

| Subject | Object |
|---------|--------|
| silva | ......... |
| ......... | mulum |
| ......... | sarcinam |
| Paulus | ......... |

**2** Choose the correct word and translate:

**(a)** Mulus (sarcina/sarcinam) portat.
**(b)** Mulum (Paulus/Paulum) portat.

**3** Choose the correct verb and translate:
**(a)** Mulus silvam non (ambulat/amat).
**(b)** Paulus in silva (portat/ambulat).
**(c)** Mulus silvam (portat/spectat).
**(d)** Non Paulus sed mulus sarcinam (portat/ambulat).

### Insight
There are no equivalent words in Latin for English *'the'* and
*'a'*. Add them to your English version as you think fit.

## Cases

'Case' is the name given to the different kinds of word-ending:

| | | |
|---|---|---|
| Nominative case | Subject | **silva, mulus** |
| Accusative case | Object, or with prepositions (e.g. **ad**) | **silvam, mulum** |
| Ablative case | 'With', 'in' used (not always) with prepositions (e.g. **cum, in**) | **silva, mulo** |

Nouns like **mulus** (e.g. **Paulus**, etc.) all have the same case endings, and nouns like **silva** (**sarcina**, etc.) have their endings in common too.

---

## Insight

The subject is in the nominative case.
The object is in the accusative case.

---

### *Est* and *sunt*

**Est** *is* and **sunt** *are* do not take objects like other verbs do. The 'object' of the verb *to be* is not on the receiving end of anything particular, but merely describes the subject. So any 'object' or rather complement of the verb 'to be' will be in the nominative case:

**Paulus monachus est.**     *Paul is a monk.*

but

**Paulus monachum spectat.**     *Paul watches the monk.*

---

## Insight

**est** = '(he/she/it) is'.
**sunt** = '(they/there) are'.

---

***Mulus lente ambulat*** *The mule walks slowly*

🔊 **CD1, TR 2, 00:44**

Paulus est monachus. Benedictus etiam est monachus. Benedictus cibum desiderat. Paulus cibum emit et ad monasterium revenit. Nunc Paulus cum mulo in silva ambulat. Cibus est in sarcina. Mulus sarcinam portat. Mulus lente ambulat et silvam spectat.

**QUICK VOCAB**

| | |
|---|---|
| **ad** | *to, towards* |
| **cibum** (*acc. of* **cibus**) | *food* |
| **desiderat** | *longs for* |
| **emit** | *buys* |
| **etiam** | *also* |
| **lente** | *slowly* |
| **monachus** | *monk* |
| **monasterium** | *monastery* |
| **nunc** | *now* |
| **revenit** | *returns* |

### Practice (II)

**1** Fill the gaps:

| Subject<br>Nominative case | Object<br>Accusative case | 'In', 'with', 'on'<br>Ablative case |
|---|---|---|
| mulus | ......... | mulo |
| ......... | Paulum | ......... |
| ......... | sarcinam | ......... |
| silva | ......... | silva |

**2** Identify the cases of the underlined nouns, and translate:
  **(a)** <u>Benedictus</u> <u>cibum</u> desiderat.
  **(b)** Mulus <u>sarcinam</u> non amat.
  **(c)** Benedictus non in <u>silva</u> est.
  **(d)** Paulus est <u>monachus</u>.

**3** Complete the words which have missing endings, and translate:

**(a)** Paul___ cum mul___ in silv___ ambulat.

**(b)** In mul___ est sarcin___.

---

## About Latin

### *The Classics*

Latin was the language spoken in Rome and the surrounding region as early as the sixth century BC and possibly earlier. The number of Latin speakers grew with the expansion of Rome's empire around the Mediterranean, and the vocabulary swelled and forms modified under the influence of languages in the new subject territories (especially Greek).

The classical Latin authors lived within a few decades either side of the life of Christ. In the first century BC Cicero sought to protect the republican government from manipulation by would-be dictators.

A compelling public speaker, his skills brought him to the attention of politicians such as Caesar and Pompey, and he was courted by them as an owner of a newspaper or television station might be today. His writing was greatly admired, and the elegance and rhetorical flair of his prose became a model for later scholars and schoolchildren to imitate. He was followed by, amongst others, the historian Tacitus, whose pointed asides on the theme of moral and aristocratic degeneration enliven his account of Rome under the early emperors. Of the poets the best known is perhaps Virgil. His story of the founding of Rome by the Trojan fugitive Aeneas emerged within a few years of publication as a political symbol and literary masterpiece. Horace, a friend of Virgil, is remembered for his Odes, four books of lyric poetry drawing on themes of love and friendship, and yearnings, never quite fulfilled, for homely contentment and rustic ease. The erotic elegies of Propertius and Tibullus echo Catullus' earlier infatuation for Lesbia and foreshadow the work of Ovid, a decade or so later. Ovid's wit and fresh invention brought new twists to the elegiac genre, and his verse was imitated more than any other by medieval writers; partly, perhaps, because copies were available, but also because of a lightness of touch which won him universal appeal.

These classics have a timeless feel about them. They have been drummed into pupils for the best part of two thousand years (less the last few decades, perhaps). They are literature's heroes and anti-heroes. If other heroes are found, more often than not they are those heroes' heroes. Classical authors have been trotted out as arbiters of good taste throughout the centuries, medieval and Renaissance, neoclassical and new wave.

This aura of permanence is reinforced by the serene grandeur of classical civilization, by the durability of buildings and statues which survive it. Much of what actually went on, however, was anything but serene and civilized. Writers and artists are known to find inspiration under duress and in times of political insecurity. So it was with some of the best Roman literature. Throughout most of the first century BC Italy suffered from political chaos and intermittent cruelty and bloodshed. **'O Tempora O Mores!'** (*What an age! What moral standards!*) cried Cicero, rounding on his peers for failing to live up to earlier times, and damning the period we have subsequently identified as one of the greatest in our history.

The classical period of Latin was a moment in the language's evolution which could not endure, for no living language can remain the same for long. The efforts of later grammarians to preserve classical Latin were a symptom of its passing. As the living, spoken language moved on, eventually evolving into French, Spanish, Italian and other Romance languages, this classical, literary Latin was preserved and 'pickled' by later generations of writers and scholars, and after the fall of the western empire, by monks in their monasteries.

Thus the rules of classical Latin, the grammar and syntax, are something of a still shot of what was essentially transitory. Nonetheless these rules are instrumental in shaping all the Latin which followed, for almost all subsequent Latinists have attempted, with different degrees of success, to remain faithful to classical norms. Where possible the Latin in this course, the grammar, syntax, idioms and pronunciation, are based on the ground rules of classical Latin, including our story set in a medieval monastery. There are some inevitable twentieth-century inventions, and a number of words are used in their medieval sense, such as **ecclesia** (*church*) and **presbyter** (*priest*).

This section of each unit contains some authentic Latin, most but not all of which is classical. The pieces are included as both a rest and a stimulant. **You are not expected to read them too closely, in fact you are advised not to!** Many of the words and endings will be unfamiliar, so be positive and accumulate what you can. With the help of the translations see what you are able to work out, then sit back and listen to the recordings, and repeat them for pronunciation practice.

## Living Latin

🔊 **CD1, TR 2, 01:22**

**1 Verberat nos et lacerat fortuna.**

(Seneca, Dial. i, 4, 12)

*Fortune batters and torments us.*

**2 Defendi rem publicam adulescens, non deseram senex.**

(Cicero, Phil. ii, 118)

*I defended the republic as a young man, I shall not desert it in
my old age.*

**3 Ubi solitudinem faciunt, pacem appellant.**

(Tacitus, Agricola xxx)

*They make a desert and call it peace.*

**4 Aurora interea miseris mortalibus almam
extulerat lucem referens opera atque labores.**

(Virgil, Aeneid xi, 182–3)

*Dawn now raised her nourishing light upon the suffering mortals and
renewed their daily grind.*

**5 O tempora, o mores! Senatus haec intellegit, consul videt.**

(Cicero, In Catilinam i, 1)

*What an age! What moral standards! The senate knows what's going
on, the consul has it right in front of his eyes.*

# TESTING YOURSELF

**1** Fill the gaps:

| Case | silva<br>*wood* | monachus<br>*monk* | sarcina<br>*bag* | cibus<br>*food* |
|---|---|---|---|---|
| Nominative<br>(subject) | silva | monachus | sarcina | cibus |
| Accusative<br>(object) | ......... | ......... | sarcinam | cibum |
| Ablative<br>(*in, on, with*) | silva | monacho | ......... | ......... |

**2** Translate into Latin:
- **(a)** Benedict is not walking in the wood.
- **(b)** The bag is on the mule.
- **(c)** The mule does not carry Paul but the bag.
- **(d)** The mule does not like the wood.

**3** Write a Latin sentence with:
- **(a)** **mulus** in the accusative;
- **(b)** **sarcina** in the ablative;
- **(c)** **Paulus** in the nominative;
- **(d)** **monachus** in the ablative.

**4** Check you know these words:
amat, ambulat, cibus, cum, desiderat, est, et, fessus, in, lentus, monachus, mulus, non, nunc, portat, sarcina, sed, silva, spectat.

# 2

# Umbrae in silva
## Shadows in the wood

In this unit you will learn about
- *Singular and plural*
- *And find out more about Latin in 'A question of rhetoric'*

### Singular and plural forms

The plural of **mulus** *mule* is **muli** if nominative (subject), **mulos** if accusative (object) or **mulis** if ablative (*in, with*, etc.). The verb (**spectat, laborat**, etc.) has an '**n**' before the final '**t**' if the subject is plural:

| | |
|---|---|
| **Mulus in agro laborat.** | *The mule is working in the field.* |
| **Muli in agro laborant.** | *The mules are working in the field.* |
| **Monachi mulos spectant.** | *The monks watch the mules.* |
| **In agro est mulus.** | *A mule is (there is a mule) in the field.* |
| **In agro sunt muli.** | *Mules are (there are mules) in the field.* |

---

**Insight**

As in English, nouns have singular and plural endings and if the subject noun is plural then the verb is plural: **muli silvam spectant** = '*the mules watch the wood*'.

---

***Mulus equos non amat*** *The mule doesn't like horses*

🔊 **CD1, TR 3**

Benedictus et Stephanus monachi sunt. Monachi in monasterio habitant. Paulus discipulus in schola est. Discipuli cum monachis in monasterio habitant. Mulus cum equis in agro habitat. Mulus saepe in agris laborat. Equi cum mulo non laborant. Equos mulus non amat.

| | |
|---:|:---|
| **agro** | *(in) a field* |
| **discipulus** | *student* |
| **equos (equus)** | *horses* |
| **habitat, habitant** | *lives, live* |
| **laborat, laborant** | *works, work* |
| **saepe** | *often* |
| **schola** | *school* |
| **sunt** | *are* |

**Practice (I)**

**1** Choose the correct words and translate:
Mulus cum (equos/equis) in agro habitat, sed (equi/equus) cum (mulum/mulo) non laborant.

**2** Choose the correct word and translate:
  **(a)** Mulus sarcinam (portat/portant).
  **(b)** Monachi in monasterio (habitat/habitant).
  **(c)** Muli non equos (amat/amant).
  **(d)** Equus in agro non (laborat/laborant).

## How to look for the subject

If there is no subject, i.e. no word in the nominative case, then we add an English pronoun (*he*, *she* or *it* if the verb is singular, *they* if plural):

| | |
|---|---|
| **In monasterio labor<u>at</u>.** | *S/he works in the monastery.* |
| **In agro habit<u>ant</u>.** | *They live in the field.* |

> **Insight**
> If a verb, e.g. **est** or **spectat**, has no noun in the nominative case then add '*he*' or '*she*' or '*they*' as subject.

Silvae, umbrae
The plural of **silva** (and nouns like **silva**) is **silvae** (nominative), **silvas** (accusative) and **silvis** (ablative):

| | |
|---|---|
| **In silv<u>is</u> sunt umbrae.** | *There are shadows in the woods.* |
| **Sarcin<u>as</u> non portat.** | *(S/he/it) does not carry the bags.* |

*Umbrae in silvis* Shadows in the woods

◀) **CD1, TR 3, 00:44**

Benedictus vinum desiderat. Paulus igitur vinum in oppido emit et ad monasterium cum mulo ambulat. Mulus vinum portat. Nunc sunt in silva. Mulus saepe in silvis ambulat, sed non silvas amat quod in silvis sunt umbrae. Mulus neque umbras neque sarcinas amat. Mulus amicos in agro desiderat.

QUICK VOCAB

| | |
|---|---|
| **amicos (amicus)** | *friends* |
| **emit** | *(s/he) buys* |
| **igitur** | *and so* |
| **in oppido** | *in the town* |
| **neque...neque** | *neither...nor* |
| **quod** | *because* |
| **umbrae (umbra)** | *shadows* |
| **vinum** | *wine* |

## Practice (II)

**1** Choose the correct words and translate:
**Mulus non (silvas/silvis) amat quod in (silvas/silvis) sunt (umbrae/umbras).**

**2** Choose the correct words and translate:
   **(a)** Sarcinae in mulo (est/sunt).
   **(b)** Umbras in silva mulus non (amat/amant).
   **(c)** Monachi sarcinas non (portat/portant).
   **(d)** Equi in silva non (habitat/habitant).

---

## About Latin

### A question of rhetoric

The classical period was a relatively brief period in the life of Latin.
It was then immortalized by the enthusiasm of later generations,
and two thousand years later the books are all we have left.
But books are all it was ever meant to be. Classical Latin was
composed on the page; it may have been brought to life by recital,
but it was a written language. We may safely assume that the
carefully weighted sentences of Cicero or the delicate rhythms of
poets were not typical of everyday conversational Latin of the time.

Latin literature was the work of an educated, erudite minority.
Authors all shared the same school texts, the same tutors, the
same tastes, the same stock of stories and myths, the same models,
Roman and Greek. Not many Romans were literate, and even

fewer were literary. Authors were either themselves members of an upper-class elite or supported by someone who was. They frequently allude to myths, heroes and episodes in their history, as though to impress us with the detail of their knowledge. But their readership, the educated Roman public, were all familiar with the material. They did not judge an author by this alone, but by the use he made of it; and this material was almost all derived from Greece.

At the beginning of the second century BC, Rome controlled parts of the western Mediterranean, and her ambitious generals were contemplating further expansion eastwards, beginning with Greece. Several Romans had already visited Greece and liked what they had sampled of the refinements of Greek culture and lifestyle. Here they found an artistic inspiration and intellectual energy unmatched by anything back home, and before long Greek art and literature found a new and enthusiastic public in Italy. Talented and educated Greeks were befriended, hired, or bought in the slave markets to guide this process of cultural transfusion, a process which gathered momentum once Rome had made the step from ally to mistress of Greece.

Political control of the eastern half of the Mediterranean had belonged to the Macedonians. Greece was once part of Alexander the Great's empire, which stretched from Greece to India and south into Egypt. Alexander's travels and conquests merged the cultures of Greece with those of the near east and north Africa, creating the 'Hellenistic' culture. The city of Alexandria in Egypt became the library of the Hellenistic world, attracting writers and artists, poets and professors. This was the Greek culture which Romans inherited and experienced first-hand, but it was not the Greek culture they aspired to.

In the fifth century BC, when Rome was still struggling to assert her independence and when the Latin language was in its infancy, Greece experienced her classical age. Having fought off the menace of Persian aggression, Athens, Sparta and other city-states (Greece was not a single country at this time) all contributed to an era of virtually unparalleled excellence in the arts, in literature, architecture, philosophy and politics. The achievements of the Athenians were the most notable, and certainly now the most visible. Having organized a union of minor states, Athens turned this into an empire, and from its revenues built the Parthenon and other buildings on the Acropolis. Abroad she ruled with the heavy hand of a despot, but at home she nurtured the world's first democratic government. In this period the dramatists Aeschylus, Sophocles, Euripides and Aristophanes wrote and produced their plays; Herodotus and Thucydides wrote their histories; and Socrates and Plato confronted politicians with arguments about power and methods of persuasion in a democratic society.

Debate, discussion, argument, a willingness to talk through issues and participate in public affairs gave impetus to Athenian democracy. But by the end of the fifth century democracy was already beginning to lose its innocence. Politicians were thought to be out for all they could get, promising the world for a taste of power. Socrates himself criticized professional teachers of rhetoric, who gave lessons in how to deliver convincing arguments (and win elections) at the expense of the substance of the argument itself. Was there a value, wondered Socrates, in persuading others of a particular course of action if we did not first have a very firm grasp of the merits of that course of action? His stubborn pursuit of the truth offended a number of powerful people, and he was put to death at the close of the fifth century.

The Athenian taste for dialogue and debate was not confined to politics and philosophy but infused their plays, histories and all their literature. No one argued more convincingly than Socrates, despite his misgivings about the power of persuasion, and his conversations were recreated by his student, Plato (we have nothing written by Socrates himself), whose dialogues were an inspiration to later students of rhetoric. Rhetoric was taught as a formal subject in Greek, Roman and medieval schools – our meaning of 'rhetoric' today shows what a lost skill speaking has become.

The Greeks were known for being good speakers, and good squabblers. The difference between a debate and a quarrel is only one of degree, and while one was a symptom of freedom, the other brought that freedom to an end. A quarrel between the two most powerful city-states, Athens and Sparta, weakened the peninsula enough for Alexander's father, Philip, to overrun it in the fourth century.

The later period of Hellenism looked back on classical Greece as a golden age, and the literati deliberately recreated and imitated earlier writers. The Romans absorbed these conventions, and thus Greek ideas, rhythms, stories, their gods even, found new fertile soil in Italy, helping to shape and develop the Latin language.

---

## Living Latin

🔊 **CD1, TR 3, 01:24**

**1  Contra quis ferat arma deos?**

(Tibullus, Elegies i, 6, 30)

*Who may take arms against the gods?*

**2  \*Nonne Socrates iniustae victoriam mortis promeruit?**

(Boethius, Consolation of Philosophy i, 3)

*Did not Socrates reap the victory of an unjust death?*

**3  Graecia capta ferum victorem cepit et artis intulit agresti Latio.**

(Horace, Epistles ii, 1, 156–7)

*When Greece was captured, she in turn captivated her untamed conqueror and introduced the arts to bumpkin Lazio.*

**4  Vivos ducent de marmore vultus.**

(Virgil, Aeneid vi, 848)

*(The Greeks) will bring to life faces from marble.*

**5  \*Si quidem deus est, unde mala? Bona vero unde, si non est?**

(Boethius, Consolation of Philosophy i, 4)

*If there is a god, how can there be evil? And how can there be good if there is not?*

\*post-classical

# TESTING YOURSELF

**1** Add the missing forms to the tables:

**(a)**

| Case | Singular | | |
|---|---|---|---|
| Nominative (subject) | **mulus** | ......... | ......... |
| Accusative (object) | ......... | **discipulum** | ......... |
| Ablative (*by, with, from, in, on*) | **mulo** | ......... | **umbra** |
| | Plural | | |
| Nominative (subject) | ......... | **discipuli** | **umbrae** |
| Accusative (object) | **mulos** | ......... | ......... |
| Ablative (*by, with, from, in, on*) | ......... | **discipulis** | **umbris** |

**(b)**

| Case | Singular | | |
|---|---|---|---|
| Nominative (subject) | **equus** | **silva** | ......... |
| Accusative (object) | ......... | ......... | **sarcinam** |
| Ablative (*by, with, from, in, on*) | ......... | ......... | ......... |
| | Plural | | |
| Nominative (subject) | ......... | ......... | ......... |
| Accusative (object) | ......... | **silvas** | ......... |
| Ablative (*by, with, from, in, on*) | ......... | ......... | ......... |

**2** Change the underlined word to the plural (if the subject is plural, the verb will be plural too), and translate:

   **(a)** Paulus saepe in agro cum <u>monacho</u> laborat.

   **(b)** <u>Sarcina</u> in mulo est.

   **(c)** <u>Discipulus</u> in monasterio habitat.

   **(d)** Mulus <u>umbram</u> non amat.

**3** Translate into Latin:

   **(a)** There are shadows in the woods.

   **(b)** The monks are not carrying bags.

   **(c)** The mule often walks in the woods.

   **(d)** The mule does not like the horses because they do not work with mules.

**4** Check you know these words:
ad, amicus, discipulus, emit, equus, habitat, igitur, laborat, quod, saepe, sunt, umbra, vinum.

**5** Identify six English words which are related to the Latin words listed above.

# 3

# Mulus gemit
The mule groans

In this unit you will learn about
- *Masculine, feminine and neuter nouns*
- *Prepositions*
- *And find out more about Latin in 'Speaking as the Romans did ...'*

### Nouns ending -er

**Presbyter** *priest*, **puer** *boy*, **liber** *book*, **magister** *master* and **ager** *field* all have endings identical to **mulus** except for the nominative singular (-er). Some lose the 'e' in the other cases:

| | Singular | | | | |
|---|---|---|---|---|---|
| Nom. | **presbyter** | **puer** | **liber** | **magister** | **ager** |
| Acc. | **presbyterum** | **puerum** | **librum** | **magistrum** | **agrum** |
| Abl. | **presbytero** | **puero** | **libro** | **magistro** | **agro** |

| | Plural | | | | |
|---|---|---|---|---|---|
| Nom. | **presbyteri** | **pueri** | **libri** | **magistri** | **agri** |
| Acc. | **presbyteros** | **pueros** | **libros** | **magistros** | **agros** |
| Abl. | **presbyteris** | **pueris** | **libris** | **magistris** | **agris** |

## Masculine, feminine and neuter

Most nouns like **silva** are feminine and those like **mulus** (and **presbyter, puer,** etc.) are masculine. There are also neuter nouns. You will need to know a noun's gender when you come to matching adjectives with the nouns they qualify.

**Neuter nouns ending -um**
**Vinum** *wine,* **monasterium** *monastery,* **oppidum** *town,* **oleum** *oil,* **ovum** *egg* and **unguentum** *perfume* also have endings similar to **mulus**: the differences are in the nominative singular, which ends -**um** (like the accusative), and the nominative/accusative plural, both of which end -**a**:

|       | Singular | Plural  |
|-------|----------|---------|
| Nom.  | **vin-um** | **vin-a** |
| Acc.  | **vin-um** | **vin-a** |
| Abl.  | **vin-o**  | **vin-is** |

## Insight
The accusative of a neuter noun always has the same ending as the nominative. So the context, not the ending, will tell you whether a neuter noun is subject or object.

These are neuter nouns, and all without exception have the same endings for both the nominative and accusative cases, so the ending alone will not tell you whether a neuter noun is subject or object. This has to be worked out from the context:

**Mulus <u>vinum</u> non amat.**   *The mule does not like wine. (object).*
**In sarcina est <u>vinum</u>.**   *In the bag is some wine. (subject).*

**Ablative case:** *'in, on, with, by, from'*

English words which commonly render the ablative are: 'in, on, with, by, from'. Sometimes the ablative is used without a preposition:

**Sarcina est <u>unguentis</u> onerosa.** *The bag is heavy <u>with perfumes</u>.*

**Cum**, *with*, is only used if it means 'in the company of'.

## Insight

The same ending can represent more than one case: e.g.
**vinum** could be nominative (subject) or accusative (object).
The context will help you decide. The shared endings key
before each part of the Latin story will list the possible cases
for each ending.

**Sarcinae onerosae** *The bags are heavy*

**◀) CD1, TR 4**

---

**Shared endings key**
(Nouns are singular, unless stated plural. Entries in bold are
   included for the first time. A vowel may be long or short, e.g.
   nominative **silva,** ablative **silvā**.)
-**um**   mulum, puerum, agrum: accusative
      **vinum: nominative or accusative**
-**a**   silva: nominative or ablative
      **vina: nominative pl. or accusative pl.**

---

Paulus et Benedictus monachi sunt. Benedictus presbyter est,
et cum ancillis in culina laborat. Paulus non presbyter sed discipulus
est. In culina et in bibliotheca et in agris laborat. Benedictus, ubi
cibum vinumque desiderat, Paulum ad oppidum mittit. Hodie
igitur Paulus mulusque ex oppido per silvam ad monasterium
reveniunt. Ager et monasterium longe absunt. Sarcinae sunt
onerosae. Sarcinae vino et ovis et oleo et unguento onerosae sunt.
Mulus gemit. Unguenta et cibum et vinum semper Benedictus
desiderat sed semper mulus portat.

| | |
|---:|---|
| **absunt** | *(they) are away, absent* |
| **ancillis (ancilla)** | *maids* |
| **bibliotheca** | *library* |
| **culina** | *kitchen* |

| | |
|---|---|
| **ex** | *from, out of* |
| **gemit** | *(s/he) groans* |
| **hodie** | *today* |
| **longe** | *far, distant* |
| **mittit** | *(s/he) sends* |
| **onerosae** | *heavy* |
| **per** | *through, across, along* |
| **-que (cibum vinumque)** | *and (food and wine)* |
| **reveniunt** | *(they) come back* |
| **semper** | *always* |
| **ubi** | *when, where* |

## Practice (I)

**1** Add the missing forms to the following tables:

| Case | Singular | | |
|---|---|---|---|
| Nominative (subject) | ager | unguentum | presbyter |
| Accusative (object) | ......... | unguentum | ......... |
| Ablative (*by, with, from, in, on*) | agro | ......... | presbytero |
| | Plural | | |
| Nominative (subject) | ......... | unguenta | ......... |
| Accusative (object) | agros | unguenta | ......... |
| Ablative (*by, with, from, in, on*) | ......... | ......... | presbyteris |

**2** Choose the correct words and translate:

**(a)** (Presbyter/presbyteri) cum (discipulos/discipulis) non (laborat/laborant).

**(b)** Sarcina (vinum/vino) et (oleo/olea) et (unguenta/unguentis) et (ovum/ovis) onerosa est.

**3** Change the underlined words into the plural, and alter any other words which are affected, and translate:

**(a)** <u>Monachus</u> in monasterio habitat.
**(b)** Mulus non <u>silvam</u> sed <u>agrum</u> amat.
**(c)** <u>Equus</u> neque in silvis neque in agris cum <u>mulo</u> laborat.
**(d)** Benedictus <u>vinum</u> et <u>unguentum</u> desiderat.

### Prepositions – ablative or accusative?

These are words which form phrases with nouns. Sometimes the noun is in the accusative case, sometimes the ablative. It depends on the preposition:

| + Accusative | | + Ablative | |
|---|---|---|---|
| **per** | *through, by way of* | **cum** | *with* |
| **in** | *into, on to* | **in** | *in, on* |
| **ad** | *to, towards* | **a(b)*** | *from, by* |
| | | **e(x)*** | *out of, away from, off* |
| | | *the extra consonant is used before a vowel |

Prepositions like 'in' which are used with either case are followed by the accusative if some motion is implied, or ablative if it is not:

| | |
|---|---|
| In terram cadit. | *S/he falls <u>on to</u> the ground.* |
| In terra iacet. | *S/he lies <u>on</u> the ground.* |
| In silvam ambulat. | *S/he walks <u>into</u> the wood.* |
| In silva ambulat. | *S/he walks <u>in</u> the wood.* |

> ### Insight
> The accusative case is for objects, and also objects of motion:
> **in silvam** = '*into the wood*', **ad monasterium** = '*to the monastery*'.

***Monachus in cucullo*** *A hooded monk*

🔊 **CD1, TR 4, 00:49**

Paulus et mulus longe a monasterio absunt. Neque silvam neque sarcinas amat mulus. 'Io!' clamat Paulus. Mulus non ambulat.

Subito equum Paulus et mulus audiunt. Deinde equum vident. Celeriter equus per viam ad Paulum mulumque venit. In equo est monachus in cucullo. Equus est territus. Equus Paulum mulumque videt et subito e via declinat. Monachus ex equo in terram cadit et equus celeriter in silvam abit. Monachus in terra iacet.

| | |
|---|---|
| **abit** | *(s/he) departs* |
| **audiunt** | *(they) hear* |
| **cadit** | *(s/he) falls* |
| **celeriter** | *quickly* |
| **clamat** | *(s/he) shouts* |
| **cucullo (cucullus)** | *hood* |
| **declinat** | *(it) swerves* |
| **deinde** | *then, next* |
| **iacet** | *(s/he) lies* |
| **io!** | *heyup!* |
| **subito** | *suddenly* |

| | |
|---|---|
| **terram (terra)** | *ground* |
| **territus** | *scared* |
| **venit** | *(s/he) comes* |
| **viam (via)** | *road* |
| **vide(n)t** | *see* |

## Practice (II)

**1** Choose the correct word and translate:
- **(a)** Monachi per (via/viam) ambulant.
- **(b)** Mulus in (agrum/agro) est.
- **(c)** Equus, a (monachos/monachis) territus, e monasterio venit.
- **(d)** Monachus ex (equum/equo) in (terra/terram) cadit.

**2** Choose the correct preposition and translate:
- **(a)** (In/Cum) silva, monachus (in/ex) equo cadit et (ab/in) terra iacet.

- **(b)** Ova (in/e) sarcina (per/in) terram cadunt.

**(c)** Mulus (e/per) silvam (in/ad) monasterium ambulat.

## About Latin

### Speaking as the Romans did ...

A recording of Cicero making a speech or Virgil reciting his poetry would be a fine thing. The best we can do twenty centuries later is tentatively reconstruct the sound of Latin, letter by letter, syllable by syllable, from various bits and pieces of evidence. Much is disputed, much open to interpretation. But we have to live with this, for no one can begin to appreciate a literature – which was written for recital – without some idea of its sound. Our reconstruction may be a somewhat incomplete jigsaw puzzle, but so too is that of Elizabethan English, and that hasn't stopped production of Shakespeare's plays.

We would be hard put to identify just one correct pronunciation in any case. Latin was the first language of the empire of Rome, which lasted for over half a millennium, and stretched from the Crimea to Spain, Edinburgh to Egypt. For centuries Latin was the language of the entire known world. Compare this with English, our international language today: is it possible to identify a single model speaker of English? If so, who? Alfred the Great? Abraham Lincoln? Nelson Mandela?

The clearest evidence we have is of the sound of the individual letters themselves. This evidence comes from ancient commentators who give detailed advice about certain sounds (that it was given at all can be taken as a symptom of variance if not change); other clues come from transliteration into and out of other languages (e.g. Greek *Kaisar* for '**Caesar**', and *Oualerios* for '**Valerius**'); also from puns and plays on words, rhymes and assonance; and from the sub-Latin, or 'Romance' languages, French, Spanish, Portuguese and Italian, of which the more isolated and conservative dialects are especially interesting – **centum**'s hard 'c', for instance, in Sardinian (*ḵentu*, a hundred).

Stress and intonation are less secure. Latin stress was probably similar to our own, where the accent falls on the penultimate syllable, or if that syllable is weak, the one before it: *Augústus*, *Cícero*. Some hold the view that the initial syllable had the weight of accent, particularly in pre-classical Latin. This idea is prompted by the weakening of first syllables when they are compounded and made second syllable: **facere, perficere; capere, recipere**. Even after the classical period we see this stress in, for example, the Italian *pellegrino* (from Latin **peregrinus**), whose initial syllable was given enough weight for the word to arrive in English as 'pilgrim'. But we should not take this first-syllable theory too far. Almost all the examples cited involve a compound with a prefix, which would naturally be stressed on first formation. Put the accent on the second syllable of a compound, and it will soon lose the prefix and revert to the simple form. Even *pellegrino* was once a compounded form, being 'a person from across the field': **per-ager-inus**.

An 'm' in the middle of a word was very similar to ours, but at the end of a word appears to lose much of its consonantal value. For instance, say **septem** (*seven*) without closing your lips on the final 'm'. It is interesting to note that many other European languages, such as Bulgarian, Dutch and German, have a nasalized ending (-m/-n) for their word for 'seven' but the Romance languages derived directly from Latin all lose it (see the table). This 'm' is also missing from some Latin inscriptions: e.g. <u>scriptum</u> est *(it was written)*: written as *scriptust*. In classical Latin poetry a final 'm' is treated like a vowel if it appears before another vowel, and is elided. In medieval Latin the final 'm' appears to be a more complete sound, no doubt reinforced by students of classical Latin learning the accusative case: a schoolmaster had to be impressed that you knew **silvam** from **silva** and so you spelt and hummed it for all it was worth.

| Latin | English | French | Spanish | Italian |
|-------|---------|--------|---------|---------|
| **unus, una** | *one* | *un, une* | *un(o), una* | *un(o), una* |
| **septem** | *seven* | *sept* | *siete* | *sette* |
| **centum** | *hundred* | *cent* | *ciento* | *cento* |

Thus the accepted view is that the final 'm' of **septem** was sounded, if openly, by educated speakers who were taught both to spell words and enunciate them until their mouths were sore; but that this sound tended to be reduced in ordinary speech, with its stress on the syllable-before-last, to the point of eventual extinction in the Romance languages.

The 'g' is a letter we probably need to look at again. The evidence points towards a hard sound, as in 'gap', although I myself suspect that this did not occur in all uses. A softer sound in some words (not the 'g' in George but closer to the modern Greek 'g') is hard to resist: *ego* (I), which evolved in Spanish as 'yo' and in Italian as 'io', may well have been closer to a plain 'y' sound than hard 'g' – or something in between. Likewise for **fugit** (escapes), in which the hard 'g' makes an oddly stumbling sound for something so lightfooted. And it's not all fanciful guesswork: **magister** (*master*, *maître* and *maestro*) crossed into German as *Meister*. Clues from the animal kingdom, whose noises are commonly onomatopoeic, remind us that snakes hiss, hens cluck, cats miaow and dogs woof: are we then to suppose that two thousand years ago cows said 'moog' (**mugire**)?

Many 'g's were no doubt hard, or harder. The recording with this course sticks to the traditional hard 'g' (as in classical Latin, not the medieval soft 'g' in genius), for we are yet to establish how many words (if any at all) are prone to this softer sound. In my view a number of words remain candidates: e.g. **reges** (kings), **frigidus** (cold), **negare** (to deny), **euge!** (hooray!), **vagitus** (wailing). These and other sounds no doubt will have varied according to region, speaker, period, and most of all the word itself. Little is known about region or period, and even less about the characteristics of individual speakers, even the ones whose works we read, most of whom admired Greek so much they wanted to reproduce it in their own language, and that too may have influenced their pronunciation of Latin.

Differences between literary and spoken Latin – or Vulgar Latin (**vulgus**: *crowd, public*) – were not confined to sound. The syntax of speech was inevitably looser and more straightforward than that of the page. There were also differences in vocabulary: **equus** was the literary man's word for *horse* (*equestrian, equine, equitation* are among the learned and 'posh' words coined after the Middle Ages), while a cart-driver made do with a **caballus** (*cheval, caballo, cavalry* and possibly *cabbie*). We shall never know how far Cicero carried his literary style into ordinary speech, but he certainly retained something of his elaborate style in letters to his friends. One thinks of Queen Victoria's famous grumble at Gladstone, the Prime Minister, telling him not to address her as if she were a public meeting.

Spoken idioms will, conversely, have in some measure been employed by writers, not so much to create a simple, plain style but to embellish a dramatic effect or intimate moment. Our unlettered cart-driver, however, would have struggled with all the allusions to Greek mythology and legends, and even in the one or two more accessible pieces, he might have found satirists firing sharpened verses at him for the din he made in going about his daily business.

In the fourth and fifth centuries AD, the early Christians gave fresh impetus to literary Latin and for a while welded it to the vulgar form. The gospels had originally been written in Greek but it was Latin translations, in particular St Jerome's bible (the Vulgate), which wooed the western world to the new religion. The language of the pulpit had to be simple and straightforward since it was aimed primarily at those with little or no schooling in literacy and rhetoric. In tandem with Christianity's populist tendency was the intellectualizing of theologians caught up in debates such as the nature of the Trinity, the 'three-in-one-ness' of the Father, Son and Holy Spirit, a controversy which fuelled the fires of early heresies, and which gave renewed life to the language of philosophy and rhetoric.

---

## Living Latin

🔊 **CD1, TR 4, 01:50**

**1  Illa quidem iurata negat, sed credere durum est.**

(Tibullus, Elegies i, 6, 7)

*She denies it under oath, but it's hard to believe her.*

**2  *Beati mites quoniam ipsi possidebunt terram.**

(St Matthew v, 4)

*Blessed are the meek for they will inherit the earth.*

**3  *Gloria in excelsis Deo et in terra pax hominibus bonae voluntatis.**

(Gloria)

*Glory be to God on high and on earth peace to men of good will.*

**4  Dum nos fata sinunt oculos satiemus amore.**

(Propertius ii, 15, 23)

*While the fates allow us let us fill our eyes with love.*

**5  Oro, si quis adhuc precibus locus, exue mentem.**

(Virgil, Aeneid iv, 319)

*I beg you, if there's still time for entreaties, change your mind.*

**6** *Non veni vocare iustos, sed peccatores in paenitentiam.

(St Luke v, 32)

*I have not come to welcome the righteous, but the sinners to repentance.*

**7** Exitiabilis superstitio rursum erumpebat, non modo per Iudaeam, originem eius mali, sed per urbem etiam quo cuncta undique atrocia aut pudenda confluunt celebranturque.

(Tacitus, Annals xv, 44)

*The deadly superstition broke out again, not only in Judaea, the source of this trouble, but also in the capital where from every corner all things sleaze-ridden and shameful ooze together and come into vogue.*

\*post-classical

# TESTING YOURSELF

**1** Add the missing forms to the tables:

| Case | Singular | | |
|---|---|---|---|
| Nominative (subject) | ......... | ......... | puer |
| Accusative (object) | silvam | ......... | ......... |
| Ablative (*by, with, from, in, on*) | ......... | mulo | puero |
| | Plural | | |
| Nominative (subject) | ......... | ......... | ......... |
| Accusative (object) | silvas | ......... | ......... |
| Ablative (*by, with, from, in, on*) | ......... | ......... | pueris |

| Case | Singular | | |
|---|---|---|---|
| Nominative (subject) | vinum | liber | ancilla |
| Accusative (object) | ......... | librum | ......... |
| Ablative (*by, with, from, in, on*) | vino | ......... | ancilla |
| | Plural | | |
| Nominative (subject) | vina | ......... | ancillae |
| Accusative (object) | vina | libros | ......... |
| Ablative (*by, with, from, in, on*) | ......... | libris | ......... |

**2** Change the underlined words into the singular, alter any other words which may be affected, and translate:
- **(a)** <u>Discipuli</u> in culinam ambulant.
- **(b)** <u>Presbyteri</u> cibum vinumque saepe desiderant.
- **(c)** Mulus per <u>silvas</u> semper venit.
- **(d)** Magister <u>libros</u>, discipuli vinum desiderant.

**3** Translate into Latin:
- **(a)** The horses work in neither the wood nor the field.
- **(b)** The monk carries the perfumes in the bag.
- **(c)** The priest walks with the students through the wood towards the monastery.
- **(d)** Students are not priests.

**4** Check you know these words:
a(b), ager, audiunt, clamat, culina, e(x), hodie, iacet, liber, magister, mittit, monasterium, oppidum, ovum, per, puer, semper, terra, ubi, venit, via, vident.

**5** Identify six English words which are related to the Latin words listed above.

# 4

## Figura feminae
### The figure of a woman

In this unit you will learn about
• **The genitive**
• **Questions**
• **And find out more about Latin in '"Anyone" for a cancan?'**

**The genitive ('of') case**

The nominative case is for subjects, the accusative for objects (and also follows some prepositions), and the ablative is the *in, on, with, by* or *from* case. Now for the genitive:

|        | Nominative | Accusative | Genitive   | Ablative |
|--------|-----------|-----------|-----------|---------|
| Sing.  | silva     | silvam    | **silvae**    | silva   |
|        | mulus     | mulum     | **muli**      | mulo    |
|        | vinum     | vinum     | **vini**      | vino    |
| Plural | silvae    | silvas    | **silvarum**  | silvis  |
|        | muli      | mulos     | **mulorum**   | mulis   |
|        | vina      | vina      | **vinorum**   | vinis   |

The genitive can almost always be translated with the preposition
'*of…*'. This may be the possessive 'of':

**Benedicti vinum**    *the wine <u>of Benedict</u> (<u>Benedict's</u> wine)*
**feminae cucullus**    *the hood <u>of the woman</u> (<u>the woman's</u> hood)*

The 'of' case may also describe a quantity:

**amphora <u>vini</u>**        *an amphora <u>of wine</u>*
**sarcina <u>ovorum</u>**      *a bag <u>of eggs</u>*

The 'of' case can be 'subjective' or 'objective':

**timor <u>Danorum</u>**   *fear <u>of the Danes</u> (either another's fear of them
or the Danes' own fear)*
**amor <u>Dei</u>**        *love <u>of God</u> (either another's love of God or God's
own love)*

........................................................................

## Insight

More shared endings: **muli** could be nominative plural
(*'mules'*) or genitive singular (*'of the mule'*). The context will
help you decide.
........................................................................

***Femina in terra iacet*** *The woman lies on the ground*

◀) **CD1, TR 5**

| **Shared endings key** | |
|---|---|
| **-i**  muli: nominative plural | **-ae**  silvae: nominative plural |
|      muli, vini: *'of …'* genitive case |      silvae: *'of …'* genitive case |

Monachus in terra iacet. Equus, ab umbris territus, e via in silvam
effugit. Vento enim folia et rami crepitant et equus, umbrarum
ramorumque timidus, nunc per silvas ad monasterium festinat.
Immotus in terra iacet monachus. Paulus ad monachum currit.
Figura tamen non monachi sed feminae est. Paulus feminam spectat.
Cucullus feminae est scissus. Paulus feminam tunica protegit.

| | |
|---:|---|
| **crepitant** | *(they) rustle* |
| **currit** | *(s/he) runs* |
| **effugit** | *(s/he) flees* |
| **enim** | *for, you see* |
| **feminam, feminae (femina)** | *woman* |

QUICK VOCAB

| | |
|---|---|
| **festinat** | *(s/he) hurries* |
| **figura** | *shape* |
| **folia (folium)** | *leaves* |
| **immotus** | *still, motionless* |
| **protegit** | *(s/he) covers* |
| **rami (ramus)** | *branches* |
| **scissus** | *torn* |
| **tamen** | *however* |
| **timidus** | *fearful* |
| **tunica** | *tunic, dress* |
| **vento (ventus)** | *wind* |

## Practice (I)

**1** Add the missing forms:

| Case | Singular | | |
|---|---|---|---|
| Nominative (subject) | **terra** | **ramus** | **folium** |
| Accusative (object) | ......... | ......... | ......... |
| Genitive (*of*) | ......... | ......... | ......... |
| Ablative (*by, with, from, in, on*) | **terra** | ......... | ......... |
| | Plural | | |
| Nominative (subject) | **terrae** | ......... | **folia** |
| Accusative (object) | ......... | **ramos** | ......... |
| Genitive (*of*) | ......... | ......... | ......... |
| Ablative (*by, with, from, in, on*) | **terris** | ......... | ......... |

**2** Add the missing endings and translate:

**(a)** Feminae in culina monasteri__ laborant.

**(b)** Ova in tunicam femin__ cadunt.

**(c)** Discipuli vinum Benedict__ bibunt.

**3** Identify the cases of the underlined nouns, and translate:

**(a)** <u>Discipuli</u> vinum <u>ancillarum</u> desiderant.

**(b)** <u>Stephanus</u> est magister <u>scholae</u>.

**(c)** Paulus est <u>Stephani</u> discipulus.

**(d)** Mulus est <u>silvarum</u> timidus.

**4** Put these nouns into the genitive singular, and genitive plural:
**(a)** ramus *branch* **(b)** ager *field* **(c)** ovum *egg* **(d)** umbra
*shadow* **(e)** ancilla *maid*

## Questions

A question may be introduced by a question word such as **ubi?**
*where?*, **quis?/qui?** *who?* and **quid?** *what?* Without such an
interrogative word to introduce the question, the suffix **-ne** is
added to the first word:

| | |
|---|---|
| **Tu-<u>ne</u> vales?** | *Are you well?* |
| **Ubi femina habitat?** | *Where does the woman live?* |
| **Cur in terra femina iacet?** | *Why is the woman lying on the ground?* |

The 'is' in the third example above is part of the verbal phrase 'is
lying', represented in Latin by **iacet** (and not **est**: see 'Verbs' in the
Introduction).

Some questions expect the answer 'yes' or 'no'. **Nonne** expects the
answer 'yes', **num** the answer 'no':

| | |
|---|---|
| <u>**Nonne**</u> **Benedictus in culina est?** | *Surely Benedict is in the kitchen?* |
| <u>**Num**</u> **Paulus est episcopus?** | *Surely Paul is not a bishop?* |

> ***Ubi sum?*** *Where am I?*

◆) CD1, TR 5, 00:50

Paulus neque videre neque audire equum feminae potest.
Equus e silvis ad monasterium festinat. Femina diu iacet immota.
Paulus est anxius et mulus trepidus. 'Te miseram!' gemit Paulus.
Femina oculos aperit et Paulum spectat. 'Nonne es mortua?' rogat
Paulus.

'Mortua? Non ita. Ubi sum? In silvis?'
'Ita vero,' inquit Paulus.
'Ubi est equus?'
'Lente, lente! Vales-ne? Vis-ne aquam bibere?'

'Non ita, tibi gratias. Equus-ne adest?'
'Non ita. Ramos umbrasque timet. Et tu, vales-ne?'
'Valeo. O malum est!' clamat femina.
'Lente! Quis es?'

| | |
|---|---|
| **adest** | *(s/he, it) is present, here* |
| **anxius** | *concerned* |
| **aperit** | *opens* |
| **aquam (aqua)** | *water* |
| **audire** | *to hear* |
| **bibere** | *to drink* |
| **diu** | *for a long time* |
| **es** | *you are* |
| **inquit** | *(s/he) says, said* |
| **ita vero** | *yes* |
| **malum est** | *it is bad! curses!* |
| **mortua** | *dead* |
| **non ita** | *no, not so* |
| **oculos (oculus)** | *eyes* |
| **potest** | *(s/he) is able, can* |
| **rogat** | *(s/he) asks* |
| **sum** | *I am* |
| **te miseram** | *you poor thing* |
| **tibi gratias** | *thank you* |
| **timet** | *(s/he, it) fears* |
| **trepidus** | *nervous* |
| **valeo (-es)** | *I am (you are) well* |
| **videre** | *to see* |
| **vis** | *you want, wish* |

QUICK VOCAB

## Insight

The present tense in English can be expressed *'he lives'* or *'he is (not) living'* or *'he does (not) live'*. The Latin is the same for all: **(non) habitat**.

So *'he is living'* = **habitat**: there is no need to add **est**.

See **Verbs** under **Essential Grammar** in the **Introduction**.

## Practice (II)

**1** Answer the questions with the correct form of the verb *to be*:
   **(a)** Quis es? ____ Paulus.
   **(b)** Qui estis? ____ Stephani discipuli.
   **(c)** Quis est? ____ episcopus.
   **(d)** Ubi sum? ____ in silva.

| | | | |
|---|---|---|---|
| sum | *I am* | sumus | *we are* |
| es | *you are* | estis | *you are* (pl.) |
| est | *s/he, it/there is* | sunt | *they/there are* |

**2** Make up questions which lead to these answers:
   **(a)** Mulus est in silva.
   **(b)** Paulus in bibliotheca laborat quod est discipulus.
   **(c)** Non ita, femina non mortua est.
   **(d)** Stephanus est magister.

## About Latin

### 'Anyone' for a cancan?

In the medieval period a 'clerical' worker was more often than not a clergyman. The Church first became active in government and administration during the latter days of the Roman empire, and became even more so after it collapsed. Libraries and schools might have died out altogether if the early monasteries had not survived to house them. Monks would sing, read and write Latin, much of which was religious and some secular. Hymns, liturgy, lives of saints, histories, charters, letters and poems all contribute to a rich variety of writing produced over more than a millennium. Sub-classical imitations were carefully crafted, and there was looser stuff too influenced by the respective native languages.

The spoken Latin of the empire had long since disintegrated into the Romance languages, intermingling with local speech habits and evolving with the peoples who spoke it. In France students of Latin have tended to pronounce Latin as they do French (e.g. 'qu' as 'k', not 'kw'). This has an interesting bearing on the origin of the word 'cancan', which is said by some to be derived from the Latin word **quamquam**. **Quamquam** usually means 'although', but the connection between 'although' and a dance is not easy to fathom. More likely is a less well-known meaning of **quamquam** – 'anyone' in the feminine, 'any girl', i.e. no fixed partner. Another theory ascribes the cancan to a 'scandalous' dance, again the origin being the Latin word **quamquam**, the scandal being a row during the Reformation: a few priests in France had adopted the pronunciation favoured in northern (and Protestant) Europe, 'kwamkwam', only to incur the severe displeasure of the French authorities. Even the pronunciation of a dying language could have life-threatening implications.

In England, as elsewhere, Latin was pronounced according to local speech habits. In the years following the Norman Conquest of 1066, English was strongly influenced by French. **'Julius Caesar'**, which was **Yoolius Ky-sser** in classical times, was pronounced **Joolius Seizer** by the many schoolmasters of French origin, and **Kikero** became **Sissero**, **Wergilius**, **Vurdgil**.

Latin is not a parent language of English, but the number of loan-words, of which many arrived via French, make it a most generous uncle. New words have one of three sources: they are either new formations, or taken from another language, or a mixture of the two. The spelling of certain words may be changed, or stabilized, at a later date (e.g. Old English *discipul* and *munuc* which were to become *disciple* and *monk*). It may be that a parent language coined the word, or itself borrowed from another source (e.g. *elephant*: Egyptian to Greek to Latin to French to English). Origins are not always clear, and there is sometimes more than one source behind a word's widespread use.

| Some loan-words taken before the Norman Conquest (1066) | Some post-1066 arrivals via French |
| --- | --- |
| *castle* **(castellum-i)** | *desire* (*désirer*/**desiderare**) |
| *disciple* **(discipulus-i)** | *oil* (*huile*/**oleum**) |
| *monk* **(monachus-i)** | *silence* (*silence*/**silentium**) |

In the eighth century Charlemagne had wanted to improve the schools within his empire, and employed an English scholar, Alcuin, to raise the standard of Latin taught in them. Similar initiatives followed over the next few centuries, culminating at the end of the Middle Ages in the Renaissance, when writers, artists and scholars were guided and inspired almost exclusively by classical models.

It was less easy to impose uniformity on the spoken language. The spoken Latin of the empire had already evolved into the vernacular languages of the Romance countries, and the Latin-as-a-second-language spoken in the medieval period became rather homeless and fragmentary. Different countries and regions could barely understand each other's use of the language, and the sound of ecclesiastical Latin was far from uniform. Even in the churches Latin was not going to last long, at least not in the countries where the Reformation was gathering momentum and allegiance to Rome would be cast aside. Latin's fading role as an international language and the continued rise of the vernacular languages was in one sense the eventual triumph of Vulgar Latin over its literary counterpart. But once retired from active life, Latin becomes provider, and feeds the vernacular languages with vast numbers of new words and expressions.

## Living Latin

🔊 CD1, TR 5, 01:43

**1** ***Nemo servus potest duobus dominis servire.***

(St Luke xvi, 13)

*No one can be a slave to two masters.*

**2** ***Quis maior est, qui recumbit an qui ministrat?***

(St Luke xxii, 27)

*Whom do we value more, the one who sits for dinner or the one who serves?*

**3** ***Alcuinum, de Britannia Saxonici generis hominem, virum undecumque doctissimum, praeceptorem habuit.***

(Einhard, Vita Karoli xxv)

*He (Charlemagne) employed Alcuin as teacher, a fellow from Britain, of Saxon blood, in every respect a most learned man.*

**4** ***Heu, cuculus nobis fuerat cantare suetus,***
   ***quae te nunc rapuit hora nefanda tuis?***
   ***Heu, cuculus, cuculus, qua te regione reliqui***
   ***infelix nobis illa dies fuerat.***

(Alcuin, Versus de Cuculo)

*Mourn the little cuckoo who liked to sing to us. What unspeakable moment snatched you from your friends? Little cuckoo, little cuckoo, where did I leave you? What a wretched day that was for us.*

**5** ***Hic Harold Rex interfectus est et fuga verterunt Angli.***

(Bayeux Tapestry)

*Here King Harold was slain and the English turned and fled.*

**6** ***Sidus clarum***
   ***puellarum,***
   ***flos et decus omnium***

**rosa veris,**
**quae videris**
**clarior quam lilium.**

(12th century anon.)

*Bright star of maidens, everything's flower and ornament, you are like a spring rose, more lovely than a lily.*

*post-classical

# TESTING YOURSELF

**1** Write sentences as answers to these questions:
   **(a)** Ubi est femina?
   **(b)** Cur equus feminae e silva festinat?
   **(c)** Ubi magister scholae laborat?
   **(d)** Quid mulus portat?

**2** Translate into Latin:
   **(a)** Are we in a wood?
   **(b)** The woman's horse is able to hear the wind.
   **(c)** The mule carries the monk's bags.
   **(d)** Surely the students do not long for Benedict's wine?

**3** Add the missing forms:

| Singular | | | |
|---|---|---|---|
| Nominative | ......... | **tunica** | ......... |
| Accusative | ......... | ......... | ......... |
| Genitive | ......... | ......... | ......... |
| Ablative | **vento** | **tunica** | ......... |
| Plural | | | |
| Nominative | **venti** | ......... | ......... |
| Accusative | ......... | **tunicas** | **ova** |
| Genitive | ......... | ......... | ......... |
| Ablative | ......... | ......... | **ovis** |

**4** Check you know these words:
adest, aqua, cur, currit, deus, diu, femina, festinat, folium, ita
vero, non ita, nonne, num, potest, quid, quis, ramus, rogat,
sum, tamen, timet, timidus, ventus.

**5** An English word which is derived from a Latin one does not
always give you the actual meaning, but it usually points
you in the right direction. From the above list identify Latin
ancestors of: *aqueduct, current, effeminate, folio, ramification,
interrogate, ventilator.*

# 5

# Egbertae filia
## Egberta's daughter

In this unit you will learn about
- *The vocative case*
- *Adjectives: -us, -a, -um*
- *And find out more about Latin in 'Reformation and Renaissance – life after death'*

### Declensions: the nominative and genitive

All nouns belong to one of five groups, or 'declensions'. Nouns like **silva**, **umbra** or **Lucia** belong to the first, while those like **mulus**, **magister** or **vinum** all belong to the second declension. **Amor** and **timor**, which appeared briefly in the previous unit, belong to the third – but more about them later. All these declensions and cases mean that some endings do double and treble duty: the ending -a, for example, might be the nominative or ablative singular of **silva**, or neuter plural of **vinum**. So to help establish a noun's declension (and therefore the endings), dictionaries show a noun's nominative and genitive endings:

First declension:      **silva, silvae**
Second declension:   **mulus, muli** (also: **puer, pueri;**
                                  **ager, agri** *a field*
                                  **vinum, vini** (neuter)

## Insight

Latin nouns are listed in dictionaries in the nominative and genitive singular.

**Lucia**

◀) **CD1, TR 6**

'Quis es? Ubi habitas?' rogat Paulus.

'In castello,' inquit femina.

'Tu-ne es Egberta, castelli domina?'

'Non Egberta, sed Egbertae filia, Lucia sum. Et tu, quis es?'

'Sum Paulus, et in monasterio habito.'

'Es presbyter?'

'Non presbyter, sed discipulus sum.'

'Episcopi-ne discipulus es?'

'Non episcopi sed Stephani.'

'Quis est Stephanus? In monasterio habitat?'

'Stephanus est monachus et scholae magister.'

'Me miseram! Ubi est ille caballus?'

'Lente! Fortasse est in agris cum monasterii equis. Age, mecum ad monasterium veni. In mulum ascendas.'

| | | |
|---|---|---|
| **age** | *come on!* | |
| **ascendas** | *you may climb* | |
| **caballus-i** [m] | *horse* | |
| **castellum-i** [n] | *castle* | |
| **domina-ae** [f] | *lady, mistress* | |
| **Egberta-ae** | *Egberta* | |
| **episcopus-i** [m] | *bishop* | |
| **filia-ae** [f] | *daughter* | |
| **fortasse** | *perhaps* | |
| **habito** (-as) (-at) | *I (you) (s/he) live* | |
| **ille** | *that* | |
| **Lucia-ae** | *Lucia* | |
| **me miseram** | *just my luck* | |
| **mecum** | *with me* | |
| **veni** | *come!* | |

QUICK VOCAB

### Practice (I)

**1** Fill the gaps:

| Nominative | Genitive |
|------------|----------|
| sarcina | sarcinae |
| umbra | ......... |
| ovum | ......... |
| puer | ......... |
| ......... | magistri |
| episcopus | ......... |
| ......... | Egbertae |
| liber | ......... |

**2** Make a list of all the nouns you have met (showing the nominative and genitive endings) similar to:
- **(a)** silva, silvae (e.g. sarcina-ae, Lucia-ae, etc.)
- **(b)** mulus, muli (e.g. episcopus-i, Paulus-i, etc.)
- **(c)** vinum, vini (e.g. ovum-i, castellum-i, etc.)

### The vocative case

Second declension nouns (those like **mulus-i**) have a special ending for when they are being spoken to. This is called the 'vocative case': **mule** for **mulus**, (**Brute** for **Brutus** in **Et tu Brute!**). Most other vocative forms are the same as the nominative, e.g. '**o Lucia**'.

#### Adjectives: *sanctus, sancta, sanctum*

> **Insight**
> An adjective can be next to the noun it describes: *'The rich bishop'* or after a verb: *'The bishop is rich'*.

Adjectives give nouns more detail or colour: a _saintly_ bishop, a _tired_ maid. A Latin adjective is said to 'agree' with the noun it describes in gender (masculine, feminine or neuter), number (singular or plural) and case (nominative, accusative, etc.):

| | |
|---|---|
| **Sanctus episcopus et ancilla fessa in agro sedent.** | _The saintly bishop and tired maid sit in the field._ |
| **Multae feminae per silvam obscuram ambulant.** | _Many women are walking through the dark wood._ |
| **Liber magnus in monasterio est.** | _The large book is in the monastery._ |

The masculine endings of adjectives like **sanct-us** are identical to those of **mul-us**, the feminine to those of **silv-a**, and neuter to those of **vin-um**. In the final example above **magnus** agrees with **liber** even though their endings are not identical: both words are nominative masculine singular.

The position of an adjective may be before or after the noun it describes. You will come across adjectives placed several words before or after the nouns they qualify, especially filia in poetry. The endings help you match the two together. Some adjectives appear after a verb (as in English):

| | |
|---|---|
| **Mulus est lentus.** | _The mule is slow._ |

## Insight

If you know the endings for **mulus**, **umbra** and **vinum** then you know the endings of adjectives like **sanctus-a-um**.

_**E silvis veniunt** They come out of the woods_

◀) CD1, TR 6, 01:07

Obscuram per silvam ad monasterium veniunt. Paulus mulum ducit. Lucia in mulo sedet. Mulus est lentus. Silva est umbrosa. Lucia Paulum rogat: 'Episcopus-ne sanctus in monasterio manet?'

'Episcopus? Nescio. Sanctus episcopus? Vel saevus?'

'Nonne est sanctus?'

'Episcopus est saevus, quod semper Stephanum nos discipulos in bibliotheca claudere iubet.'

'Discipuli-ne estis boni studiosique?'

'Certe, semper.'

'Num vos discipuli semper boni estis? Fortasse mali, ignavi, somnulenti estis.'

'Mali? Ignavi? Nos? Iocosa es.'

'Cur in silva ambulas? Cur studiosus in bibliotheca non laboras?'

'Episcopus certe est malus, gulosus, saevus, vinolentus ....'

'Ssst. Maledicis. Episcopus est Egbertae avunculus.'

'Vero? Episcopus est cognatus Egbertae? Quid ergo? Hic, o Domina, est mulus. Mulus est cognatus equorum qui in monasterii agris habitant, eho mule?' Paulus ridet. Sed neque Lucia neque mulus ridet. Nunc enim mulus et Luciam et onerosas cibo multo vinoque sarcinas portat. 'Ignoscas, o Lucia!' inquit Paulus. Per silvas silentio procedunt. Mox magnos monasterii muros vident et e silvis in agros veniunt.

| | |
|---|---|
| **ambulas** | *you walk* |
| **avunculus-i [m]** | *uncle* |
| **bonus-a-um** | *good* |
| **certe** | *certainly, yes* |
| **claudere** | *to lock* |
| **cognatus-i [m]** | *kinsman* |
| **ducit** | *(s/he) leads* |
| **eho** | *eh* |
| **et... et** | *both... and* |
| **gulosus-a-um** | *greedy* |
| **hic** | *here* |
| **ignavus-a-um** | *lazy* |
| **ignoscas** | *forgive (me), sorry* |
| **iocosus-a-um** | *full of jokes, humorous* |
| **iubet** | *(s/he) orders, tells* |
| **laboras** | *you work* |

| | |
|---|---|
| **magnus-a-um** | *great, large* |
| **maledicis** | *you slander* |
| **malus-a-um** | *troublesome, bad* |
| **manet** | *(s/he) stays* |
| **mox** | *soon, presently* |
| **multus-a-um** | *much, many* |
| **murus-i** [m] | *wall* |
| **nescio** | *I don't know* |
| **nos** | *us* |
| **num** | *surely… not* |
| **obscurus-a-um** | *dark* |
| **procedunt** | *(they) go forward* |
| **qui** | *who* |
| **quid ergo?** | *so what?* |
| **ridet** | *(s/he) laughs* |
| **saevus-a-um** | *cruel, mean* |
| **sedet** | *(s/he) sits* |
| **silentium-i** [n] | *silence* |
| **somnulentus-a-um** | *sleepy* |
| **studiosus-a-um** | *hard-working* |
| **umbrosus-a-um** | *full of shadows* |
| **vel** | *or* |
| **veniunt** | *(they) come* |
| **vero** | *indeed* |
| **vinolentus-a-um** | *fond of wine* |
| **vos** | *you* |

## Insight

Adjectives agree with the nouns they describe, i.e. show the same case, gender and number (singular or plural). The endings are often exactly the same – but not always: e.g. **liber magnus** (*'a large book'*).

### Practice (II)

**1** Fill each gap with the appropriate form of **furiosus** *angry* and **sanctus** *saintly*: (**fugat** = *chases*)

**(a)** Bestiae _____
Christianos _____ fugant.

**(b)** Christianus _____
bestias _____ fugat.

**(c)** Christianum _____
bestiae _____ fugant.

**2** Change the underlined words to the plural form (other endings should be changed if affected) and translate the new version:

**(a)** <u>Bestia</u> furiosa sanctum monachum spectat.

**(b)** <u>Liber</u> magnus in bibliotheca est.

**(c)** <u>Discipulus</u> ignavus <u>mulum</u> furiosum in <u>agro</u> videt.

**(d)** <u>Monachus</u> somnulentus in bibliotheca non laborat.

# About Latin

## Reformation and Renaissance – life after death

The Renaissance was a 'rebirth', a renewal of interest in classical literature and art. Many Greek and Latin books which had previously been ignored or unknown were brought to light and translated. There were imitations as well as translations, and original works were written in the authors' own languages which echoed classical precedents in form or content. Schoolmen and scholars redoubled their efforts to introduce classical standards of grammar and syntax, and medieval Latin as a living language was all but laid to rest, helped on its way by the Reformers' distrust of anything Roman. Latin, in its classical form, had achieved immortality: dead languages do not change, and the linguistic rules which govern their use will always remain the same.

The translation of classical texts into English demanded a wider range of vocabulary than it was able to supply. There were not the words to express the many new ideas of religion, astronomy, science and philosophy which were stimulated by the interest in these ancient texts, and often the simplest solution was to import a word direct from the Latin or Greek. Many of these words in time lost their foreign status, and became part of our language (some with slight modifications, e.g. **splendidus** was first *splendidious* and then settled as *splendid*). The anglicized pronunciation of these loan-words will in turn have influenced our pronunciation of original Latin.

Latin was very closely caught up in the religious conflicts in the sixteenth century. It was, after all, the language of the Church, where it had survived as a spoken language for over a thousand years. Latin was a symbol of all things Roman, and since scholars were being strangled, burnt and beheaded for denying or affirming Rome, it's no small mercy that Latin survived at all. In England, classical scholars took sides in the dispute over the correct language for the liturgy – Sir John Cheke spoke out against Latin and assisted Cranmer with his Book of Common Prayer. Some wanted to follow the lead of the Dutch scholar, Erasmus, and recreate a more authentic classical sound. Others wanted most of all to rid Latin of its association with the Church. Thus the sound of Latin, now deprived of its status as an independent, if ritualized, language, lived for a brief while in a limbo of learned good intentions before slipping into the stream of English and a pronunciation along the lines of our own speech habits.

A further complication is the famous 'vowel shift' which occurred in English at this time. Vowel quantities of Latin-derived words had been changing since pre-Conquest times. **Pater**, for instance, has a short 'a' in Latin which was lengthened on arrival in English, possibly by association with the long 'a' in 'father'. The vowel shift then brought about a further change, leaving us with the 'pay-ter' we hear in period dramas. Through change of quantity or vowel shift or both, we now have in English (and, until as late as the nineteenth century, in Latin): **bone-us** from **bonus** (classical pronunciation: 'bonnus'); **mise-er** from **miser** ('missair'), *fil-ial* from **filius** ('feelius'), *wine* from **vinum** ('weenum').

If Latin in this country was somewhat anglicized, it is even more pertinent to say English was Latinized. Coining new words became something of a fad, beyond the requirement of scientists and translators. Some loan-words which had settled into English, many having arrived via French, were reformed to make them resemble the original Latin ones more closely. We now have many cases of pairs of words, which have subsequently developed different meanings:

| Latin | Pre-1500 | Post-1500 |
| --- | --- | --- |
| **securus** | *sure* | *secure* |
| **computare** | *count* | *compute* |
| **desiderare** | *desire* | *desiderate* |

Not all these later additions survived (e.g. *desiderate*). Some words were respelt and replaced the earlier forms altogether – a headache for all those who struggle with spelling:

| Latin | Pre-1500 | Post-1500 |
|---|---|---|
| **dubium** | *doute* | *doubt* |
| **septem** | *set* (French) | *sept* (French) |
| **subtilis** | *sutil* | *subtle* |

Some Latin-derived words can appear dry and pompous. Comic writers from Shakespeare onwards have had plenty of mileage from unnecessarily tortuous circumlocutions. In the sixteenth century one poor fellow closed a letter to someone he hoped to impress with 'I relinquish to fatigate your intelligence …'. However, quirk and affectation aside, Latin has proved to be a rich source of new words. Some loan-words have settled in so well that you would not notice their origin, and their crispness and nuance help to give English its unequalled richness and variety.

---

## Living Latin

◀) **CD1, TR 6, 03:04**

**1** *Ne nos inducas in tentationem, sed libera a malo.**

(Pater Noster)

*Do not lead us into temptation but free us from evil.*

**2** *Beati pauperes, quia vestrum est regnum Dei.**

(St Luke vi, 20)

*Blessed are the poor, for yours is the kingdom of God.*

**3** Sequitur clades, forte an dolo principis incertum (nam utrumque
auctores prodidere), sed omnibus quae huic urbi per violentiam
ignium acciderunt gravior atque atrocior.

(Tacitus, Annals xv, 38)

*A disaster followed – whether accidental or by Nero's hand no one
knows (both versions have their supporters) – but this city had never
experienced a more serious or damaging fire.*

**4** Eorum multitudo ingens haud proinde in crimine incendii quam
odio humani generis convicti sunt.

(Tacitus, Annals xv, 44)

*A large number of Christians were condemned, not so much on any
charge of arson but because of their aversion to the human race.*

**5** Quamquam adversus sontis et novissima exempla meritos
miseratio oriebatur, tamquam non utilitate publica sed in
saevitiam unius absumerentur.

(Tacitus, Annals xv, 44)

*Despite their guilt and the deserved severity of their punishment,
people began to feel pity because their destruction was not so much
in the interests of the public but rather for the sadistic amusement of
one man.*

**6** Pervaserat rumor ipso tempore flagrantis urbis inisse eum
domesticam scaenam et cecinisse Troianum excidium.

(Tacitus, Annals xv, 39)

*A rumour circulated that at the very time of the fire in Rome Nero had
gone on to his stage in the palace and sung of the Fall of Troy.*

*post-classical

# TESTING YOURSELF

**1** Fill the gaps:

| Latin | English | Derivative(s) |
|-------|---------|---------------|
| **ovum-i** | *egg* | oval |
| **lucidus-a-um** | *bright* | ......... |
| **murus-i** | ......... | ......... |
| **bestia-ae** | ......... | ......... |
| **folium-i** | ......... | ......... |
| **dubium-i** | *doubt* | ......... |
| **loquax** | *talkative* | ......... |
| **vir-i** | *man* | ......... |
| **iratus-a-um** | *angry* | ......... |

**2** Change the underlined words into the plural and alter any other words which are affected, and translate:
 **(a)** <u>Monachus</u>-ne ignavus in agris laborat?
 **(b)** Num <u>discipulus</u> cognatus Luciae est?
 **(c)** Paulus magistri <u>librum</u> in bibliotheca spectat.
 **(d)** Num Benedictus <u>ancillae</u> avunculus est!

**3** Write out **sanctus-a-um**, singular and plural, in all the cases you have met so far.

**4** Check you know these words:
 bestia-ae, bonus-a-um, domina-ae, ducit, episcopus-i, fessus-a-um, iubet, lentus-a-um, magnus-a-um, malus-a-um, manet, mox, multus-a-um, murus-i, ridet, saevus-a-um, sanctus-a-um, sedet, vero.

**5** Identify the Latin ancestor of *very* from the above list.

**6** What is the difference in meaning between **fugat** and **fugit**?

**7** During the Renaissance many new adjectives were coined from Latin roots. Identify the English meanings of the Latin nouns below, and the English adjective derived from the Latin word:

| e.g. *noctes* | <u>nights</u> | <u>nocturnal</u> |
|---|---|---|
| **noctes** | *son* | |
| **canis** | *church* | |
| **culina** | *house* | |
| **decem** | *sun* | |
| **domus** | *brother* | |
| **ecclesia** | *nights* | |
| **filius** | *mother* | |
| **frater** | *dog* | |
| **mater** | *cattle* | |
| **sol** | *ten* | |
| **boves** | *kitchen* | |

**8** Translate into Latin:
   **(a)** Surely the bishop is not greedy?
   **(b)** The tired students often sit in the field.
   **(c)** Is the lady furious, Stephen?
   **(d)** Do mules work in the dark wood?

# 6

## In amphitheatro saevitia
## Cruelty in the amphitheatre

In this unit you will learn about
- *Verbs:* potest, vult, debet
- *Infinitives*
- *Adjectives:* -er, -era, -erum
- *And find out more about Latin in 'Latin wanted – dead or alive'*

### Adjectives: *miser, misera, miserum* wretched

The endings of these adjectives are almost identical to those
of **sanct-us-a-um** but for the nominative masculine singular
(cf. **presbyt<u>er</u>** and **mul<u>us</u>**). So **mulus miser, mulum miserum,
femina misera, feminam miseram**, etc.

### Verbs: *potest, vult, debet*

|        | is/are able | want(s) | ought, owe(s) |
|--------|-------------|---------|----------------|
| *s/he* | **potest**  | **vult** | **debet**     |
| *they* | **possunt** | **volunt** | **debent**   |

These verbs are usually followed by an infinitive (an infinitive of an
English verb is formed with 'to...', e.g. *to see*, *to believe*, *to say*.

**Abbatissa cantare non potest.**   *The abbess is unable to sing.*
**Pecuniam dare debent.**   *They ought to give some money.*

## Insight

The infinitive of a verb in English begins with *'to'*: *'to eat'*, *'to drink'*, etc.

### Latin infinitives -re

| amat | s/he loves | amare | to love |
|------|-----------|--------|---------|
| videt | s/he sees | videre | to see |
| scribit | s/he writes | scribere | to write |
| audit | s/he hears | audire | to hear |
| facit | s/he makes | facere | to make, do |

The five verbs above each represent a different group (or conjugation). With the exception of irregular verbs like **esse** and **posse**, all Latin verbs belong to one of these five conjugations.

### *In bibliotheca* In the library

◄ CD1, TR 7

| **Shared endings key** | |
|---|---|
| **-o** | mulo, vino: ablative |
| | **mulo, vino: dative ('to… / for…')** |
| **-ae** | silvae: genitive, nominative plural |
| | **silvae: dative ('to… / for…')** |
| **-is** | mulis, silvis, vinis: ablative plural |
| | **mulis, silvis, vinis: dative plural ('to… / for…')** |

Est meridies. Discipuli Stephanusque sunt in bibliotheca. Scholae magister discipulis historiam Christianorum bestiarumque narrat.

'Christiani multi in amphitheatro occisi sunt. Romani pro suffragiis populi ludos faciebant et magnam opulentiam ostentare volebant. Miseros Christianos! Pagani semper videre multam saevitiam volunt. Ludos in amphitheatro spectabant etiam docti, qui eos non saevos sed ineptos existimabant. Nulla enim victimis erat misericordia. Nunc nobis libri non ludi sunt grati, eho Paule? Age, Paulus-ne nobis recitare potest? Paule? Ubi est Paulus?'

'Quando Christiani, o Domine, in amphitheatro paganos mutilaverunt?' rogavit Augustinus ex discipulis unus.

'Ubi est Paulus?' inquit Stephanus qui eum non audit.

'Hodie Paulus in culina laborat,' inquit Augustinus.

'Quid? Cur Paulus in culina laborare vult? Adesse in schola debet. Paulus enim non coquus sed discipulus est.'

| | |
|---|---|
| **adesse** | to be here |
| **amphitheatrum-i** [n] | amphitheatre |
| **bestia-ae** [f] | beast |
| **Christianus-i** [m] | Christian |
| **coquus-i** [m] | cook |
| **debet** | (s/he) ought |
| **doctus-i** [m] | learned man |
| **dominus-i** [m] | lord, sir |
| **eos** | them |
| **erat** | (s/he, it, there) was |
| **eum** | him |
| **existimabant** | (they) thought |
| **faciebant** | (they) prepared |
| **gratus-a-um** | pleasing |
| **historia-ae** [f] | story |
| **ineptus-a-um** | foolish |
| **laborare** | to work |
| **ludus-i** [m] | game, show |
| **meridies** | midday |
| **miseros Christianos!** | wretched Christians |
| **mutilaverunt** | (they) did mutilate |
| **narrat** | (s/he) tells, relates |
| **nobis** | to us, for us |
| **nulla misericordia(-ae)** | no pity |
| **occisi sunt** | were killed |
| **opulentia-ae** [f] | wealth |
| **ostentare** | to show |
| **paganus-i** [m] | pagan |
| **populus-i** [m] | people |
| **pro** [+abl.] | in return for |
| **quando** | when |

| | |
|---|---|
| **qui** | *who* |
| **recitare** | *to recite, read aloud* |
| **rogavit** | *(s/he) asked* |
| **Romanus-i** [m] | *a Roman* |
| **saevitia-ae** [f] | *cruelty* |
| **spectabant** | *(they) used to watch* |
| **suffragium-i** [n] | *vote* |
| **unus** | *one* |
| **victima-ae** [f] | *victim* |
| **volebant** | *(they) wanted* |
| **vult, volunt** | *(s/he) wants, (they) …* |

## Practice (I)

Choose the correct words and translate:

**(a)** Monachi abbatissam videre non (debet/possunt).

**(b)** Abbatissa in culina laborare (debet/volunt) sed in ecclesia monachos spectare (vult/possunt).

**Accusative of exclamation: *Miseros christianos! Me miserum!***

The phrases are both in the accusative without on the face of it being objects. This expression is called the 'accusative of exclamation'. The use of the accusative suggests they are implied objects of a hidden verb.

**Dative case:** *'to, for'*

This is the last of the cases to be studied. If the genitive is the 'of' case, the ablative the 'by, with, in, on' or 'from' case, then the dative may be known as the 'to' or 'for' case. 'To' a place, or 'towards' somewhere, is expressed by **ad** followed by the accusative (e.g. **ad monasterium** *to(wards) the monastery*). Otherwise 'to' something or someone is represented by the dative case:

| | |
|---|---|
| **Augustinus <u>Paulo</u> amicus est.** | *Augustine is friendly <u>to Paul</u> (or Augustine is Paul's friend).* |
| **Non <u>culinae</u> sed <u>scholae</u> est Pauli oboedientia!** | *Not <u>to the kitchen</u> but <u>to the school</u> is Paul's duty!* |

The word in the dative is commonly an indirect, not direct, object of a verb:

| | |
|---|---|
| **Paulus <u>Benedicto</u> cibum vinumque portat.** | *Paul is bringing food and wine for <u>Benedict</u>.* |

**Cibum vinumque** is the object in the accusative, and **Benedicto** the indirect object in the dative.

......................................................................

## Insight

The dative case usually represents an indirect object:
**monachus pecuniam <u>abbatissae</u> dat** = *'the monk gives money <u>to the abbess</u>'*.

......................................................................

|  | Nominative | Accusative | Genitive | Dative | Ablative |
|---|---|---|---|---|---|
| Sing. | silva | silvam | silvae | **silvae** | silva |
|  | mulus | mulum | muli | **mulo** | mulo |
|  | vinum | vinum | vini | **vino** | vino |
| Plural | silvae | silvas | silvarum | **silvis** | silvis |
|  | muli | mulos | mulorum | **mulis** | mulis |
|  | vina | vina | vinorum | **vinis** | vinis |

The dative has a small overlap with the genitive in so far as the dative may also show possession. The genitive is generally attached to another noun (e.g. **magister scholae**), whereas the dative is affected by a verb (often the verb 'to be'). The genitive tends to emphasize the possessor, and where the dative is used, the emphasis is on the thing(s) possessed:

**Sunt Benedicto unguenta.**  *The perfumes are to/for Benedict (Benedict has perfumes).*

'To' or 'for' will help you find the meaning of the dative, but these prepositions are sometimes not appropriate in a final English version. A word in the dative should be taken closely with the verb – be this an indirect object, possessive or whatever.

## Insight

The dative can show possession. The person in possession is in the dative: **Augustino est liber** = *'the book is Augustine's/for Augustine'.*

### Augustinus

🔊 **CD1, TR 7, 01:09**

Mox Stephanus e culina revenit. 'Paulus non in culina laborat sed in silvis vacat.'

'Ex oppido revenit,' inquit Augustinus, qui Paulo est amicus. 'Paulus cibum vinumque ex oppido portat.'

'Cibum vinumque? Quis iussit Paulum ad oppidum ire et cibum vinumque emere?'

'Et oleum et ova et unguenta,' inquit Augustinus.

'Unguenta? Sumus monachi! Et ova? Hic multa sunt ova.'

'Non satis Benedicto, o Magister,' inquit Augustinus. 'Paulus Benedicto cibum vinumque semper dat. Paulus culinae servus est.'

'Neque coquo neque culinae sed magistro et scholae est Pauli oboedientia,' clamavit miser magister.

'Sed nunc Paulus Benedicto est servus,' inquit Augustinus, 'et in culina cum ancillis laborat.'

'In culina cum ancillis?'

'Etiam-ne nos possumus in culina laborare, Domine?'
'St! Tacete! Ad libros! Ubi eram?'
'In culina cum ancillis?' rogant discipuli.
'Me miserum! Ah ... in amphitheatro eram.'

QUICK VOCAB

| | |
|---|---|
| **clamavit** | *wailed* |
| **dat** | *(s/he) gives, is giving* |
| **emere** | *to buy* |
| **eram** | *I was* |
| **ire** | *to go* |
| **iussit** | *(s/he) told, ordered* |
| **miser-a-um** | *wretched* |
| **oboedientia-ae** [f] | *duty* |
| **possumus** | *we are able, can* |
| **satis** | *enough* |
| **servus-i** [m] | *serf, slave* |
| **St!** | *Sssh!* |
| **tacete!** | *be quiet!* |
| **vacat** | *(s/he) is idle* |

## Practice (II)

**1** Add the missing forms to the tables:

| Singular | | | |
|---|---|---|---|
| Nominative | ......... | ......... | ......... | **oleum** |
| Accusative | **agrum** | ......... | ......... | ......... |
| Genitive | **agri** | ......... | **culinae** | ......... |
| Dative | ......... | **coquo** | ......... | ......... |
| Ablative | ......... | ......... | ......... | **oleo** |
| Plural | | | |
| Nominative | ......... | ......... | ......... | ......... |
| Accusative | ......... | ......... | ......... | ......... |
| Genitive | ......... | ......... | **culinarum** | **oleorum** |
| Dative | **coquis** | ......... | ......... | ......... |
| Ablative | **agris** | ......... | ......... | ......... |

**2** Put each noun in its correct form and translate:

    **(a)** (Ancilla/Ancillae) (discipulos/discipulis) cibum portat.

    **(b)** Discipulus non (episcopi/episcopo) sed (abbatissae/
        abbatissa) unguentum dat.

**3** Change the underlined words to the singular (other
   endings should be changed if affected) and translate the
   new version:

    **(a)** Episcopus historiam monasterii <u>presbyteris
        monachisque</u> narrat.

    **(b)** <u>Discipuli</u> ignavi Luciam spectant.

    **(c)** Miser mulus sarcinas <u>onerosas</u> semper portat.

    **(d)** Cur <u>ancillae</u> cum <u>monachis</u> laborare debent?

## About Latin

### Latin wanted – dead or alive?

After the Renaissance Latin survived as the language of scholars
and intellectuals, and with Greek was a fertile source for scientists
and innovators looking for new words and names. The majority
of these are unwieldy and obscure, though shorter ones were also
coined, sometimes for wider commercial impact. A scientist will
deliberately choose a long-winded word which has little appeal
to the rest of us because he has to be as precise as he can. Any
word which spills into everyday use, where it may pick up further,
figurative meanings (e.g. *magnet, radical, livid*), will lose its
specialist value.

Some Latin-derived words mean much the same as a native English
word, though tend to be more formal: someone who admits he
is 'culpable' is almost too clever to be given the blame (**culpa**); to
'concur' (**concurrere**) is somehow not as supportive as 'agree'. But
this gives the wrong impression of the Latin language, and not an
entirely representative one of its influence on English. There are
also countless shorter words derived from Latin, many via French,
whose origins we hardly notice. Examples with Latin ancestors
in the last few passages are: *vacant, data, servile, labour, wine,
doctor, popular, spectator, unit, history, obscure* and *mural*.
Some Latin words have been absorbed in their original form,
e.g *aborigine, agenda, arena, computer, deficit, facsimile, genius,
junior, miser, rabies, recipe, referendum, series, squalor, status,
video* and *virus*.

The correct form of the plural of Latin-derived words remains
debatable. For instance, Latin-derived words which end *-um* in
the singular change to *-a* in the plural (e.g. *curriculum, curricula*);
others are similar according to declension and form. The trouble
with this rule is its inconsistency. Some loan-words like *circus*
and *area* already had ordinary English plurals before the influx
of further loan-words during the Renaissance. Others such as

*affidavit* (*s/he has affirmed*) and *recipe* (*take...* i.e. ingredients, the first word of cooking instructions) are nouns now but in Latin were verbs. The plural of these can hardly be **affidaverunt** and **recipite**, which are the respective plural forms in Latin. Should we be receiving **boni** in place of *bonuses*? *Referendums* is heavier on the ear than *referenda*, but *agendum* is a rather unwieldy singular form of *agenda* (and *agendas*, the 'plural of a plural', is now commonplace).

A number of Latin-derived words and phrases are current in legal and other technical uses of English. Recently there has been a move to rid the language of such obscure archaisms, but will the awkward phrases or forgettable acronyms which may replace them be an improvement? In any case, **ad hoc, status quo** and **et cetera** can scarcely be called Latin any more. These words and phrases are now part of English. And this is a good point to move on, for the purpose of this course is not to pick over Latin's lifeless present, but sample the living past.

---

## Living Latin

🔊 **CD1, TR 7, 02:22**

**1** *****Si monumentum quaeris circumspice.**

(Epitaph of Christopher Wren in St Paul's Cathedral)

*If you seek a memorial, look around you.*

**2** *****Nihil est in intellectu quod non fuerit in sensu.**

(Locke, 17th century)

**Excipe: nisi ipse intellectus.**

(Leibnitz, 17th/18th century)

*There is nothing in the mind which exists separate from the senses.*
*With one exception: the mind itself.*

3 *Floreas longum, America, o beata,
  libera et felix vigeas in aevum.

(Samuel Wilson c.18th century)

*Blessed America, long may you flourish, and enjoy your freedom and good fortune far into the future.*

4 *Inter Vietnamiam et Civitates Americae Unitas
  relationes diplomaticae coniunguntur. De ea re praesidens
  Bill Clinton oratione sollemni in Aedibus Albis die Martis habita
  nuntiavit.

(The Finnish Broadcasting Company, Nuntii Latini)

*Diplomatic relations between Vietnam and the United States of America are being restored. On that matter President Bill Clinton made an announcement in a formal speech in the White House on Tuesday.*

*post-classical

# TESTING YOURSELF

**1** Make a phrase which is current in English with these words:
  **(a)** initium-i (*beginning*), ab
  **(b)** annus-i (*year*), dominus-i (*lord, master*)
  **(c)** vita-ae (*life*), curriculum-i (*course*)
  **(d)** ceterus-a-um (*other, rest*), et
  **(e)** nausea-ae (*sickness*), ad
  **(f)** infinitus-a-um (*endless*), ad

**2** Rewrite these sentences, changing the underlined words into the plural, and translate:
  **(a)** <u>Bestia-ne</u> <u>Christianum</u> in amphitheatro devorat?
  **(b)** <u>Monachus</u> bonus ludos saevos non amat.
  **(c)** Paulus-ne <u>coquo</u> cibum vinumque semper portat?
  **(d)** Cur discipulo <u>librum</u> magister dat?

**3** Add the missing forms to the table:

|  | Singular | | |
|---|---|---|---|
| Case | **paganus-i** [m]<br>*pagan* | **oppidum-i** [n]<br>*town* | **bestia-ae** [f]<br>*animal* |
| Nominative | ......... | ......... | ......... |
| Accusative | ......... | ......... | ......... |
| Genitive | ......... | oppidi | bestiae |
| Dative | ......... | ......... | ......... |
| Ablative | pagano | ......... | ......... |
|  | Plural | | |
| Nominative | ......... | ......... | ......... |
| Accusative | ......... | oppida | bestias |
| Genitive | paganorum | ......... | ......... |
| Dative | ......... | ......... | ......... |
| Ablative | ......... | ......... | ......... |

**4** Translate into Latin:

   **(a)** Paul gives much food to the cook.

   **(b)** The student ought to walk not with the maids but with the monks.

   **(c)** The monks want to watch the games but have to work in the monastery.

   **(d)** Is Lucia able to work in the kitchen?

**5** Check you know these words:
amphitheatrum-i, ancilla-ae, annus-i, dat, debet, dominus-i, etiam, facit, gratus-a-um, miser-a-um, narrat, populus-i, qui, recitat, satis, scribit, unus-a-um, vita-ae, vult.

**6** How many English words can you make by matching the prepositions on the left with the stems on the right – e.g. *pre* + *fer* = *prefer*, *preference*, etc.?

| | |
|---|---|
| **ad** (*to*) | **dic-** (*say*) |
| **con-, com-, coll-** (*with, together*) | **duc-** (*bring*) |
| | **fer-** (*carry, bear*) |
| **contra-** (*against*) | **habit-** (*live*) |
| **de-** (*down, from*) | **iac-/jac-** (*lie*) |
| **e(x)-** (*out, from*) | **labor-** (*work*) |
| **in-, im-** (*in, on*) | **mit-** (*send*) |
| **per-** (*through*) | **port-** (*carry*) |
| **pre-** (*before*) | **scrib-** (*write*) |
| **pro-** (*forward*) | **ven-** (*come*) |
| **re-** (*back*) | |
| **sub-** (*under, beneath*) | |
| **trans-** (*across*) | |

**7** Does **persona non grata** mean **(a)** an ungrateful cleric; **(b)** someone out of favour; **(c)** pay now, no credit?

# Revision i (Units 1–6)

**1** Identify the correct form of the nouns in brackets (the nominative and genitive forms are given):

**(a)** Abbatissa (bestia-ae) sanctam timet.

**(b)** Ova in (episcopus-i) ignavum cadunt.

**(c)** Liber Augustini non
(discipulus-i) furiosis sed (ancilla-ae)
gratus est.

**(d)** (Benedictus-i) gulosus
unguenta (abbatissa-ae)
odorae desiderat.

**2** Rewrite these sentences, changing underlined words to
the plural if they are singular, or to the singular if plural.
Translate the new version.

**(a)** <u>Monachus</u> muros monasterii videre potest.

**(b)** Misera <u>ancilla</u> semper in <u>culina</u> laborat.

**(c)** <u>Puer</u> <u>mulo</u> cibum dat.

**(d)** Cur est <u>abbatissa</u> in bibliotheca?

**(e)** Ludos <u>monachi</u> non spectant.

**(f)** <u>Episcopi</u>-ne in <u>monasteriis</u> habitant?

**(g)** <u>Monachus</u> <u>feminae</u> aquam dat.

**3** What do these words mean?

| saepe | igitur | ad |
|-------|--------|------|
| enim | cum | ubi |
| quod | nunc | ex |
| cur | nonne | per |
| semper | mox | hodie |

**4** Translate into Latin:
- **(a)** Are the students tired?
- **(b)** An evil monk cannot live in the monastery.
- **(c)** The furious master gives books to the wretched students.
- **(d)** The mistress's daughter is unable to work in the kitchen. Surely she ought not to walk with the students?
- **(e)** Can the horses hear the mule in the wood? He is bringing the horses' food to the monastery.

**5** Fill the table with the correct forms of **magnus-a-um** *large, great*:

|  | Masculine | Feminine | Neuter |
|---|---|---|---|
| Singular | | | |
| Nominative | ......... | ......... | ......... |
| Accusative | ......... | ......... | ......... |
| Genitive | ......... | ......... | ......... |
| Dative | ......... | ......... | ......... |
| Ablative | ......... | ......... | ......... |
| Plural | | | |
| Nominative | ......... | ......... | ......... |
| Accusative | ......... | ......... | ......... |
| Genitive | ......... | ......... | ......... |
| Dative | ......... | ......... | ......... |
| Ablative | ......... | ......... | ......... |

**6** Pronounce the following words in the recommended classical manner:

| | | |
|---|---|---|
| bonus | miser | bona fide |
| data | Cicero | angelus |
| pater | mater | et cetera |
| alibi | circus | recipe |
| alias | pauper | veto |
| video | agenda | genius |

**7** What do these nouns mean?
- **(i)** aqua-ae, bestia-ae, domina-ae, femina-ae, filia-ae, silva-ae, terra-ae, umbra-ae, via-ae, vita-ae.
- **(ii)** annus-i, deus-i, dominus-i, episcopus-i, equus-i, filius-i, liber-bri, magister-tri, monachus-i, mulus-i, murus-i, populus-i, puer-i, servus-i, ventus-i.
- **(iii)** folium-i, oppidum-i, ovum-i, silentium-i, vinum-i.

**8** If you know **deus-i**, can you work out what **dea-ae** means?

**9** What do these adjectives mean?
bonus-a-um, fessus-a-um, gratus-a-um, ignavus-a-um, iratus-a-um, lentus-a-um, magnus-a-um, malus-a-um, miser-a-um, multus-a-um, obscurus-a-um, saevus-a-um, sanctus-a-um.

**10** Is vespa-ae **(a)** a wasp; **(b)** an abbreviated version of ancient evensong; **(c)** an early medieval form of bicycle?

# 7

## Puer cum diabolo ambulat
## The boy walks with the devil

In this unit you will learn about
- *Third declension nouns*
- *And find out more about Roman gods in 'Di immortales'*

### Nouns: third declension

So far you have met the first declension (nouns like **silva**) and the second declension (nouns like **mulus**, **magister** and **vinum**). Now for the third. These nouns have many different nominative forms, but the genitive (remember a dictionary will give this form as well) of *all* third declension nouns is **-is**. The genitive will also show you the noun's stem as it appears in all cases other than the nominative, e.g.

**abbas, abbatis** (*stem:* **abbat-**) **abbot**
**arbor, arboris** (*stem:* **arbor-**) **tree**
**pater, patris** (*stem:* **patr-**) **father**
**virgo, virginis** (*stem:* **virgin-**) **maiden, girl**

> **Insight**
> Nouns of the third declension have various different endings in the nominative, but always end **-is** in the genitive.

| Singular | | | | |
|------|------|------|------|------|
| Nom. | abbas | arbor | pater | virgo |
| Acc. | abbat-em | arbor-em | patr-em | virgin-em |
| Gen. | abbat-is | arbor-is | patr-is | virgin-is |
| Dat. | abbat-i | arbor-i | patr-i | virgin-i |
| Abl. | abbat-e | arbor-e | patr-e | virgin-e |

| Plural | | | | |
|------|------|------|------|------|
| Nom. | abbat-es | arbor-es | patr-es | virgin-es |
| Acc. | abbat-es | arbor-es | patr-es | virgin-es |
| Gen. | abbat-um | arbor-um | patr-um | virgin-um |
| Dat. | abbat-ibus | arbor-ibus | patr-ibus | virgin-ibus |
| Abl. | abbat-ibus | arbor-ibus | patr-ibus | virgin-ibus |

## Practice (I)

**1** Translate the underlined nouns into Latin in their correct case:

- **(a)** with the <u>abbots</u>
- **(b)** in the <u>trees</u>
- **(c)** of the <u>maiden</u>
- **(d)** for the <u>father</u>
- **(e)** with the <u>abbot</u>
- **(f)** of the <u>trees</u>
- **(g)** with the <u>father</u>
- **(h)** for the <u>maidens</u>
- **(i)** the <u>father's</u>
- **(j)** he sees the <u>abbot</u>

**2** Identify the English meanings of each noun (look them up in the back if necessary):

**(a)**

| | |
|---|---|
| superstitio, superstitionis | *sun* |
| virtus, virtutis | *love* |
| pax, pacis | *mind* |
| mens, mentis | *peace* |
| sol, solis | *virtue* |
| amor, amoris | *superstition* |

**(b)**

| | |
|---|---|
| miles, militis | *ox* |
| homo, hominis | *soldier* |
| bos, bovis | *mother* |
| panis, panis | *man* |
| rex, regis | *king* |
| mater, matris | *bread* |

**3** Rewrite these sentences, changing underlined words to the plural if they are singular, or to the singular if plural. Translate the new version.

  **(a)** <u>Rex</u> in monasterio non habitat.
  **(b)** Monachus <u>bovem</u> in silva videre potest.
  **(c)** Virtutem <u>matris</u> laudant.
  **(d)** <u>Amicus</u>-ne <u>abbatis</u> <u>gratus</u> est <u>militi</u>?

  **O di immortales!** *Oh immortal gods!*

◀) **CD1, TR 8**

| **Shared endings key** | |
|---|---|
| **-is** silvis, mulis, vinis: dat. pl. or abl. pl. | **-e** 3rd declension: ablative |
|     3rd declension: genitive |     mule, Paule: vocative |
| **-i** muli: nom. pl.; muli: vini: genitive | **-um** mulum: acc. |
|     3rd declension: dative |     vinum: nom. or acc. |
| **-es** 3rd declension: nom. pl. or acc. pl. |     3rd declension: gen. pl. |

Stephanus discipulis fessis Romae historiam adhuc narrabat. 'At Romanis erant multi dei deaeque. Iuppiter deus erat caeli, Diana silvarum et venationis, Mars belli et militum, Venus amoris,

Neptunus aequoris, Apollo solis et carminum. Quomodo autem possumus, ut dicit unus ex sanctis, "commemorari omnia nomina deorum et dearum?" Quis vero sapiens piusque in tot deos credere potest?'

'Liberum amo!' susurravit Augustinus.

'Quid?'

'Nihil, Magister.'

'Quid dixisti?'

'Librum amo.'

'Bene. Mox librum recitabis exscribesque. Ubi eram? ... Dei deaeque ergo in fabulis male se gerebant, et nunc nobis illae superstitiones sunt exempla turpitudinis. Neque enim virtutem laudabant neque animas hominum curabant. Deus tamen, creator terrae caelique hominumque bestiarumque, semper nos omnes curat. "Num," ut dicit sanctus Boethius, "Deus facere malum potest?" Nos sumus omnes semper carissimi Deo...'

'Magister, ecce Paulus!' Augustinus clamavit.

'... fortasse praeter Paulum. Ubi est ille delinquens?' inquit Stephanus, et ad fenestram festinavit. 'Nihil videre possum nisi boves ovesque.'

'Paulus sub arboribus cum virgine ambulat.'

'Cum virgine?' Stephanus Paulum et Luciam conspexit. 'Mehercule,' inquit, 'illa est virgo!' et statim discipuli libros reliquerunt et ad fenestram festinaverunt. 'Ad libros, o inepti, ad libros! Cibum vinumque scilicet! Paulus modo cum ancillis modo cum virgine vacat. O di immortales!'

| | |
|---:|:---|
| **adhuc** | *still* |
| **aequor-is** [n] | *water, sea* |
| **aliquis** | *someone* |
| **amo** | *I love* |
| **amor-is** [m] | *love* |
| **anima-ae** [f] | *soul* |
| **at** | *but, yet* |
| **autem** | *however* |
| **bellum-i** [n] | *war* |
| **bene** | *fine* |

QUICK VOCAB

| | |
|---|---|
| **caelum-i** [n] | *heaven, sky* |
| **carissimus-a-um** | *very dear, special* |
| **carmen-inis** [n] | *song, poem* |
| **clamavit** | *(s/he) shouted* |
| **commemorari** | *to remember, relate* |
| **conspexit** | *(s/he) caught sight of* |
| **creator-is** [m] | *creator* |
| **credere** | *to believe* |
| **curabant** [+acc.] | *(they) cared for* |
| **curat** [+acc.] | *(s/he) cares for* |
| **dea-ae** [f] | *goddess* |
| **deus-i** (n.pl.: **di**) [m] | *god* |
| **di immortales** | *immortal gods* |
| **dicit (dixisti)** | *(s/he) says (you said)* |
| **ecce** | *look* |
| **exemplum-i** [n] | *example, proof* |
| **exscribes** | *you will write out* |
| **facere** | *to do, make* |
| **fenestra-ae** [f] | *window* |
| **festinaverunt** | *(they) hurried* |
| **fortasse** | *perhaps* |
| **homo-inis** [m] | *man* |
| **illa** | *that, she* |
| **illae** | *those* |
| **ille delinquens** | *that delinquent* |
| **Iuppiter** | *Jupiter* |
| **laudabant** | *(they) praised* |
| **liber-bri** [m] | *book* |
| **Liber-i** [m] | *Liber, god of wine* |
| **male se gerebant** | *(they) conducted themselves badly* |
| **mehercule!** | *well I be Hercules!* |
| **miles-itis** [m] | *soldier* |
| **modo... modo** | *one minute ... the next* |
| **narrabat** | *(s/he) was recounting* |
| **nihil** | *nothing* |
| **nisi** | *except* |
| **nomina** [acc.] [n] | *names* |

| | |
|---|---|
| **omnia** [n.pl.] | *all* |
| **pius-a-um** | *pious, dutiful* |
| **possum (possumus)** | *I am able (we…)* |
| **praeter** [+acc.] | *except, besides* |
| **quomodo** | *how* |
| **recitabis** | *you will recite* |
| **reliquerunt** | *(they) left* |
| **sapiens** | *wise* |
| **scilicet!** | *my foot!* |
| **sol-is** [m] | *sun* |
| **sub** [+abl.] | *beneath* |
| **superstitio-nis** [f] | *superstition* |
| **susurravit** | *(s/he) whispered* |
| **tot** | *so many* |
| **turpitudo-inis** [f] | *disgraceful behaviour* |
| **ut** | *as* |
| **vacat** | *(s/he) idles* |
| **venatio-nis** [f] | *hunt* |
| **virtus-tutis** [f] | *courage, virtue* |

## The third declension: neuter nouns *-us, -en*

Like all neuter nouns, the nominative and accusative endings are the same, with the plural always -**a**. Do not confuse nouns like **mulus** with third declension neuter nouns like **tempus**. Having learned the ending -**um** to be the object ending of -**us**, you now have to recognize that -**us** may be an object ending itself! The genitive, dative and ablative endings are the same as those of other third declension nouns:

| | **tempus** *time* | **carmen** *song, poem* |
|---|---|---|
| | Singular | |
| Nom. | tempus | carmen |
| Acc. | tempus | carmen |
| Gen. | temporis | carminis |
| Dat. | tempori | carmini |
| Abl. | tempore | carmine |

| Plural | | |
|---|---|---|
| Nom. | **tempora** | **carmina** |
| Acc. | **tempora** | **carmina** |
| Gen. | **temporum** | **carminum** |
| Dat. | **temporibus** | **carminibus** |
| Abl. | **temporibus** | **carminibus** |

## Insight

All neuter nouns and adjectives end **-a** in the nominative and accusative plurals.

### Practice (II)

**1** Identify the English meanings of each noun:

| | |
|---|---|
| opus, operis | *name* |
| nomen, nominis | *task* |
| munus, muneris | *body* |
| corpus, corporis | *gift* |

**2** Translate into Latin:
  **(a)** the names of the abbots
  **(b)** mother's gifts
  **(c)** many tasks
  **(d)** the bodies of the beasts
  **(e)** the songs of the abbot
  **(f)** (with) pleasing songs

*Paulus cum diabolo ambulat* Paulus walks with the devil

◀)) **CD1, TR 8, 02:13**

| **Shared endings key** | |
|---|---|
| **-us** tempus: nom. or acc.<br>mulus: nom. | **-a** tempora, carmina: nom. or acc. pl.<br>silva: nom. or abl.<br>vina: nom. pl. or acc. pl. |

In culina ancillae strenuae cenam magnam parant; nam hodie abbatem ex abbatum convocatione exspectant. Aliae igitur potiones aliae carnem aliae panem aliae crusta aliae fruges parant. Deinde operibus fessae in horto requiescunt.

Mox Paulum et Luciam conspexerunt. 'Quis est illa? Quid est puellae nomen?' rogavit una ex ancillis.

'Filia est Comitis Karoli, nomine Lucia,' inquit alia. Nunc ancillae possunt videre abbatissam abbatemque qui Luciam salutant. Interea Benedictus culinam intravit.

'Age, tempus fugit!' clamavit coquus. 'Ubi sunt unguenta vinaque? Ubi est ignavus servus?'

'Hic est puer, Pater Benedicte, nunc Paulus adest.'

'Dico vobis, puer ille ignavus cum diabolo ambulat ... Sancta Maria! Paulus cum abbatissa ambulat? Num abbatissa salutem dicit puero? Quid fit? Nunc puer abbati salutem dicit! Dic mihi, nam scire volo: quis est illa virgo? Est-ne puer nunc magnus et abbati amicus? Paulo gratiam et munera praebeo, sed quid ille puer Benedicto dat?'

'Ecce, nunc venit.'

'Videre est credere.'

Una ancillarum e culina ad Paulum festinavit. 'Age, Paule, Pater Benedictus sarcinas desiderat!'

Paulus 'ubi Patris Benedicti,' inquit, 'est temperantia?'

| | |
|---|---|
| **adest** | *(s/he) is here* |
| **age** | *come on!* |
| **alia** | *another (person)* |
| **aliae... aliae** | *some... others* |
| **amicus-i** [m] | *friend* |
| **caro, carnis** [f] | *flesh, meat* |
| **cena-ae** [f] | *dinner* |
| **comes-itis** [m] | *count* |
| **conspexerunt** | *(they) caught sight of* |
| **convocatio-nis** [f] | *conference* |
| **crustum-i** [n] | *pastry, cake* |
| **dat** | *(s/he) gives* |
| **diabolus-i** [m] | *devil* |

QUICK VOCAB

| | |
|---|---|
| **dic mihi** | *tell me* |
| **dico vobis** | *I tell you* |
| **exspectant** | *(they) wait for* |
| **festinavit** | *(s/he) hurried* |
| **frux-gis [f]** | *fruit* |
| **fugit** | *(s/he/it) flees, flies* |
| **gratia-ae[f]** | *favour* |
| **hic** | *here* |
| **hortus-i [m]** | *garden* |
| **ille [m], illa [f]** | *he/she, that* |
| **interea** | *meanwhile* |
| **intravit** | *(s/he) entered* |
| **Karolus-i [m]** | *Charles* |
| **nam** | *for* |
| **panis-is [m]** | *bread* |
| **parent** | *(they) prepare* |
| **possunt** | *(they) are able* |
| **potio-nis [f]** | *drink* |
| **praebeo** | *I give, offer* |
| **qui** | *who* |
| **quid fit?** | *what's going on?* |
| **requiescunt** | *(they) relax* |
| **salutant** | *(they) greet* |
| **salutem dicit** | *(s/he) says hello* |
| **scire** | *to know* |
| **strenuus-a-um** | *energetic* |
| **temperantia-ae [f]** | *restraint* |
| **volo** | *I want* |

---

## Living Latin

🔊 **CD1, TR 8, 04:00**

### *Di immortales* Immortal gods

Countless stories from Greek mythology were unravelled in Latin and with them came their gods: Zeus, Aphrodite, Ares, Hephaistos and Artemis were absorbed and further embellished in Jupiter, Venus, Mars, Vulcan and Diana. These pagan gods were not only pagan, they were immoral. The stories about them were so appealing to the monks that after overcoming resistance they came to settle on monastic shelves as allegories, not heresies.

**1** Vulcan, the god of the forge, finds his wife Venus is having a fling with Mars, the god of war. So using his skills, Vulcan sets a trap.

**Ut venere torum coniunx et adulter in unum,**
**arte viri vinclisque nova ratione paratis**
**in mediis ambo deprensi amplexibus haerent.**
**Lemnius extemplo valvas patefecit eburnas**
**inmisitque deos; illi iacuere ligati**
**turpiter, atque aliquis de dis non tristibus optat**
**sic fieri turpis; superi risere diuque**
**haec fuit in toto notissima fabula caelo.**

(Ovid, Metamorphoses iv, 182–9)

*When his wife and her adulterer came together on the couch, by his skill and with the chains which he had so cleverly set up, they were both caught fast in each other's arms. Immediately the Lemnian god opened the ivory doors and let in the other gods: there the two lay in their shaming bondage – and one of the gods, who were much tickled, wished he could be so ashamed. The gods laughed, and for a long time this story went the rounds of heaven.*

**2** In another story Venus gently brings her husband round to her way of thinking.

**Dixerat et niveis hinc atque hinc diva lacertis**
**cunctantem amplexu molli fovet. Ille repente**
**accepit solitam flammam, notusque medullas**
**intravit calor et labefacta per ossa cucurrit.**

(Virgil, Aeneid viii, 387–90)

*Venus finished speaking, and slipping her snow-white arms this way and that, wraps him up in a cuddle. He hesitates. Then suddenly he felt that familiar rush and recognized the glow as it penetrated his innermost core flickering through his trembling bones.*

**3**  Lucretius, a poet-philosopher and contemporary of Cicero, had little time for the gods.

**Quippe ita formido mortalis continet omnis,**
**quod multa in terris fieri caeloque tuentur**
**quorum operum causas nulla ratione videre**
**possunt ac fieri divino numine rentur.**

(Lucretius, De rerum natura i, 151–4)

*There's no question all mortals are repressed by fear: they see many phenomena on earth and in the sky which they are unable to account for with any rational explanation, so they imagine them to be the work of gods.*

# TESTING YOURSELF

**1** Fill the gaps:

| Case | corpus, corporis [n] *body* | homo, hominis [m] *man, person* | potio, potionis [f] *drink* |
|---|---|---|---|
| | Singular | | |
| Nominative | corpus | ......... | ......... |
| Accusative | ......... | hominem | ......... |
| Genitive | ......... | ......... | potionis |
| Dative | corpori | ......... | ......... |
| Ablative | ......... | ......... | ......... |
| | Plural | | |
| Nominative | ......... | ......... | ......... |
| Accusative | corpora | ......... | potiones |
| Genitive | ......... | hominum | ......... |
| Dative | ......... | ......... | ......... |
| Ablative | ......... | ......... | ......... |

**2** Rewrite these sentences, making the underlined words plural:
   **(a)** <u>Munus</u> discipuli dominae gratum est.
   **(b)** Num magister in <u>superstitionem</u> credit?
   **(c)** Augustinus <u>carmen</u> <u>virgini</u> recitat.
   **(d)** <u>Monachus</u> pacem, <u>miles</u> bellum desiderat.

**3** Translate into Latin:
  **(a)** Who is the goddess of love? Is it Diana?
  **(b)** The abbess walks with Father Benedict into the wood.
  **(c)** Are the maiden's songs pleasing to the abbot?
  **(e)** Why does Benedict always long for meat, bread and cakes?

**4** Check you know these words:
  abbas-atis, age!, amor-is, anima-ae, arbor-is, bellum-i, bene, bos-vis, caelum-i, carmen-inis, cena-ae, corpus-oris, gratia-ae, homo-inis, hortus-i, interea, mater-tris, miles-itis, munus-eris, nam, nihil, nomen-inis, opus-eris, panis-is, pater-tris, pax-cis, rex-gis, tempus-oris, virgo-inis.

**5** From the words in 4, list the following:
  **(a)** all nouns like **silva** (1st declension)
  **(b)** all nouns like **mulus** (2nd declension)
  **(c)** all nouns like **vinum** (2nd declension neuter)
  **(d)** all neuter 3rd declension nouns, like **carmen** or **tempus**
  **(e)** all other 3rd declension nouns.

# 8

# Nos fortunatos!
## How lucky we are!

In this unit you will learn about
- *Verbs: first and second conjugations*
- *And find out more about Latin authors in 'Brotherly love'*

**Present tense:** *amo* I love, *amare* to love

| | |
|---|---|
| *I love (am loving/do love)* | **am-o** |
| *you* (singular) *love (are loving/do love)* | **am-as** |
| *s/he, it loves (is loving/does love)* | **am-at** |
| *we love (are loving/do love)* | **am-amus** |
| *you* (plural) *love (are loving/do love)* | **am-atis** |
| *they love (are loving/do love)* | **am-ant** |

## Insight
For more about verbs see **Essential Grammar** in the **Introduction**.

### Practice (I)

**1** All these verbs belong to the first conjugation, and have endings like **amo, amare**. Match each one to its English meaning (look in the vocabulary section if necessary). See also the Index of Grammar Support on p. 300 to find the meaning of grammatical terms used in this book.

**(a)**

| | |
|---|---|
| ambulo-are | *think* |
| desidero-are | *watch* |
| habito-are | *prepare* |
| laboro-are | *greet* |
| paro-are | *ask* |
| puto-are | *walk* |
| rogo-are | *live* |
| saluto-are | *work* |
| specto-are | *long for** |

**(c)**

| | |
|---|---|
| curo-are | *ride* |
| damno-are | *fly* |
| do-are | *stand* |
| devoro-are | *explain* |
| equito-are | *whisper* |
| explico-are | *eat* |
| sto-are | *give* |
| susurro-are | *care for/look after** |
| volito-are | *condemn* |

**(b)**

| | |
|---|---|
| intro-are | *tell/narrate* |
| laudo-are | *recite* |
| monstro-are | *save/preserve* |
| mutilo-are | *beg/pray* |
| narro-are | *enter* |
| oro-are | *show/point out* |
| recito-are | *tolerate* |
| servo-are | *mutilate* |
| tolero-are | *praise* |

**(d)**

| | |
|---|---|
| aestimo-are | *show off* |
| canto-are | *punish* |
| castigo-are | *sing* |
| clamo-are | *preach* |
| exspecto-are | *hurry* |
| festino-are | *wait for** |
| ostento-are | *estimate/value* |
| praedico-are | *shout* |
| vaco-are | *be empty, idle* |

---

### Insight

The two forms of the present tense in English (*'she watches'* and *'she is watching'*) are expressed the same in Latin: **spectat**. Likewise in the plural: *'they watch'* or *'they are watching'* = **spectant**.

---

*These Latin verbs take an object in the <u>accusative</u> even though the English has a preposition to complete the meaning: e.g. **mulum curat** *s/he cares for the mule.*

**2** Translate the underlined verbs into Latin:

**(a)** They <u>wait for</u> the student.

**(b)** We <u>praise</u> the monk.

**(c)** He <u>is idle</u>.

**(d)** You <u>are working</u>, boys.

**(e)** I <u>am reciting</u> a poem.

**(f)** They <u>whisper</u>.

**(g)** He does not <u>ride</u>.

**(h)** They <u>are preparing</u> dinner.

**(i)** She <u>greets</u> Augustine.

**(j)** Horses do not <u>fly</u>.

**(k)** The bishop <u>is preaching</u>.

**(l)** The cook <u>looks after</u> the wine.

**(m)** Why are you <u>punishing</u> the student, Stephen?

**Present tense:** *moneo* I warn, *monere* to warn

The endings of verbs like **amare** and those like **monere**
are very similar but for the 'a' and 'e'. **Amare** belongs to the
first conjugation, **monere** to the second (there are five conjugations
in all, the third, fourth and fifth all being fairly similar).

| | |
|---|---|
| *I warn (am warning/do warn)* | **mon-eo** |
| *you* (singular) *warn (are warning/do warn)* | **mon-es** |
| *s/he, it warns (is warning/does warn)* | **mon-et** |
| *we warn (are warning/do warn)* | **mon-emus** |
| *you* (plural) *warn (are warning/do warn)* | **mon-etis** |
| *they warn (are warning/do warn)* | **mon-ent** |

## Practice (II)

**1** Match each verb to its English meaning:

**(a)**

| | |
|---|---|
| debeo-ere | *remain/stay* |
| doceo-ere | *lie* |
| doleo-ere | *order* |
| habeo-ere | *have* |
| iaceo-ere | *teach* |
| iubeo-ere | *grieve* |
| maneo-ere | *owe/ought* |

**(b)**

| | |
|---|---|
| respondeo-ere | *fear* |
| rideo-ere | *laugh/smile* |
| sedeo-ere | *sit* |
| taceo-ere | *be silent* |
| teneo-ere | *see* |
| timeo-ere | *hold* |
| video-ere | *reply* |

**2** Translate the underlined verbs into Latin:
- **(a)** <u>We sit</u> in the field.
- **(b)** <u>They fear</u> the woods.
- **(c)** <u>She is warning</u> the maids.
- **(d)** <u>Are you laughing</u>, students?
- **(e)** <u>We stay</u> in the monastery.
- **(f)** <u>Do they reply</u>?
- **(g)** <u>Are you teaching</u> the students, Stephen?
- **(h)** <u>They grieve</u> in the church.

***Quanti diligentiam aestimas?*** *How much do you value hard work?*

◀) CD1, TR 9

| Shared endings key |
|---|
| **-es** 3rd declension: nom. pl.   **-as** 1st declension: acc. pl. (silvas)<br>or acc. pl. |
| **mones:** 'you...' (s.)                    **amas:** 'you...' (s.) |

'Sancti igitur,' inquit Stephanus, 'exempla nobis virtutum et pagani vitiorum monstrant. Sancti nos vitam bonam, pagani malam, docent. Carmina quidem Romana superstitionibus fabulisque deorum sunt plena; sed nonne poetae deos esse falsos putaverunt? Lucretius certe in illos non credidit et originem superstitionum sic explicat: "*Formido mortales continet omnes*". Nunc poetarum opera magni aestimamus et in monasterii bibliotheca servamus: fabulas enim sicut allegorias tolerabimus nec damnabimus. Nos fortunatos! Nunc multos carminum libros in bibliotheca habemus. Nunc ergo ad legendum … hoc opus, hic labor est.'

'Cur tibi soli mortui poetae sunt grati, o Pater Stephane?' inquit Augustinus. 'Poeta Martialis olim dicebat: "*Nec laudas nisi mortuos poetas*".'

'Hodie, o pueri, opus non Martialis sed Vergilii recitabimus:
"*Aurora interea miseris mortalibus almam extulerat lucem referens opera atque labores …*" Quis est ille?'

'Ignoscas, Pater Stephane.'

'Paule? Nunc ades? O male discipule! Cur lascive in silvis vacas ubi in bibliotheca adesse debes? Dolebis certe, o puer, et te castigabo.'

'Magister, erat puella in silva.'

'Ita vero.'

'Saucia erat.'

'Saucia, puto, amore.'

'Ex equo cecidit, Magister.'

'Cecidit scilicet, puer. Unde? De caelo? Equus-ne in caelo volitabat? Ut poma de arboribus sic virgines de caelo cadunt?' Alii discipuli rident.

'Magister, vera tibi dico.'

'Vera? O tempora o mores! Putas-ne studia esse nugas? Quanti diligentiam aestimas?'

'Magni, Pater Stephane, magni.'

'O Paule, magister non saevus sum, sed diligentiam te docebo. Vides-ne hunc librum?'

'Video, Magister.'

'Hodie liber est exscribendus; etiam in noctem, si necesse est, laborabis.'

'Hodie?'

| | |
|---|---|
| **ad legendum** | *to (our) reading* |
| **agamus** | *we should do* |
| **alii** | *the other (pl)* |
| **allegoria-ae** [f] | *allegory* |
| **'Aurora…'** | *see Unit 1* |

| | |
|---|---|
| **cadunt** | *(they) fall* |
| **cecidit** | *(s/he) fell* |
| **certe** | *at least, of course* |
| **credidit** | *(s/he) believed* |
| **de** [+abl.] | *from, about* |
| **dicebat** | *(s/he) said* |
| **diligentia-ae** [f] | *attentiveness* |
| **ergo** | *so, therefore* |
| **exemplum-i** [n] | *example, precedent* |
| **exscribendus-a-um** | *to be written out* |
| **fabula-ae** [f] | *story* |
| **falsus-a-um** | *false* |
| **'formido...'** | *see Unit 7* |
| **fortunatus-a-um** | *happy, lucky* |
| **hoc... hic** | *this... this* |
| **hunc** | *this* |
| **in illos** | *in them* |
| **laborabis** | *you will work* |
| **labor-is** [m] | *work* |
| **lascive** | *wantonly* |
| **magni** | *much, greatly* |
| **mortuus-a-um** | *dead* |
| **nec** | *and...not* |
| **nugae-arum** [pl.] | *trifles, nonsense* |
| **o tempora o mores!** | *see Unit 1* |
| **olim** | *once (upon a time)* |
| **origo-inis** [f] | *origin* |
| **paganus-i** [m] | *pagan* |
| **plenus-a-um** [+abl.] | *filled (with)* |
| **poeta-ae** [m] | *poet* |
| **pomum-i** [n] | *fruit* |
| **putaverunt** | *(they) thought* |
| **quanti** | *how much, at what value* |
| **quidem** | *in fact* |
| **saucius-a-um** | *wounded, smitten* |
| **si** | *if* |
| **sic** | *thus* |
| **sicut** | *just as, as if* |
| **solus-a-um** | *only, alone* |

| | |
|---|---|
| **studium-i** [n] | *study* |
| **tibi** [dative] | *(to) you* |
| **tolero-are** | *endure, support* |
| **unde** | *from where* |
| **ut** | *as* |
| **vita-ae** [f] | *life* |
| **vitium-i** [n] | *vice* |
| **volitabat** | *(s/he, it) was flying* |

## Future tense: *amo, amare; moneo, monere*

The future tense is expressed in English with the help of auxiliaries (*shall, will, going to*). In Latin there's only one word to cover the pronoun (*I, you, he*, etc.) and the tense itself. So, not so many words to remember, but once more the inevitable endings; at least they are the same for both verbs:

| Future | | | |
|---|---|---|---|
| *I shall love* | **ama-bo** | *I shall warn* | **mone-bo** |
| *you* (s.) *will love* | **ama-bis** | *you* (s.) *will warn* | **mone-bis** |
| *s/he, it will love* | **ama-bit** | *s/he, it will warn* | **mone-bit** |
| *we shall love* | **ama-bimus** | *we shall warn* | **mone-bimus** |
| *you* (pl.) *will love* | **ama-bitis** | *you* (pl.) *will warn* | **mone-bitis** |
| *they will love* | **ama-bunt** | *they will warn* | **mone-bunt** |

## Practice (III)

**1** Identify the correct endings of **canto, cantare** and **iaceo, iacere**:

    **(a)** Corpus in terra ____

**(b)** Pater Benedictus ____

**2** Translate the underlined verbs into Latin:
- **(a)** <u>She will warn</u> the abbot.
- **(b)** <u>Will they love</u> the songs?
- **(c)** <u>We shall praise</u> courage.
- **(d)** <u>You</u>, boys, <u>will sit</u> in the garden.
- **(e)** Paul, <u>will you sing</u> to me?
- **(f)** <u>We shall order</u> the students to recite the songs.
- **(g)** The abbot <u>will preach</u> in the church.
- **(h)** Now <u>you will see</u> the bishop, Father Stephen.
- **(i)** <u>We shall stay</u> in the monastery.

**Quis philosophus esse vult?** *Who wants to be a philosopher?*

◀) **CD1, TR 9, 02:25**

Lucia et abbatissa et episcopus prope portam monasterii stant, ubi equos raedamque exspectant. Mox abbas e monasterio venit et eis vale dicit; deinde duo famuli viatoribus equos et raedam e stabulo ducunt. Lucia tamen ipsa non equitabit quod adhuc convalescit, sed cum abbatissa in raeda sedebit. Nunc episcopus in equum ascendit et sub arbores cum raeda equitat.

Interea in bibliotheca Paulus et Augustinus adhuc laborant; duos enim Stephanus iussit regulam monachorum per totum diem exscribere. Nunc Augustinus e fenestra viatores monasterium relinquentes conspexit: 'Illic tua virgo monasterium relinquit. Eam-ne videre vis?'

'Num adhuc vacas, Augustine? Opus perficere debemus,' inquit Paulus.

'Scribere est lentum et difficile: "*Nam vigilare leve est, pervigilare grave est*", ut dicit Martialis. Ecce illa virgo: est abbati abbatissaeque amica; etiam, puto, opulenta. Et tu, Paule, scientiam an pecuniam habere vis? an amorem?'

'Sst! Nunc est scribendum.'

'Quis philosophus vel theologus esse vult? Ego volo divitias habere:

> *Disputet philosophus vacuo cratere,*
> *sciat quia minus est scire quam habere.'*

| | |
|---|---|
| **amica-ae** [f] | *girlfriend* |
| **an** | *or* |
| **conspexit** | *(s/he) caught sight of* |
| **deinde** | *then* |
| **dicit** | *(s/he) says* |
| **per totum diem** | *all day long* |
| **difficile** | *difficult* |
| **disputet** | *let (him/her) dispute* |
| **divitiae-arum** [pl.] | *riches* |
| **ducunt** | *(they) bring* |
| **duos** | *two* |
| **eam** | *her* |
| **eis** | *to them* |
| **exscribere** | *to write out* |
| **famulus-i** [m] | *attendant* |
| **grave** | *serious* |
| **illic** | *over there* |
| **iussit** | *(s/he) told, ordered* |
| **leve** | *unimportant* |
| **Martialis-is** | *Martial* |
| **minus** | *less* |
| **opulentus-a-um** | *well-heeled, rich* |
| **pecunia-ae** [f] | *money* |
| **perficere** | *to finish* |
| **pervigilare** | *to lie awake all night* |
| **philosophus-i** [m] | *philosopher* |
| **porta-ae** [f] | *gate* |
| **prope** [+acc.] | *near* |
| **quam** | *than* |

| | |
|---|---|
| **quia** | *that* |
| **raeda-ae** [f] | *carriage* |
| **regula-ae** [f] | *rule* |
| **relinquentes** | *leaving* |
| **relinquit** | *(s/he) leaves* |
| **sciat** | *let (him/ her) know* |
| **scientia-ae** [f] | *knowledge* |
| **scribendus-a-um** | *should be written* |
| **stabulum-i** [n] | *stable* |
| **sub** [+acc./abl.] | *under* |
| **theologus-i** [m] | *theologian* |
| **tuus-a-um** | *your* |
| **ut** | *as* |
| **vacuo cratere** | *with an empty bowl* |
| **vale dicit** | *(s/he) says goodbye* |
| **vel** | *or* |
| **viator-is** [m] | *traveller* |
| **vigilare** | *to lie awake* |
| **vis** | *you want* |

## Living Latin

🔊 **CD1, TR 9, 03:39**

### Brotherly love

**1** The 'republic' of ancient Rome was an oligarchy of aristocrats tempered by public elections of questionable influence. From time to time ambitious individuals upset the balance of this oligarchy, only for it to be restored by a concession or something underhand. However, in the first century BC, Julius Caesar and Octavian each gained supreme power having survived the efforts of Pompey to oppose one, and Mark Antony the other. Octavian defeated Antony (and Cleopatra) at the battle of Actium in 32 BC, and consolidated his authority, taking the name 'Augustus'. He was succeeded by Tiberius, Tiberius by Caligula, Caligula by Claudius, and Claudius by Nero, and so a dynasty of emperors was created.

Under the emperors the façade of republican government continued with elections, consulships and meetings of the senate, but a revolution of power had occurred, from oligarchy of nobles to an absolute ruler influenced by counsellors and favourites. Political rivalries within the republic had seldom been resolved without bloodshed, and although the absolute power of an emperor may not have pleased what was left of the old republican nobility, many less influential people will have welcomed the security and safety which a single authority brought.

Even the murder of Nero's step-brother, Britannicus, failed to excite much reaction beyond the walls of the dining-room where he was poisoned:

**(Nero) ut erat reclinis et nescio similis solitum ita ait per comitialem morbum quo prima ab infantia adflictaretur Britannicus, et redituros paulatim visus sensusque. Ita post breve silentium repetita convivii laetitia. Nox eadem necem Britannici et rogum coniunxit, proviso ante funebri paratu, qui modicus fuit. In campo tamen Martis sepultus est adeo turbidis imbribus, ut vulgus iram deum portendi crediderit adversus facinus cui plerique etiam hominum ignoscebant, antiquas fratrum discordias et insociabile regnum aestimantes.**

(Tacitus, Annals xiii, 16–17)

*Nero just lay there feigning ignorance, and remarked that Britannicus had suffered from epilepsy since childhood and this was one of the symptoms; little by little, he told them, Britannicus would recover his sight and senses. And so, after a brief silence, the jollity of dinner was resumed. Britannicus meanwhile was buried the same night, since arrangements for the funeral – a rather modest one – had been taken care of. He was buried in the Field of Mars amid such a violent rainstorm that ordinary folk believed it to be a sign of the gods' anger.*

*Most people condoned the murder, putting it down to age-old feuds of brothers and a power which could not be shared.*

**2** Worldly politics seem very distant to the poet Martial, who lived during Nero's reign. His problems start with his neighbour – a teacher:

**Vicini somnum non tota nocte rogamus:**
**nam vigilare leve est, pervigilare grave est.**
**Discipulos dimitte tuos. Vis, garrule, quantum**
**accipis ut clames, accipere ut taceas?**

(Martial, Epigrams ix, 68, 9–12)

*We neighbours do not ask for sleep all night long: some loss of sleep is neither here nor there, but to lie awake the whole night is no joke. Dismiss your students. Tell me, you chatterbox, do you want to earn as much as you are paid to make your din – just to keep quiet?*

**3** Virgil, Horace and other poets were considered 'classics' almost while they were still alive. The 'dead poets' society' is something Martial is not quite ready to join:

**Miraris veteres, Vacerra, solos**
**nec laudas nisi mortuos poetas.**
**Ignoscas petimus, Vacerra: tanti**
**non est, ut placeam tibi, perire.**

(Martial, Epigrams viii, 69)

*You like only the ancient poets, Vacerra, and give no acclaim unless they are dead. Pray forgive me, Vacerra, but I don't wish to die just to keep you happy.*

# TESTING YOURSELF

**1** Change the underlined verbs into the future tense and translate:

    **(a)** Equi in caelo <u>volitant</u>.

    **(b)** In ecclesia <u>sedeo</u>.

    **(c)** Discipulos somnulentos <u>castigant</u>.

    **(d)** Lucia mihi in ecclesia <u>susurrat</u>.

**2** Change the underlined verbs into the present tense and translate:

    **(a)** O Domina, cur <u>dolebis</u>?

    **(b)** Philosophiam te <u>docebo</u>, o Paule.

    **(c)** Labores in agris non <u>tolerabimus</u>.

    **(d)** Nonne, o Virgo, Augustinum <u>amabis</u>?

**3** Fill the gaps:

| Case | **munus** [n] **muneris** *gift* | **labor** [m] **laboris** *toil* | **allegoria** [f] **allegoriae** *allegory* | **deus** [m] **dei** *god* |
|---|---|---|---|---|
| Singular | | | | |
| Nominative | ......... | **labor** | **allegoria** | **deus** |
| Accusative | ......... | ......... | ......... | **deum** |
| Genitive | ......... | **laboris** | ......... | ......... |
| Dative | ......... | ......... | **allegoriae** | ......... |
| Ablative | **munere** | ......... | ......... | ......... |
| Plural | | | | |
| Nominative | ......... | ......... | **allegoriae** | **dei (di)** |
| Accusative | **munera** | ......... | ......... | ......... |
| Genitive | ......... | **laborum** | ......... | ......... |
| Dative | ......... | ......... | ......... | ......... |
| Ablative | ......... | ......... | ......... | ......... |

**4** Translate into Latin:
   **(a)** The abbess will prepare a large dinner.
   **(b)** Are the students still working in the library?
   **(c)** What are you whispering, Lucia?
   **(d)** They will grieve in the church.

**5** Check you know these words:
   aestimo-are, ambulo-are, amica-ae, amicus-i, canto-are,
   clamo-are, curo-are, debeo-ere, deinde, do-dare, doceo-ere,
   ergo, doleo-ere, fabula-ae, falsus-a-um, habeo-ere, iaceo-ere,
   iubeo-ere, labor-is, laboro-are, maneo-ere, minus, monstro-
   are, mortuus-a-um, nisi, olim, oro-are, paro-are, pecunia-ae,
   plenus-a-um, respondeo-ere, rideo-ere, servo-are, si, studium-i,
   sub, susurro-are, taceo-ere, teneo-ere, timeo-ere, tuus-a-um,
   video-ere.

**6** From the words in 5, list the following:
   **(a)** all verbs like **amo-are** (1st conjugation)
   **(b)** all verbs like **moneo-ere** (2nd conjugation)

**7** What is the difference in meaning between **vita-ae** and **via-ae**?

# 9

**Quis in silva ululat?**
Who is howling in the wood?

In this unit you will learn about
- *Adjectives like* omnis
- *Verbal adjectives*: -ndus, -nda, -ndum *(gerundives)*
- *And find out more about Latin authors in*
  'Speculator amicae'

### Third declension adjectives

Adjectives like **sanctus** have endings identical to the nouns **mulus**, **silva** and **vinum**, and agree with the noun they qualify. A noun and adjective in agreement may have matching endings, e.g. **mul<u>us</u> bon<u>us</u>** *a good mule*, but not always so, e.g. **virgo laet<u>a</u>** *a cheerful maiden*, or **magn<u>um</u> op<u>us</u>** *a great work*.

There are some adjectives which do not have endings like **sanctus**, but are similar to third declension nouns. The ablative usually ends **-i**, and the neuter singular **-e**, otherwise they are identical to the third declension. There is no difference between masculine and feminine forms:

| Case | Masc./Fem. | | Neuter |
|------|------------|------|--------|
| | | **omnis** *all, every* | |
| | | Singular | |
| Nom. (+ voc.) | **omn-is** | | **omn-e** |
| Acc. | **omn-em** | | **omn-e** |
| Gen. | | **omn-is** | |
| Dat. | | **omn-i** | |
| Abl. | | **omn-i** | |
| | | Plural | |
| Nom. | **omn-es** | | **omn-ia** |
| Acc. | **omn-es** | | **omn-ia** |
| Gen. | | **omn-ium** | |
| Dat. | | **omn-ibus** | |
| Abl. | | **omn-ibus** | |

## Insight

Adjectives like **omnis** have endings very similar to third declension nouns, except they end **-i** in the ablative as well as dative singular, and **-e** in the neuter nominative and accusative singular.

### Practice (I)

**1** Translate into Latin:

- **(a)** (with) all the students
- **(b)** a brief song
- **(c)** difficult tasks
- **(d)** of humble monks
- **(e)** disgraceful superstition
- **(f)** a soft tunic
- **(g)** for the brave soldiers
- **(h)** a sweet mistress

**2** Match the Latin and English adjectives:

**(a)**

| | |
|---|---|
| brevis | *brief* |
| facilis | *disgraceful* |
| fortis | *serious* |
| gravis | *soft* |
| humilis | *easy* |
| levis | *humble* |
| mollis | *trivial* |
| nobilis | *brave* |
| turpis | *noble* |

**(b)**

| | |
|---|---|
| crudelis | *slender* |
| difficilis | *sweet* |
| gracilis | *cruel* |
| mirabilis | *terrible* |
| terribilis | *sad* |
| tristis | *useful* |
| utilis | *marvellous* |
| dulcis | *difficult* |
| fidelis | *faithful* |

**Regula monachorum** *The rule of the monks*

◀) CD1, TR 10

Augustinus de Lucia adhuc cogitat: 'Tua amica monasterium
reliquit, et ex oculis evanuit,' Paulo inquit Augustinus.
　'Illa non amica est mea.'
　'Non tua vero? Bene. Ego virginem salutabo. Quis scit? Fortes
Fortuna adiuvat, ut dicunt poetae.'
　'O satis poetarum, Augustine; opus perficere debes.'
　'Dulcis amica, tu es mirabilis, et me Cupido inflammat amore.
Carmina tibi, Lucia, dedicabo ... vel hoc Propertii: *Dum nos fata
sinunt oculos satiemus amore.* Vel hoc Catulli: *Vivamus mea Lucia
atque amemus.*'
　'Satis carminum, amice! Nunc exscribendum, si tibi placet,
silentio.'
　'Ignoscas si tibi sum molestus,' inquit Augustinus, et librum
spectat. Omnes paginae sunt abbatum monachorumque regulis plenae.
Stephanus discipulos duos monachorum regulas exscribere iusserat
omnes. 'Num totum librum exscribere debeo?' rogavit Augustinus.
　'Ita vero,' respondit Paulus, et Augustinus tandem scribere
incipit: I... *Dominum Deum diligere.* II... *Non occidere.* III... *Non
adulterare.* IV... *Non facere furtum.* V... *Mortuum sepelire.*
VI... *Iniuriam non facere.* VII... *Inimicos diligere.* VIII... *Non*

*falsum testimonium dicere. IX… Nudum vestire. X… Infirmum
visitare. XI… Non esse superbum. XII… Invidiam non exercere.
XIII… Castitatem amare. XIV… Non esse vinolentum…*
'Io Benedicte!' *et cantat:* 'Bibat ille, bibat illa, bibat servus
et ancilla.'

| | |
|---|---|
| **adiuvat** | *(s/he) helps* |
| **amemus** | *let us love* |
| **bibat** | *let [him/her] drink* |
| **castitas-tatis** [f] | *chastity* |
| **Catullus-i** | *Catullus* |
| **cogito-are** | *think* |
| **Cupido-inis** | *Cupid* |
| **diligere** | *to love* |
| **dum** | *while, as long as* |
| **evanuit** | *(s/he) has vanished* |
| **fatum-i** [n] | *fate* |
| **furtum-i** [n] | *theft* |
| **hoc** | *this* |
| **incipit** | *(s/he) begins* |
| **infirmus-a-um** | *sick* |
| **inflammo-are** | *inflame* |
| **inimicus-i** [m] | *enemy* |
| **iniuria-ae** [f] | *harm* |
| **invidia-ae** [f] | *grudge, jealousy* |
| **iusserat** | *(s/he) had ordered* |
| **meus-a-um** | *my* |
| **molestus-a-um** | *troublesome* |
| **occidere** | *to kill* |
| **oculus-i** [m] | *eye* |
| **pagina-ae** [f] | *page* |
| **placeo-ere** | *please* |
| **Propertius-i** | *Propertius* |
| **reliquit** | *(s/he) has left* |
| **rogavit** | *(s/he) asked* |
| **satiemus** | *let us fill* |
| **satis** | *enough* |
| **scit** | *(s/he) knows* |

| | |
|---|---|
| **sepelire** | *to bury* |
| **silentium-i** [n] | *silence* |
| **sinunt** | *(they) allow* |
| **superbus-a-um** | *proud* |
| **tandem** | *at last* |
| **tu** [nom.] | *you* |
| **tuus-a-um** | *your* |
| **vestire** | *to clothe* |
| **vinolentus-a-um** | *fond of booze* |
| **vivamus** | *let us live* |

## Adjectives ending -*ndus, -nda, -ndum*

The girl's name 'Amanda' comes from the Latin for 'to-be-loved':

**virgo amanda**                    *a girl to be loved*

**Amandus-a-um** is an adjective with the same endings as **sanctus-a-um**. It is formed from a verb (**amo, amare**) but behaves exactly like an adjective, agreeing with its noun in number, case and gender. It is called a 'gerundive', and usually carries a sense of obligation ('should', 'ought', 'must'):

**Virgo amanda est.**                *The girl is to be loved*
                                     *(ought to be loved).*
**Stephanus monendus est.**          *Stephen is to be warned*
                                     *(should be warned).*

A gerundive is always <u>passive</u>. This means the subject is 'done to', not the 'doer' (i.e. in the examples above, **virgo** is loved, not doing the loving, and **Stephanus** is to be warned, not doing the warning).

The first conjugation (-**are** verbs) end -**andus**, all the remainder -**endus**:

**amandus-a-um**
**monendus-a-um**
**agendus-a-um**, *etc.*

### Practice (II)

**1** Match the Latin phrases to their English meanings:

| | |
|---|---|
| **carmen non audiendum** | *a monk to be praised* |
| **abbatissa reverenda** | *a maid to be admired* |
| **opera agenda** | *an abbess to be revered* |
| **monachus laudandus** | *an abbot to be revered* |
| **munera dividenda** | *gifts to be distributed* |
| **verba addenda** | *a song not to be heard* |
| **abbas reverendus** | *tasks to be done* |
| **ancilla miranda** | *words to be added* |

**2** Identify the correct form of the gerundive, and translate:

e.g. **Ancilla (laudo, laudare, laudandus-a-um) est.**
**Ancilla <u>laudanda</u> est.** *The maid should be praised.*

**(a)** Abbas (audio, audire, audiendus-a-um) est.

**(b)** Milites non (amo, amare, amandus-a-um) sunt.

**(c)** Opus (perficio, perficere, perficiendus-a-um) est.

**Ohe, libelle!** *Whoa, little book!*

🔊 **CD1, TR 10, 02:08**

Nunc Paulus opere perfecto abiit, sed Augustinus adhuc scribit:
... *XXVII... diem iudicii timere. XXVIII... veritatem ex corde et ore proferre. XXIX... nihil amori Christi praeponere. XXX... honorare omnes homines. XXXI... dolum in corde non tenere. XXXII... contentionem non amare...* '...scribere est difficile,' inquit, et carmen Martialis murmurat: '*Ohe, iam satis est, ohe, libelle,*' nec multo post obdormit.

'Eho! Ubi est regula?' clamat Stephanus, 'Dormis-ne, Augustine?' et e somno Augustinum excitat.

'Regula? Immo, o Domine, non dormio.'

'Nunc regula est perficienda!'

'Ita vero Pater Stephane. Cogitabam de regulis.'

'Cogitabas an dormiebas?'

'Ignoscas, Domine. Ego fessus sum.' Subito Stephanus et

Augustinus horrendum clamorem audiunt. Unus ex monachis in monasterio magna voce ululare incipit.

'Quis est ille? Audivisti-ne?' Stephanus ad fenestram festinavit.

'Illic Theodorus e silva currit. Cur Theodorus territus est?' et Stephanus celeriter bibliothecam reliquit.

| | |
|---|---|
| **abiit** | *(s/he) went away* |
| **audivisti** | *you heard* |
| **clamor-is [m]** | *shout, cry* |
| **cogitabam, cogitabas** | *I was thinking, you ...* |
| **contentio-nis [f]** | *dispute, competition* |
| **cor-dis [n]** | *heart* |
| **currit** | *(s/he) runs* |
| **de [+abl.]** | *about* |
| **dolus-i [m]** | *deceit* |
| **dormiebas** | *you were sleeping* |
| **dormio, dormis** | *I am sleeping, you ...* |
| **excito-are** | *wake, arouse* |
| **honoro-are** | *honour* |
| **horrendus-a-um** | *fearful, to be feared* |
| **iam** | *now, already* |
| **immo** | *no, on the contrary* |
| **iudicium-i [n]** | *trial, judgment* |
| **libellus-i [m]** | *little book* |
| **murmuro-are** | *murmur* |
| **nec multo post** | *not long afterwards* |
| **obdormit** | *(s/he) falls asleep* |
| **ohe** | *whoa* |
| **opere perfecto** | *with the task completed* |
| **os, oris [n]** | *mouth* |
| **praeponere** | *to prefer* |
| **proferre** | *to put forward* |
| **scribit** | *(s/he) writes* |
| **somnus-i [m]** | *sleep* |
| **ululo-are** | *howl* |
| **veritas-tatis [f]** | *truth* |
| **vox, vocis [f]** | *voice* |

# Living Latin

◀) CD1, TR 10, 03:24

*Speculator amicae* One who spies on his mistress

The earliest erotic poetry which has survived is the work of Catullus, whose ill-starred passion for Lesbia fills his lyrics with hungry love mixed with bitter reproaches. Then we have the impassioned seriousness of Propertius, whose rough and tumble with Cynthia delighted the men and women of ancient Rome; so too the elegies of his contemporary Tibullus, whose yearning submission to his mistress makes him as loving as any of the poets. Last, and possibly most popular of all, comes Ovid: his sometimes frivolous and leering wit disguises a poet who was, he tells us, happily married and unpromiscuous.

**1** Propertius spies on his mistress:

Mane erat, et volui, si sola quiesceret illa,
  visere: at in lecto Cynthia sola fuit.
Obstipui: non illa mihi formosior umquam
  visa, neque ostrina cum fuit in tunica,
ibat et hinc castae narratum somnia Vestae,
  neu sibi neve mihi quae nocitura forent:
talis visa mihi somno dimissa recenti.
  Heu quantum per se candida forma valet!
'Quid? tu matutinus,' ait, 'speculator amicae?
  Me similem vestris moribus esse putas?
Non ego tam facilis: sat erit mihi cognitus unus,
  vel tu vel si quis verior esse potest.
Apparent non ulla toro vestigia presso,
  signa volutantis nec iacuisse duos.
Aspice ut in toto nullus mihi corpore surgat
  spiritus admisso notus adulterio.'
Dixit, et opposita propellens savia dextra
  prosilit in laxa nixa pedem solea.

**Sic ego tam sancti custos retrudor amoris:**
  **ex illo felix nox mihi nulla fuit.**

(Elegies ii, 29B)

*It was early, and I desired to see her, to see if she slept alone: but
there was Cynthia by herself in bed. I was taken aback: never has she
looked more stunning, not even when she went in her purple gear to
chaste Vesta to report her dreams, in case they might bring harm to
her or me: this is how she looked freshly arisen from sleep. What power
such natural beauty holds!*

*'Oh?' she says, 'do you lark about spying on your mistress? Do you judge
me by your standards? I'm not so free and easy: one lover is plenty,
yourself maybe, or another if there's one more true. You'll find no trace of
rough and tumble in this bed, no sign of a couple's frolicsome contortions.
See for yourself: my body is quite calm without the adulterer's breathless
panting flagrante delicto.' With that, she waved away my lunging kisses,
slipped into loose sandals and was gone. Thus am I, the guardian of so
heavenly a love, rejected: since then I've not had a single happy night.*

**2**  Catullus reflects on his girl's faithlessness:

**Nulli se dicit mulier mea nubere malle**
  **quam mihi, non si se Iuppiter ipse petat.**
**Dicit: sed mulier cupido quod dicit amanti,**
  **in vento et rapida scribere oportet aqua.**

(Poems lxx)

*My girl says she wants to marry no one other than me. Not even
if Jupiter himself should ask. That's what she says. But what a girl
says to an eager lad is best inscribed in the breeze and swift-flowing
streams.*

**3**  The piece below is part of a letter written in the twelfth century
by Héloise to her former tutor, lover, and husband, Abelard.
Her uncle had taken violent and cruel exception to their match
(Abelard was castrated), and Héloise lived the remainder of her
life in a nunnery.

**\*Missam ad amicum pro consolatione epistulam, dilectissime, vestram ad me forte quidam nuper attulit. Quam ex ipsa statim tituli fronte vestram esse considerans, tanto ardentius eam coepi legere, quanto scriptorem ipsum charius amplector, ut cuius rem perdidi, verbis saltem tanquam eius quadam imagine recreer.**

(From *Mediaeval Latin*, ed. K.P. Harrington, University of Chicago Press, 1997)

*Dearest, a letter you sent to a friend pouring out your feelings happened recently to fall into my hands. I knew it was yours the moment I saw your writing on the envelope, and a desire to read it seized me, much as I desire to have its author in my arms. I may not have him in person, but at least his words give some sort of picture to refresh me.*

\*post-classical

# TESTING YOURSELF

**1** Rewrite these sentences, changing underlined words to the plural, if they are singular, or to the singular if plural. Translate the new version.

    **(a)** Magna <u>cena</u> in culina paranda est.

    **(b)** Dulces <u>dominae</u> semper audiendae sunt.

    **(c)** Turpis <u>discipulus</u> excitandus est.

    **(d)** Humiles <u>servi</u> etiam laudandi sunt.

    **(e)** Cur <u>abbates</u> reverendi sunt?

**2** Translate into Latin:

    **(a)** We will dedicate the song to the brave soldiers and the humble maid.

    **(b)** I grieve, because Lucia will inflame me with love but will not love me.

    **(c)** Now the girl will sing a sweet song, and the boys will relate the history of the monastery.

**3** Write out all the endings, singular and plural, masculine, feminine and neuter of **(a)** dulcis **(b)** agendus.

**4** Check you know these words:
bibo-ere, brevis, dormio-ire, dulcis, facilis, fatum-i, gravis, horrendus-a-um, iam, invidia-ae, meus-a-um, mirabilis, oculus-i, omnis, scribo-ere, somnus-i, superbus-a-um, tandem, tristis, turpis, veritas-tatis, vivo-ere, vox-cis.

**5** From the words in 4, list all the adjectives with endings like **omnis**.

**6** What do people wear who dribble when they drink?

# 10

**Lacrimae in monasterio**
Tears in the monastery

In this unit you will learn about
- *Third, fourth and mixed conjugations*
- *Irregular verbs:* sum, possum, volo
- *Numbers*
- *And find out more about Latin authors in 'Miserabile corpus'*

### Present tense: third, fourth and mixed conjugations

The third and fourth conjugations are quite similar. A 'mixed' conjugation which shares endings with both the third and fourth conjugations only has a few verbs, though these are frequently used (e.g. **capio**, **capere** and compounds, **recipio**, **accipio**, etc.; and **facio**, **facere** and compounds, **perficio**, etc.).

| | Third | Fourth | Mixed |
|---|---|---|---|
| | **mitt-ere** *to send* | **aud-ire** *to hear* | **cap-ere** *to take, capture* |
| *I* | mitt-o | aud-io | cap-io |
| *you* (s.) | mitt-is | aud-is | cap-is |
| *s/he, it* | mitt-it | aud-it | cap-it |
| *we* | mitt-imus | aud-imus | cap-imus |
| *you* (pl.) | mitt-itis | aud-itis | cap-itis |
| *they* | mitt-unt | aud-iunt | cap-iunt |

## Insight

There are five kinds (conjugations) of regular verbs. The first two (**amare** and **monere**) are quite similar; the other three (**mittere, audire, capere**) are also similar to each other.

### Practice (I)

**1** Translate the underlined verbs into Latin:
   **(a)** She <u>sends</u> a gift.
   **(b)** We <u>capture</u> the soldier.
   **(c)** They <u>hear</u> a song.
   **(d)** I <u>capture</u> the beast.
   **(e)** They <u>send</u> a book.
   **(f)** You <u>are hearing</u> the abbot, students.
   **(g)** We <u>send</u> money.
   **(h)** Do you <u>hear</u> Paul, Augustine?

**2** Match each verb to its English meaning (look them up if necessary):

   **(a)**

   | third conjugation: | |
   | --- | --- |
   | curro-ere | write |
   | dico-ere | leave |
   | duco-ere | lead |
   | lego-ere | run |
   | rego-ere | say |
   | relinquo-ere | rule |
   | scribo-ere | read |

   **(b)**

   | third conjugation: | |
   | --- | --- |
   | ascendo-ere | live |
   | credo-ere | do |
   | bibo-ere | fall |
   | cado-ere | climb |
   | emo-ere | buy |
   | ago-ere | drink |
   | vivo-ere | believe |

   **(c)**

   | fourth conjugation: | |
   | --- | --- |
   | venio-ire | feel |
   | dormio-ire | know |
   | scio-ire | bury |
   | sentio-ire | open |
   | sepelio-ire | sleep |
   | aperio-ire | come |

   **(d)**

   | mixed conjugation: | |
   | --- | --- |
   | facio-ere | regain/accept |
   | fugio-ere | complete |
   | incipio-ere | make |
   | perficio-ere | begin |
   | recipio-ere | flee |

**3** Translate the underlined verbs into Latin:

(a) I <u>am reading</u> Augustine's book.

(b) <u>Are they running</u> into the church?

(c) The abbot <u>writes</u> all the rules.

(d) We <u>are beginning</u> to live!

(e) <u>Are they burying</u> a monk?

(f) Why <u>are they fleeing</u> from the monastery?

(g) <u>Are you drinking</u> wine in the kitchen, maids?

(h) Who <u>is coming</u>?

(i) They do not <u>hear</u> the abbess.

*Miserabile corpus* The pitiable corpse

◄)) CD1, TR 11

---

**Shared endings key**

**-is** silvis, mulis, vinis: dat. pl. or abl. pl.   **-o** mulo: dat. or abl.
   3rd declension: genitive           **all verbs:** 'I...'
   mitti(ti)s, audi(ti)s, capi(ti)s:
   'you...'

---

Post Theodori mortem – fortuitam, ut dicit abbas, sed quis potest scire? – multae erant lacrimae. Theodorus enim fuerat monachus pius et omnibus amicus. Timor autem per monasterium agrosque vulgatus est. Monachi multos dies erant pavidi tacitique.

Nunc in schola discipulis pauca verba de Theodori morte Stephanus dicit. Postea magister tristis e Vulgato legit:

'*Hoc autem dico, fratres, quoniam caro et sanguis regnum Dei possidere non possunt ...*'

Paulus per fenestram spectat et mortem Theodori contemplat. Quis eum occidere voluisset? Fuerat amicus omnibus, vir pius et humilis. Erat rumor. Dani? Num Dani Theodorum trucidaverunt? Dani in regione iam viginti annos non visi erant.

'...*Ubi est, mors, victoria tua? Ubi est, mors, stimulus tuus?*' Stephanus campanam per monasterium resonantem audit et legere desinit. 'Nunc corpus Theodori sepeliemus, o pueri,' inquit, 'et vos

unam horam sine me laborabitis et opera perficietis,' et per genas
lacrimas fundens bibliothecam relinquit.

QUICK VOCAB

| | |
|---|---|
| annus-i [m] | year |
| campana-ae [f] | bell |
| caro, carnis [f] | flesh |
| Danus-i [m] | Dane, Viking |
| desino-ere | leave off, abandon |
| dies [nom./acc.] | days |
| fortuitus-a-um | accidental |
| frater-tris [m] | brother |
| fuerat | (s/he) had been |
| fundens | pouring |
| genae-arum [f] | cheeks |
| hora-ae [f] | hour |
| lacrima-ae [f] | tear |
| mors, mortis [f] | death |
| paucus-a-um | few |
| pavidus-a-um | fearful |
| possideo-ere | occupy |
| post [+acc.] | after |
| postea | afterwards |
| quoniam | since |
| regio-nis [f] | region |
| regnum-i [n] | kingdom |
| resonantem | resounding |
| rumor-is [m] | rumour, gossip |
| sanguis-inis [m] | blood |
| sine [+abl.] | without |
| stimulus-i [m] | sting |
| tacitus-a-um | silent, quiet |
| timor-is [m] | fear |
| trucidaverunt | (they) murdered |
| tuus-a-um | your |
| unus-a-um | one |
| verbum-i [n] | word |
| victoria-ae [f] | victory |

| | |
|---|---|
| **viginti** | *twenty* |
| **vir-i** [m] | *man* |
| **visi erant** | *(they) had been seen* |
| **voluisset** | *had wanted* |
| **Vulgatum-i** [n] | *the Vulgate* |
| **vulgatus est** | *was spread abroad* |

## Numbers 1–20, 100, 1000

| | |
|---|---|
| **unus*** | *one* |
| **duo*** | *two* |
| **tres*** | *three* |
| **quattuor** | *four* |
| **quinque** | *five* |
| **sex** | *six* |
| **septem** | *seven* |
| **octo** | *eight* |
| **novem** | *nine* |
| **decem** | *ten* |
| **undecim** | *eleven* |
| **duodecim** | *twelve* |
| **tredecim** | *thirteen* |
| **quattuordecim** | *fourteen* |
| **quindecim** | *fifteen* |
| **sedecim** | *sixteen* |
| **septendecim** | *seventeen* |
| **duodeviginti** | *eighteen* |
| **undeviginti** | *nineteen* |
| **viginti** | *twenty* |
| **centum** | *hundred* |
| **mille (milia)** | *thousand (thousands)* |

*Most numbers have fixed endings, like **viginti**; a few have endings which change (e.g. **unus, una, unum; duo, duae; tres, tria**).

## Accusative of duration

The accusative case is used to express a length of time. Thus above we have **multos dies** *for many days*, **viginti ann<u>os</u>** *for twenty years* and **un<u>am</u> hor<u>am</u>** *for one hour*.

# Future tense: third, fourth and mixed conjugations

The future of the first two conjugations have the endings -**bo**, -**bis**, -**bit**, etc. The third, fourth and mixed are different, all sharing the letter **e** in the ending:

|          | mitt-ere<br>*to send* | aud-ire<br>*to hear* | cap-ere<br>*to take, capture* |
|----------|-----------|-----------|-----------|
| *I*       | mitt-am   | audi-am   | capi-am   |
| *you* (s.) | mitt-es   | audi-es   | capi-es   |
| *s/he, it* | mitt-et   | audi-et   | capi-et   |
| *we*       | mitt-emus | audi-emus | capi-emus |
| *you* (pl.) | mitt-etis | audi-etis | capi-etis |
| *they*     | mitt-ent  | audi-ent  | capi-ent  |

## Insight

The first two conjugations (**amare** and **monere**) share future endings: -**bo**, -**bis**, -**bit**, -**bimus**, -**bitis**, -**bunt**. The other three conjugations (**mittere**, **audire**, **capere**) all share the future endings: -**am**, -**es**, -**et**, -**emus**, -**etis**, -**ent**.

### Irregular verbs: *sum, possum, volo*

It is one of the laws of language that rules and regular forms have exceptions. Irregular verbs are amongst the most commonly used:

|          | **esse** *to be* | **posse** *to be able*<br>Present | **velle** *to want* |
|----------|--------|---------|--------|
| *I*       | sum    | possum   | volo    |
| *you* (s.) | es     | potes    | vis     |
| *s/he, it* | est    | potest   | vult    |
| *we*       | sumus  | possumus | volumus |
| *you* (pl.) | estis  | potestis | vultis  |
| *they*     | sunt   | possunt  | volunt  |

| | | Future | | |
|---|---|---|---|---|
| I | **ero** | **potero** | **volam** |
| you (s.) | **eris** | **poteris** | **voles** |
| s/he, it | **erit** | **poterit** | **volet** |
| we | **erimus** | **poterimus** | **volemus** |
| you (pl.) | **eritis** | **poteritis** | **voletis** |
| they | **erunt** | **poterunt** | **volent** |

The compound forms of **esse** (**abesse, adesse**) share the same irregular endings.

## Insight

A verb ending **-et** (pl. **-ent**) could be either the present of the second conjugation (**monet** = 's/he warns'); or future of the third, fourth and mixed conjugations (**audiet** = 's/he will hear').

### Practice (II)

**1** Translate the underlined verbs into Latin:
   **(a)** She <u>will send</u> a gift.
   **(b)** We <u>shall capture</u> the beasts.
   **(c)** They <u>will hear</u> a song.
   **(d)** She <u>is sitting</u> in the church.
   **(e)** <u>Will</u> you <u>hear</u> the abbot, students?
   **(f)** They <u>will be able</u> to see us.
   **(g)** Do you <u>want</u> to come, Paul?
   **(h)** We <u>shall be present</u> in the monastery today.

### How to recognize a conjugation

| Conjugation | First person | Infinitive | How to recognize the conjugation |
|---|---|---|---|
| first | **am-o** | **am-are** | the infinitive ending **-are** |
| second | **mon-eo** | **mon-ere** | the infinitive **-ere**, and the **e** in the present |
| third | **mitt-o** | **mitt-ere** | same infinitive as **monere** but no **e** in the present |

| Conjugation | First person | Infinitive | How to recognize the conjugation |
|---|---|---|---|
| fourth | **aud-io** | **aud-ire** | the **i** in the present, with infinitive **-ire** |
| mixed | **cap-io** | **cap-ere** | the **i** in the present, with infinitive **-ere** |

### Practice (III)

**1** To which conjugation do the following verbs belong?

(a) aperio-ire     (g) bibo-ere

(b) oro-are     (h) scio-ire

(c) incipio-ere     (i) perficio-ere

(d) dico-ere     (j) video-ere

(e) satio-are     (k) laudo-are

(f) retineo-ere     (l) vivo-ere

*Hic iacet Theodorus* Here lies Theodorus

◆) CD1, TR 11, 02:00

'Miserum Theodorum,' inquit Paulus, per fenestram exsequias Theodori spectans. Pluit; monachi miserabile corpus Theodori ex ecclesia portant et abbas exiguam pompam ducit.

Discipuli libros relinquunt et per fenestram pompam spectant. 'Ecce, Theodorum sepelient sub arborem ubi nobis fabulas narrabat,' inquit unus. 'Cur omnes monachi non adsunt? Cur eum tam cito sepeliunt?' rogavit alter. 'Quis Theodorum occidit?' rogavit tertius.

> HIC IACET THEODORUS
> MONASTERII HUIUS
> MONACHUS QUI IN ANNO
> VICESIMO ET QUINTO
> MORTUUS NUNC CUM
> DEO IN PACE REQUIESCIT

'Quis scit?' respondit Paulus.

'Quando sciemus?' rogavit Augustinus.

'Abbas proxima nocte eum vidit,' inquit Paulus. 'Fortasse Stephano dicet.'

'*Soles occidere et redire possunt. Nobis cum semel occidit brevis lux, Nox est perpetua una dormienda,*' murmurat Augustinus, e Catulli libello recitans.

'O miserum Theodorum!' inquit Paulus. Ecce, nunc corpus in terram demittunt.' Nunc aliquis flere incipit.

Mox abbas et monachi in ecclesiam reveniunt praeter Stephanum qui prope sepulcrum orat. Adhuc pluit; mox vocem Stephani iterum iterumque gementem audiunt.

| | |
|---:|:---|
| **aliquis** | *someone* |
| **alter** | *another* |
| **cum semel** | *as soon as* |
| **demitto-ere** | *lower* |
| **eum** | *him* |
| **exiguus-a-um** | *slender, scant* |
| **exsequiae-arum** | *funeral* |
| **fleo-ere** | *weep* |
| **gementem** | *groaning* |
| **huius** | *of this* |
| **iterum** | *again* |
| **libellus-i** [m] | *book* |
| **lux-cis** [f] | *light, life* |
| **miserabilis-e** | *pitiable* |
| **murmuro-are** | *murmur* |
| **nox, noctis** [f] | *night* |
| **occidit** | *(s/he) kills, killed or falls/fell* |
| **occido-ere** | *fall* |
| **perpetuus-a-um** | *unending* |
| **pluit** | *it is raining* |
| **pompa-ae** [f] | *procession* |
| **praeter** [+acc.] | *except, besides* |
| **proximus-a-um** | *nearest, previous* |
| **quando** | *when* |
| **redeo-ire** [irreg.] | *return* |
| **rogavit** | *(s/he) asked* |
| **sepulcrum-i** [n] | *grave* |
| **sol-is** [m] | *sun, day* |
| **spectans** | *watching* |
| **tam cito** | *so quickly* |
| **tertius-a-um** | *third* |
| **vicesimo et quinto** | *in the twenty-fifth* |

QUICK VOCAB

## Living Latin

***Miserabile corpus*** *The pitiable corpse*

🔊 **CD1, TR 11, 04:02**

**1** The Aeneid of Virgil is regarded by many as the Latin poem
with the most breadth and range, reaching all corners of the
soul with moments of love, friendship, loyalty, suffering,
fulfilment and despair. In this scene below, the Trojans bring
the corpse of Pallas back to his father, Evander:

**At non Evandrum potis est vis ulla tenere,**
**sed venit in medios. Feretro Pallanta reposto**
**procubuit super atque haeret lacrimansque gemensque,**
**et via vix tandem vocis laxata dolore est:**
**'Non haec, o Palla, dederas promissa parenti,**
**cautius ut saevo velles te credere Marti.**
**Haud ignarus eram quantum nova gloria in armis**
**et praedulce decus primo certamine posset.**
**Primitiae iuvenis miserae bellique propinqui**
**dura rudimenta, et nulli exaudita deorum**
**vota precesque meae!'**

(Virgil, Aeneid xi, 148–58)

*Nothing could restrain Evander who came out into the middle of the*
*throng. The bier was put down and he knelt over Pallas. He clung to*
*him, and wept and groaned, and hoarse with grief could barely speak:*

*'O Pallas, are these the promises you gave your father, that you take*
*care of yourself in the savage fighting? I was all too aware of the lure*
*of honour in a man's first battle, and the first sweet taste of glory in*
*untried combat. What a wretched coming-of-age, what a cruel start to*
*a war so close to home. Not one of the gods listened to my prayers or*
*vows!'*

**2**  Life is short, so let's make it sweet, says Catullus:

Vivamus, mea Lesbia, atque amemus,
rumoresque senum severiorum
omnes unius aestimemus assis.
Soles occidere et redire possunt:
nobis cum semel occidit brevis lux,
nox est perpetua una dormienda.
Da mi basia mille, deinde centum,
dein mille altera, dein secunda centum,
deinde usque altera mille, deinde centum.

(Poems v, 1–9)

*Come my Lesbia, let's live, let's love, and never mind the chatter of old frowning bores – they're not worth tuppence. The sun may go down and return, but for us when our brief peep of light goes out, a single night awaits of unbroken sleep. So give me a thousand kisses, then a hundred, then I'll take another thousand, and another hundred, and then yet another thousand, and one more hundred.*

# TESTING YOURSELF

1 Change the underlined verbs to the future tense, and translate:
    **(a)** Monachus mulos duos in silvam <u>ducit</u>.
    **(b)** Hodie discipuli labores <u>perficiunt</u>.
    **(c)** Monasterium-ne <u>relinquimus</u>?
    **(d)** Augustinum audire non <u>possum</u>.

2 Change the underlined verbs to the present tense, and translate:
    **(a)** In superstitiones non <u>credam</u>.
    **(b)** Me amica <u>inflammabit</u> amore.
    **(c)** Carmina-ne Augustini <u>audies</u>?
    **(d)** Discipuli tres e Vulgato <u>legent</u>.

3 Translate into Latin:
    **(a)** The maids always want to hear Augustine's songs!
    **(b)** Lucia is already able to read, sing and work in the fields.
    **(c)** We shall care for the souls of both humble serfs and great kings.
    **(d)** Why are twenty monks fleeing out of the wood?

4 Write out these nouns, all cases, singular and plural: **opus, operis; nox, noctis** (gen.pl.: **noctium**); **fabula, fabulae; sepulcrum, sepulcri; annus, anni**.

5 Identify the Latin ancestor shared by *mile*, *millennium* and *millimetre*.

6 How many months in the year were there when September, October, November and December were first named?

7 Check you know these words:
ago-ere, aperio-ire, cado-ere, capio-ere, credo-ere, dico-ere, duco-ere, emo-ere, facio-ere, fleo-ere, frater-tris, fugio-ere, incipio-ere, iterum, lacrima-ae, lego-ere, lux-cis, miserabilis,

mors-tis, nox-ctis, perficio-ere, perpetuus-a-um, proximus-
a-um, regio-onis, regnum-i, rego-ere, sanguis-inis, scio-ire,
sentio-ire, sepelio-ire, sol-is, timor-is, verbum-i, victoria-ae.

**8** From the words in 7 above, list the following:
    **(a)** all verbs like **mitto-ere** (third conjugation)
    **(b)** all verbs like **audio-ire** (fourth conjugation)
    **(c)** all verbs like **capio-ere** (mixed conjugation).

# 11

# Libera nos a malo
## Deliver us from evil

In this unit you will learn about
- *Imperfect tense*
- *Adjectives: -ens*
- *Present participles*
- *And find out more about Latin in 'Yaysoos in chaylo'*

### Past tense: imperfect

The present tense describes this moment or current period, the future tense is for a future event, and all the remaining tenses are past ones. The imperfect tense describes a past event which was habitual, recurrent or lasting for a while. The name 'imperfect' means unfinished:

| | |
|---|---|
| **Discipuli ante cenam in ecclesia <u>cantabant</u> sed Augustinus carmina <u>legebat</u>.** | *Before dinner the students <u>used to sing/were singing</u> in the church, but Augustine <u>would read/was reading</u> his poetry.* |

There are different ways to express this tense in English: 'used to sing', 'were singing', 'was reading' and 'would read' may all be used to represent the imperfect. A simple past might do as well, as in 'Every day the students <u>sang</u> in the church'.

The endings of this tense are common to all verbs:

|  | **am-are** *love* | **mon-ere** *warn, advise* | **mitt-ere** *send* |
|---|---|---|---|
| *I* | ama-bam | mone-bam | mitte-bam |
| *you* (s.) | ama-bas | mone-bas | mitte-bas |
| *s/he, it* | ama-bat | mone-bat | mitte-bat |
| *we* | ama-bamus | mone-bamus | mitte-bamus |
| *you* (pl.) | ama-batis | mone-batis | mitte-batis |
| *they* | ama-bant | mone-bant | mitte-bant |

|  | **aud-ire** *hear* | **cap-ere** *take, capture* |
|---|---|---|
| *I* | audie-bam | capie-bam |
| *you* (s.) | audie-bas | capie-bas |
| *s/he, it* | audie-bat | capie-bat |
| *we* | audie-bamus | capie-bamus |
| *you* (pl.) | audie-batis | capie-batis |
| *they* | audie-bant | capie-bant |

Exceptions are **sum, esse** (and compounds: **adsum, absum, possum**):

| *I was* | **eram** | *I was able/could* | **poteram** |
|---|---|---|---|
| *you* (s.) *were* | **eras** | *you* (s.) *were able/could* | **poteras** |
| *s/he, it was* | **erat** | *s/he, it was able/could* | **poterat** |
| *we were* | **eramus** | *we were able/could* | **poteramus** |
| *you* (pl.) *were* | **eratis** | *you* (pl.) *were able/could* | **poteratis** |
| *They were* | **erant** | *they were able/could* | **poterant** |

### *In ecclesia* In church

◄) CD2, TR 1

Nec multo post Theodori exsequias, multi in ecclesia aderant.
Ecclesia candelis incensique fragrantia plena erat. Abbas ipse
cum monachis missam celebrabat. Lucia iuxta matrem in primis
subselliis inter magnas familias sedebat. Post nobiles erant peregrini
et agricolae et pueri et ancillae et servi. Abbas ad aram in veste
purpurea splendens stabat et monachi discipulique post aram in
choro cantabant.

'*Pater noster, qui es in caelis...*' cantare abbas incipiebat.
Omnes discipuli cantabant praeter Augustinum, qui dormiebat
quod Stephanus eum per totam noctem epistulas sancti Pauli ad
Corinthios exscribere iusserat. Augustinus poenas dabat quod in
schola carmina Catulli, non epistulas sancti Pauli, legebat.

'*Et ne nos inducas in tentationem, sed libera nos a malo,*' abbas
cantabat.

QUICK VOCAB

| | |
|---|---|
| **agricola-ae** [m] | *farmer* |
| **ara-ae** [f] | *altar* |
| **candela-ae** [f] | *candle* |
| **celebro-are** | *celebrate* |
| **chorus-i** [m] | *choir* |
| **Corinthi-orum** | *Corinthians* |
| **epistula-ae** [f] | *letter* |
| **eum** | *him* |
| **exscribo-ere** | *write out* |
| **familia-ae** [f] | *family* |
| **fragrantia-ae** [f] | *odour* |
| **incensum-i** [n] | *incense* |
| **inter** [+acc.] | *among* |
| **ipse** | *himself* |
| **iusserat** | *(s/he) had ordered* |
| **iuxta** [+acc.] | *next to* |
| **libera** | *free, deliver* |

| | |
|---|---|
| **missa-ae** [f] | *mass* |
| **ne... inducas** | *do not lead us into* |
| **noster** | *our* |
| **peregrinus-i** [m] | *foreigner, pilgrim* |
| **poenas do-are** | *to pay the penalty, be punished* |
| **primus-a-um** | *first* |
| **purpureus-a-um** | *purple* |
| **qui** | *who* |
| **splendeo-ere** | *be bright, resplendent* |
| **subsellium-i** [n] | *pew, bench* |
| **tentatio-nis** [f] | *temptation* |
| **vestis-is** [f] | *clothing* |

## Practice (I)

**1** Translate the underlined verbs into Latin (all verbs should be in the imperfect):

- **(a)** She <u>used to love</u> the student.
- **(b)** They <u>were listening</u> to their mother.
- **(c)** We <u>would send</u> food to the slaves.
- **(d)** Where <u>were</u> you, Paul?
- **(e)** I <u>could</u> see all the students in the church.
- **(f)** She always <u>warned</u> us.
- **(g)** All the poems of Catullus <u>were</u> in the book.

**2** Put the underlined verbs into the imperfect and translate:

- **(a)** <u>Pluit</u>. (pluit, pluere)
- **(b)** Miserabile corpus in terra <u>iacet</u>. (iaceo-ere)
- **(c)** Carmina Catulli <u>legimus</u>. (lego-ere)
- **(d)** Monachum prope ecclesiam <u>sepeliunt</u>. (sepelio-ire)
- **(e)** Virgo <u>flet</u>. (fleo-ere)

### Adjectives ending *-ens*

You have already met adjectives like **sanctus** and **omnis**. You will also come across adjectives like **omnipotens** or **prudens**. These are third declension adjectives, similar to **omnis**. Most of the cases have a 't' and extra syllable:

| Case | Masc./Fem. | prudens *wise* | Neuter |
|------|------------|----------------|--------|
| | | Singular | |
| Nom. | **prud-ens** | | **prud-ens** |
| Acc. | **prud-entem** | | **prud-ens** |
| Gen. | | **prud-entis** | |
| Dat. | | **prud-enti** | |
| Abl. | | **prud-enti** | |
| | | Plural | |
| Nom. | **prud-entes** | | **prud-entia** |
| Acc. | **prud-entes** | | **prud-entia** |
| Gen. | | **prud-entium** | |
| Dat. | | **prud-entibus** | |
| Abl. | | **prud-entibus** | |

### Present participles

A participle is a cross between an adjective and a verb. It has the function of an adjective but is formed from a verb. A participle agrees with its subject noun in case, gender and number (sing. or plural):

**Lucia <u>Paulum</u> <u>natantem</u> vidit.**     *Lucia saw <u>Paul</u> <u>swimming</u>.*

**Natantem** is the present participle of **nato, natare** and agrees with **Paulum**, the object of **vidit**. Unlike an ordinary adjective, a present participle can have an object of its own:

**Paulus Danos <u>silvam</u>**     *Paul saw the Danes leaving*
**relinquentes vidit.**      *<u>the wood</u>.*

**Relinquentes** is the present participle of **relinquo, relinquere,** here in the accusative masculine plural because it agrees with **Danos,** and has an object of its own: **silvam.**

A present participle can be translated in different ways:

*Lucia saw Paul who/while he was swimming.*
*Paul saw the Danes who/as they were leaving the wood.*

These participles all share the endings of **prud-ens.** Participles of verbs from the first conjugation, like **amare,** have an **a** in place of the **e** in the ending:

| | | |
|---|---|---|
| amo-are | **am-ans** | *loving* |
| moneo-ere | **mon-ens** | *advising, warning* |
| mitto-ere | **mitt-ens** | *sending* |
| audio-ire | **audi-ens** | *listening (to), hearing* |
| capio-ere | **capi-ens** | *taking, capturing* |

## Insight

Present participles are adjectives created from verbs (in English they end '*-ing*') and have endings like the adjective **prudens.**

### Adjectives as nouns

The traditional 'parts of speech' (i.e. nouns, verbs, adjectives, etc.) from time to time adopt each other's roles. If your grasp of these is still a little shaky, pursue them in the Essential Grammar section of the Introduction and through the **Index of grammar** support at the end of the book.

Nouns are frequently used as adjectives in English, especially by newspaper editors (e.g. 'Government sex scandal cover up'). Conversely we use adjectives as nouns: 'The good, the bad, and the ugly'.

Latin adjectives (and participles) also act as nouns:

**<u>Nobiles</u> in ecclesia sedent.**  *The <u>nobles</u> are sitting in the church.*
**Ille qui proximus**  *He who is standing next to <u>the one-</u>*
**<u>dormienti</u> stat.**  *<u>who-sleeps.</u>*

***Insolentes monachi*** *The insolent monks*

🔊 **CD2, TR 1, 01:11**

In ecclesia Lucia Paulum et Augustinum, qui adhuc dormiebat, conspexit. Iam Augustinus stertere incipiebat. Paulus Augustinum excitare volebat quod Stephanum eum spectantem videre poterat.

In primis subselliis Egberta filiam furtim spectantem unum ex discipulis qui in choro cantabant conspexit.

'Lucia, quid spectas?' susurravit Egberta.

'Nil, praeter illum, qui dormit, discipulum,' Lucia respondit. Iam Paulus etiam Luciam spectabat.

'Quis est ille puer qui te spectat?' rogavit mater.

'Quis puer?'

'Puer ille qui proximus dormienti stat,' inquit Egberta ridens. 'Eho, nunc abbas praedicabit.' Egberta tamen ridere desiit ubi Benedictum se ipsam spectantem conspexit. 'Insolentissimos monachos!' susurravit Egberta, et Karolus, coniunx, eam audiens rogavit: 'Mea carissima, vales-ne?'

Interea Stephanus Augustinum dormientem adhuc stertentemque spectabat. Paulus Stephanum spectabat et 'Cave, Augustine!' susurravit, 'nunc est cantandum.'

'Abi!' respondit magna voce Augustinus. 'Volo dormire.' Omnes in ecclesia vocem eius audire poterant.

'*Ora pro nobis peccatoribus,*' cantabat abbas, palmas ad caelum tendens.

| | |
|---|---|
| **abi** | *go away!* |
| **carissimus-a-um** | *dearest* |
| **cave** | *look out* |
| **coniunx-gis [m/f]** | *husband/wife* |
| **conspexit** | *(s/he) caught sight of* |
| **desiit** | *(s/he) stopped* |
| **eam** | *her* |
| **eius** | *his/her* |
| **furtim** | *secretly* |
| **illum [acc.]** | *that one, him* |
| **ipsam** | *her(self)* |
| **nil (nihil)** | *nothing* |
| **nunc est cantandum** | *it is time to sing (lit. now it is to be sung)* |
| **ora pro nobis peccatoribus** | *pray for us sinners* |
| **palma-ae [f]** | *palm* |
| **proximus-a-um** | *next, nearest* |
| **quis** | *who, which* |
| **respondit** | *(s/he) replied* |
| **se** | *her (him/them) self* |
| **sterto-ere** | *snore* |
| **te [acc.]** | *you* |
| **tendo-ere** | *stretch* |
| **valeo-ere** | *to be well* |
| **volebat** | *(s/he) wanted* |

QUICK VOCAB

### Practice (II)

**1** Choose the correct form for each gap from: **praedicans,
praedicantem, praedicantes, dormiens, dormientem,
dormientes**:

**(a)** Discipuli abbatem
in ecclesia _____
audiebant.

**(b)** Omnes monachi
discipulos _____ videre
poterant.

**2** Change the underlined word to the plural if singular, or
singular if plural, and translate:
**(a)** Egberta <u>ova</u> e sarcina cadentia videt.
**(b)** Lucia <u>monachos</u> in ecclesia cantantes audiebat.
**(c)** Paulus cum <u>discipulo</u> stertenti sedebat.
**(d)** Abbatissa cibum <u>monachis</u> dormientibus non dabit.
**(e)** Benedictus <u>ancillam</u> in culina susurrantem audiebat.
**(f)** <u>Femina</u> Theodorum in silva currentem videre poterat.

## Living Latin

🔊 **CD2, TR 1, 02:26**

### 'Yaysoos in chaylo'

Latin was finally dropped from Catholic liturgy in 1960s, ending an unbroken line of Latin from the Church's earliest days, though hymns, prayers and chants are still sung in some churches. In the centuries before printing presses, churches were the centres of learning where books were copied and kept, and churchmen found pleasure in classical Latin literature; but the primary use of the language was to observe the ritual and get the Christian message across to the local brethren. Each region of the Christian domain will have had its own mix of Latin and local speech habits, evolving over many centuries. The pronunciation will have varied from country to country and priest to priest. In 1912 Pope Pius X, frustrated by the disparate sounds of Latin across Europe, encouraged the clergy everywhere to adopt what was then the Italian pronunciation of Latin. Hence 'Yaysoos', 'bone-us' and 'chaylum' for *Jesus*, *bonus* and *caelum*.

**1** The Vulgate was the first full Latin version of the Bible, translated by St Jerome at the end of the fourth century.

\*Hoc autem dico, fratres, quoniam caro et sanguis regnum Dei possidere non possunt: neque corruptio incorruptelam possidebit. In momento, in ictu oculi, in novissima tuba: canet enim, et mortui resurgent incorrupti, et nos inmutabimur. Oportet enim corruptibile hoc induere incorruptelam: et mortale hoc induere inmortalitatem, tunc fiet sermo qui scriptus est: Absorta est mors in victoria. Ubi est, mors, victoria tua? Ubi est, mors, stimulus tuus?

(St Paul, Corinthians i, 15; 50, 52–5)

*This I tell you, brothers, that flesh and blood cannot inherit the kingdom of God: neither will the perishable possess immortality. In a moment, in the twinkling of an eye, at the last call of the trumpet: for it will sound, and the bodiless dead will rise, and we shall be changed; for this matter must lose its perishability, and this mortality become immortal; then the saying which is written will come to pass: 'Death is swallowed up in victory. Where, death, is your victory? Where, death, is your sting?'*

**2**  St Benedict was a contemporary of Jerome. His order has survived centuries of religious conflict, and there are now monasteries all over Europe.

**\*Cellerarius monasterii eligatur de congregatione sapiens, maturus moribus, sobrius, non multum edax, non elatus, non turbulentus, non iniuriosus, non tardus, non prodigus, sed timens Deum, qui omni congregationi sit sicut pater.**

(Regula sancti Benedicti, xxxi)

*A procurator for the monastery should be picked from the community, a prudent fellow of mature character, sober, without a great appetite, with no pretensions, not a trouble-maker, not one who causes harm, punctual, parsimonious, and fearing the Lord; a man who may be a father to the community.*

**3**  Monks of the middle ages were not too immersed in pious abstinence and godly spirituality to overlook the pleasures of life. Refuge from the rigours of monasticism was found in the bottle, with girlfriends, and with the pen. Many anonymous verses have survived, some of which were parodies of formal, ecclesiastical Latin:

**\*Bibat ille, bibat illa,
bibat servus et ancilla,
bibat hera, bibat herus:
ad bibendum nemo serus.**

*Let him drink and her drink, and the serf have one, the maid too, and the mistress, and the master – no one's too late for a jugful.*

\*post-classical

# TESTING YOURSELF

**1** Write a sentence with:
- **(a)** the present participle of **devoro-are**;
- **(b)** the present participle of **ululo-are**;
- **(c)** the present participle of **bibo-ere**;
- **(d)** the gerundive of **audio-ire**.

**2** Translate into Latin:
- **(a)** Augustine was sleeping for twelve hours.
- **(b)** Wise teachers always used to drink with students.
- **(c)** Lucia, could you hear the mule drinking in the field?
- **(d)** The students were watching the abbot leading a procession out of the church.

**3** Fill each gap with the corresponding form in the correct tense:

|         | Infinitive | Present  | Future     | Imperfect   |
|---------|-----------|----------|------------|-------------|
| *love*  | amare     | amamus   | amabimus   | amabamus    |
| *hear*  | audire    | audit    | audiet     | audiebat    |
| *work*  | laborare  | ......... | laborabitis | laborabatis |
| *send*  | ......... | mitto    | ......... | mittebam    |
| ......... | ......... | venis    | venies     | veniebas    |
| *write* | ......... | ......... | scribent   | .........   |
| *take*  | ......... | capit    | ......... | .........   |
| ......... | timere    | ......... | timebis    | .........   |
| *give*  | ......... | dat      | ......... | .........   |
| *open*  | ......... | aperio   | ......... | .........   |
| ......... | ......... | vident   | ......... | .........   |
| ......... | ......... | laudamus | ......... | .........   |
| *do*    | facere    | ......... | ......... | faciebat    |
| *teach* | ......... | docetis  | ......... | .........   |

**4** Check you know these words:
agricola-ae, ara-ae, carus-a-um, coniunx-gis, ecclesia-ae,
epistula-ae, iubeo-ere, libero-are, n(ih)il, nunc, peccator-is,
peregrinus-i, post, praeter, primus-a-um, quis, vestis-is.

**5** Think of some English words which are derived in part at least
from **coniunx**, **ecclesia** and **primus**.

# 12

# In manus tuas commendo spiritum meum
Into your hands I commend my spirit

In this unit you will learn about
- *Perfect tense*
- *Personal pronouns:* ego, tu, nos, vos
- Meus, tuus, noster, vester *(my, your, our, your [pl])*
- *And find out more about Latin in 'The murder in a cathedral'*

### Past tense: perfect

The perfect ('finished', 'perfected') is a past tense describing an action which is more momentary or instantaneous than that of the imperfect. In general the imperfect points us to the action itself, the perfect to the completion of the action (and therefore what comes next). In the two examples below, the same English verbal phrase is used to translate both tenses. But in one, the 'hurrying' is a singular, momentary, completed event, and in the other a recurring one.

Perfect

**Stephanus ad fenestram festinavit.**  *Stephen <u>hurried</u> to the window.*

## Imperfect

**Stephanus ad fenestram saepe festinabat.**

*Stephen often <u>hurried</u> (used to hurry) to the window.*

## Perfect endings

|  | am-are<br>*love* | mon-ere<br>*warn, advise* | mitt-ere<br>*send* |
|---|---|---|---|
| *I* | amav-i | monu-i | mis-i |
| *you* (s.) | amav-isti | monu-isti | mis-isti |
| *s/he, it* | amav-it | monu-it | mis-it |
| *we* | amav-imus | monu-imus | mis-imus |
| *you* (pl.) | amav-istis | monu-istis | mis-istis |
| *they* | amav-erunt | monu-erunt | mis-erunt |

|  | and-ire<br>*hear* | cap-ere<br>*take, capture* |
|---|---|---|
| *I* | audiv-i | cep-i |
| *you* (s.) | audiv-isti | cep-isti |
| *s/he, it* | audiv-it | cep-it |
| *we* | audiv-imus | cep-imus |
| *you* (pl.) | audiv-istis | cep-istis |
| *they* | audiv-erunt | cep-erunt |

In the perfect tense the endings of the verbs are not the only parts to change. Some verbs have a different stem. Try to remember it when you look the verb up.

| ambulo | ambulare | ambulavi | I (have) walked |
|---|---|---|---|
| laudo | laudare | laudavi | I (have) praised |
| habeo | habere | habui | I (have) had |
| video | videre | vidi | I saw, have seen |
| scribo | scribere | scripsi | I wrote, have written |
| dico | dicere | dixi | I (have) said |
| venio | venire | veni | I came, have come |
| facio | facere | feci | I (have) made, did, have done |
| sum | esse | fui | I have been, was |

144

### Practice (I)

**1** Translate into Latin (in the perfect tense):
  **(a)** He has walked.
  **(b)** They saw.
  **(c)** We have come.
  **(d)** I have taken.
  **(e)** You (s.) have warned.
  **(f)** He heard.
  **(g)** We have sent.
  **(h)** She advised.

**2** Change the underlined verbs to the corresponding perfect form, and translate:
  **(a)** Monachus servo <u>dicit</u>.
  **(b)** Ancillas in culina <u>laudamus</u>.
  **(c)** Dani-ne omnia monasteria <u>capiunt</u>?
  **(d)** Epistulam episcopo <u>scribis</u>?

*Si munimentum quaeris, circumspice* If you seek protection, look around you

◀) CD2, TR 2

Adhuc abbas in ecclesia praedicabat: '... Hic, in ecclesia, ubi sedemus, ubi oramus, ubi Deum laudamus, est vestra securitas. Si igitur munimentum quaeritis, circumspicite. Ecce tectum! Ecce magni muri! Hic in ecclesia vos curavimus, nunc vos curamus, et post mortem animas vestras semper curabimus. Aedificatum lapidibus monasterium centum annos hic stetit et hic stabit annos mille! Hic sunt omnia tuta. Quod vestras animas illud vestras res custodire potest. Iterum vobis dico: in ecclesia non solum animae sed etiam res sunt tutae. Scitis-ne cur haec dicam?

Rumores quosdam audivimus, non quidem confirmatos, sed tamen referendos. Nihil nos vidimus. Alieni-ne in silvis adfuerunt? Vidit-ne alienos in silva Theodorus? Quis nunc dicere potest? Theodorum miserum! Theodorus saltem in caelo cum angelis requiescit. Cras, ergo, si vultis esse securi, boves oves equi mulique in monasterii agros adducendi sunt. Si vobis placet, etiam res vestras in monasterio relinquatis. Vel autem, si mavultis, res vestras retinere licet, sed cavete.'

| | |
|---|---|
| aedificatus-a-um | built |
| alienus-i [m] | stranger |
| angelus-i [m] | angel |
| bos-vis [m/f] | ox |
| cavete | take care |
| centum | hundred |
| circumspicite | look around |
| confirmatus-a-um | confirmed |
| cras | tomorrow |
| custodio-ire | guard, watch over |
| haec [n.pl.] | these things |
| hic | here |
| lapis-idis [m] | stone |
| licet | it is permitted |
| mavultis | you prefer |
| mille | thousand |
| munimentum-i [n] | protection |
| murus-i [m] | wall |
| non solum ... sed etiam | not only ... but also |
| ovis-is [f] | sheep |
| placet | it pleases |
| quaero-ere | seek |
| quidem | indeed |
| quod ... illud | that which ... that... |
| quosdam | certain, unspecified |
| refero, referre | report |
| relinquatis | you may leave |
| requiesco-ere | rest |

| | |
|---:|:---|
| **res** [f] | *things, possessions* |
| **saltem** | *at least* |
| **securitas-tatis** [f] | *peace of mind* |
| **securus-a-um** | *sure, secure* |
| **sto-are, steti** | *stand* |
| **tectum-i** [n] | *ceiling* |
| **tutus-a-um** | *safe* |
| **vester-tra-trum** | *your* |
| **vos, vobis** [dat.] | *you (pl.)* |

**Personal pronouns: *Ego, tu, nos, vos***

They are only used in the nominative case for emphasis, because subject pronouns are implied in the ending of a verb (if there is no subject noun):

**Danos non vidimus.**　　　　*We did not see the Danes.*
<u>**Nos**</u> **nihil vidimus.**　　　　<u>*We*</u> *saw nothing.*

Pronouns are words used in place of nouns (**pro** is the Latin word for *in place of*):

| | I/me | you (s.) | we/us | you (pl.) |
|------|---------|----------|-------------------|--------------------|
| Nom. | **ego** | **tu** | **nos** | **vos** |
| Acc. | **me** | **te** | **nos** | **vos** |
| Gen. | **mei** | **tui** | **nostri/** | **vestri/** |
| | | | **nostrum** | **vestrum** |
| Dat. | **mihi/mi** | **tibi** | **nobis** | **vobis** |
| Abl. | **me** | **te** | **nobis** | **vobis** |

The preposition **cum** with often follows rather than precedes a pronoun, and is attached to it: **nobiscum** *with us*, **mecum** *with me*.

## 'My', 'your', 'our'

The possessive adjectives **meus, mea, meum** *my*, **tuus, tua, tuum** *your* (s.) have endings like **sanctus-a-um**, as do the plural equivalents **noster, nostra, nostrum** *our* and **vester, vestra, vestrum** *your* (pl.) with the exception of the nominative masculine singular (-**er**):

| | |
|---|---|
| *my* | **meus-a-um,** etc. |
| *your* (sing.) | **tuus-a-um,** etc. |
| *our* | **noster, -tra, -trum,** etc. |
| *your* (pl.) | **vester, -tra, -trum,** etc. |

**Da mi basia mille** *Give me a thousand kisses*

◀)) **CD2, TR 2, 01:30**

'Nunc, o amici, est optandum,' abbas adhuc praedicabat. 'Nos monachi, qui in monasterio habitamus, scientiae artium vitarum animarum sumus custodes. Deo volente, nos vigilantes capita bonaque vestra bene curabimus. Nunc, igitur, si dormire sine cura vultis, hodie in monasterium bona vestra capitaque adducenda sunt.' Abbatis vox e somno Augustinum excitavit.

'Dormire?' inquit Augustinus. 'Ego certe dormire sine cura volo.'

'St.' susurravit Paulus. 'Dani prope monasterium visi sunt.'

'Non credo!' inquit Augustinus. 'Cuius est fama?'

'Stephani.'

'Stephani? Si elephantus iuxta Stephanum sedeat, magister noster eum non agnoscat.'

'Immo. Theodorus ante mortem Danos in silvis ipse vidit et Stephano dixit.' Augustinus Paulum non audivit sed Luciam in primo subsellio spectabat: 'Da mi basia,' murmuravit Augustinus.

'Quid?'

'Da mi basia mille'.

'St. Taceas.'

'Deinde usque altera mille.'

'Equidem tibi nulla basia dabo,' ridebat Paulus.

'Eheu!' gemuit Augustinus, 'Illa te solum spectat, te solum amat. *Ille mi par esse deo videtur, ille, si fas est, superare divos.*'

'Quis est ille?' rogavit Paulus.

'Tu.'

'Ego?'

'Ita vero.' inquit Augustinus. 'Cupido est saevus. Me miserum. *Certas habuit puer ille sagittas.*'

'Io satis carminum!' exclamavit Paulus.

'*Rosa veris, quae videris clarior quam lilium,*' murmuravit Augustinus. Subito Pater Stephanus apparuit:

'Augustine et Paule, hodie ambo vos mecum ad Patrem Ricardum venietis,' inquit magister. 'Ille vos severissime verberabit.'

'Nos? Cur?' rogavit Augustinus.

'Semper in ecclesia estis garruli. Vos antea admonui. Nunc poenas dabitis.'

'Ignoscas nobis. Te oro, Magister, ne nos ducas ad Ricardum. Si tibi placet, rursum regulam monachorum exscribam.'

'O Sancta Maria!'

'Te oramus.'

'O molesti pueri ... esto. Sed si vos iterum susurrantes in ecclesia videbo, ambo verberandi eritis. Totus liber est exscribendus – hodie.'

'Ut vis, Magister.'

'St. Nunc cum ceteris discipulis cantandum est.'

Tandem abbas praedicare desiit. Omnes 'Deo gratias,' responderunt et cantare inceperunt.

| | |
|---|---|
| **agnoscat** | *would recognize* |
| **altera** | *another* |
| **ante(a)** | *before(hand)* |
| **appareo-ere-ui** | *appear* |
| **ars-tis [f]** | *art, skill* |
| **basium-i [n]** | *kiss* |
| **caput, capitis [n]** | *head, capital* |
| **certus-a-um** | *sure, unerring* |
| **clarior** | *more lovely* |
| **cuius** | *whose* |
| **cura-ae [f]** | *anxiety, stress* |

QUICK VOCAB

| | |
|---|---|
| **custos-dis** [m/f] | *guardian* |
| **da** | *give!* |
| **deinde** | *then, next* |
| **deo volente** | *with God willing* |
| **divus-i** [m] | *god* |
| **equidem** | *indeed, to be sure* |
| **esto** | *so be it* |
| **fama-ae** [f] | *story, report* |
| **fas** | *not blasphemous* |
| **garrulus-a-um** | *talkative* |
| **gemo-ere-ui** | *groan* |
| **illa** [f] | *she, that* |
| **ille** [m] | *he, that* |
| **immo** | *no* |
| **io** | *hey* |
| **ipse** | *he himself* |
| **lilium-i** [n] | *lily* |
| **molestus-a-um** | *troublesome* |
| **ne ducas** | *do not take* |
| **opto-are** | *choose* |
| **par** | *equal* |
| **quae videris** | *you who seem* |
| **quam** | *than* |
| **quid** | *what* |
| **rosa-ae** [f] | *rose* |
| **rursum** | *again* |
| **sagitta-ae** [f] | *arrow* |
| **scientia-ae** [f] | *knowledge* |
| **sedeat** | *were to sit* |
| **severissime** | *very severely* |
| **supero-are** | *surpass* |
| **usque** | *and on to* |
| **ver-is** [n] | *spring* |
| **verbero-are** | *beat* |
| **videtur** | *(s/he) seems* |
| **vigilans** | *watchful* |
| **visi sunt** | *were seen* |
| **vita-ae** [f] | *life* |

## Practice (II)

Rewrite the words in brackets in their correct forms:

**(a)** In ecclesia (nos) monachi (vester) pecuniam custodiemus.

**(b)** Ubi est (meus-a-um) vinum? Ancillae-ne vinum (vos) dederunt?

**(c)** (Meus-a-um) carmina (tu) dare volo.

**(d)** Gratias (tu), multas gratias.

## Living Latin

◄) CD2, TR 2, 04:07

### The murder in a cathedral

The sacrosanctity of a church in the Middle Ages was taken for granted. Refugees from the bloodiest conflicts might seek sanctuary in a church and even the least godfearing of soldiers would think twice before breaking it. The majority of people lived very parochial lives. The local church was one of the few stone buildings some might ever see. Here was a solid fortress for their protection, and a symbol of permanence and life everlasting. A church was, in both senses, a building you could have faith in.

Cathedrals were even more imposing, and some still stand out in today's urban skylines. How much more impressive when all around them lay wooden houses and thatched huts. Canterbury Cathedral was the scene of Thomas Becket's murder in the twelfth century, a shocking episode because an archbishop was hacked to death – in a cathedral.

This is an abbreviated version of the account by an eyewitness to Thomas' murder, William FitzStephen*:

**1**  The monks persuade Thomas to come into the church.

**Quid nisi timor et tremor venerunt super nos monachos, clericos et socios archiepiscopi? Sed bonus ille Thomas contemptor mortis erat.**

*Nothing but fear and trembling came over us monks, clerics, and companions of the archbishop. But the good Thomas was disdainful of death.*

**2**  The assassins arrive.

**Iturus ad aram superiorem, iam quattuor gradus ascenderat, cum ecce ad ostium claustri, quo veneramus, primus adest Reginaldus Ursonis loricatus, ense evaginato, et vociferans, 'Nunc huc ad me, homines regis!' Nec multo post adduntur ei tres socii eius, similiter loricis contecti corpora et capita praeter oculos solos, ensibus nudatis.**

*He was about to go up to the upper altar and had already gone up four steps, when there by the door to the cloister, where we had entered, stood the first of them, Reginaldus Ursonis, in full armour, sword drawn, shouting, 'Now follow me, men of the king!' A moment later his three accomplices joined him, their bodies and heads covered with armour except for their eyes alone, and their swords drawn.*

**3**  'Where is the traitor?'

**Clamavit aliquis, 'Ubi est proditor?' Ille: 'Ecce ego, non proditor, sed presbyter Dei; et miror, quod in tali habitu ecclesiam Dei ingressi estis. Quid placet vobis?' Unus sicarius, 'Ut moriaris.' At ille: 'Et ego in nomine Domini mortem suscipio, et animam meam et ecclesiae causam Deo et beatae Mariae et sanctis huius ecclesiae patronis commendo. Absit ut propter gladios vestros fugiam.'**

*One of them shouted: 'Where is the traitor?' He replied: 'Here I am, no traitor, but a priest of God; and I am surprised that you have entered the house of God in such attire. What is your business?' One of the murderers said: 'To kill you.' He replied: 'I embrace death in the name of the Lord, and I commend my soul and the cause of the church to God, to Blessed Mary and to the patron saints of this church. Don't think that I will run from your swords.'*

**4** His death.

**Quidam eum plano ense caedebat inter scapulas, dicens, 'Fuge; mortuus es.' Ille immotus perstitit, et cervicem praebens, se Domino commendabat. 'In manus tuas, Domine, commendo spiritum meum.' Datur in caput eius ictus secundus. Super dextram cecidit, ad dextram Dei iturus.**

*One of them whipped him across his shoulders with a flat blade, saying, 'Run; you are a dead man.' He didn't budge but stood his ground, and offering his neck he entrusted himself to the Lord. 'Into your hands, O Lord, I commend my spirit.' A second blow struck his head. He fell to the right, on his way to the right hand of God.*

*post-classical

# TESTING YOURSELF

**1** Fill each gap with the corresponding form in the correct tense:

|         | Infinitive | Present  | Future    | Imperfect | Perfect    |
|---------|------------|----------|-----------|-----------|------------|
| *walk*  | ambulare   | ambulat  | ......... | ......... | ambulavit  |
| *come*  | venire     | venimus  | ......... | ......... | venimus    |
| ....... | .........  | .........| laudabitis| ......... | laudavistis|
| *teach* | .........  | doceo    | ......... | ......... | docui      |
| ....... | .........  | dicis    | dices     | ......... | .........  |
| ....... | .........  | .........| .........| scribebant| .........  |
| *take*  | .........  | .........| capiemus  | ......... | .........  |
| ....... | videre     | .........| videbunt  | ......... | .........  |
| *be*    | .........  | .........| erit      | ......... | fuit       |

**2** Rewrite these sentences making underlined words plural (if singular) and singular (if plural), and translate:
  **(a)** O Augustine, mihi dulce <u>carmen</u> tuum leges?
  **(b)** Miser Stephanus cum <u>discipulo</u> in bibliotheca semper laborabat.
  **(c)** Lucia-ne <u>peregrinos</u> in silva audivit?
  **(d)** <u>Ancilla</u> nos monuit.

**3** Translate into Latin (use the perfect for all past tenses):
  **(a)** Students, did Theodorus walk with you in the wood?
  **(b)** Augustine, did you hear the abbot preaching?
  **(c)** I saw the abbess whispering to the cook.
  **(d)** Paul, did you write a letter to Lucia?

**3** English doesn't give many clues to the meaning of these words. How many do you know?
adhuc, autem, bene, certe, deinde, enim, ergo, et...et, etiam, fortasse, igitur, nam, neque...neque, quidem, quoniam, rursum, saepe, semper, sic, sine, subito, tamen, tandem, vel.

# Revision ii (Units 7–12)

**1** Fill the gaps with the correct form (tense and person) of one of:
canto-are-avi, devoro-are-avi, dormio-ire-ivi, scribo-ere,
scripsi, video-ere, vidi.

**(a)** Abbatissa nobis
\_\_\_\_ (*future*).

**(b)** Monachi \_\_\_\_
(*present*) **quod
multum cibum
vinumque** \_\_\_\_
(*perfect*).

**(c)** Multos Danos
in silva \_\_\_\_
(*perfect*)!

Multos Danos in silva.......!

**(d)** Paulus epistulam Luciae ____ (*present*).

2 Identify the future, imperfect and perfect forms of the underlined verbs:
  **(a)** In bibliotheca discipulus carmina <u>recitat</u>.
  **(b)** Discipuli <u>rident</u>.
  **(c)** O ancillae, Danos <u>auditis</u>?
  **(d)** Epistulam Luciae <u>scribo</u>.

3 Choose the correct form of the gerundive:
  **(a)** Peregrini multas linguas (doceo-ere) sunt.
  **(b)** Nunc corpus miserabile est (sepelio-ire).
  **(c)** Discipuli mali non (laudo-are) sunt.
  **(d)** Epistula non in ecclesia sed in bibliotheca est (scribo-ere).

4 Choose the correct form of the present participle:
  **(a)** Monachus in terram cecidit e silva (fugio-ere).
  **(b)** Abbatem ex monasterio pompam (duco-ere) spectavi.
  **(c)** Amicos nostros in ecclesia (sedeo-ere) vidimus.
  **(d)** Discipulus virgines in horto (canto-are) audivit.

5 Write out the following nouns in all five cases, singular and plural: **annus-i, vita-ae, oppidum-i, potio-nis, clamor-is, tempus-oris**

6 Translate into Latin:
  **(a)** Did you hear the maiden's song, Father Stephen?
  **(b)** The bishop was preaching to all the monks.

**(c)** Soon we shall bury the monk's pitiable corpse.

**(d)** The cook was drinking wine with the sad student all night long.

**7** Group the English words with their Latin ancestor:

| | | |
|---|---|---|
| **hospes, hospitis** | sure | dainty |
| **caput, capitis** | predicate | dish fancy host |
| **discus-i** | fantasy hotel | disco |
| **dignitas, dignitatis** | cattle hospital | computer |
| **phantasia-ae** | secure disk | |
| **praedico-are** | hospice chapter | |
| **blasphemo-are** | capital | count |
| **securus-a-um** | blaspheme discus blame | chattel |
| **computo-are** | hostel dignity | preach |

**8** Give the English meaning and also the genitive singular of these nouns:
amor, ars, basium, bos, caput, carmen, coniunx, cura, frater, frigus, homo, labor, lux, mater, miles, murus, nomen, nox, panis, pax, tectum, tempus, timor, ventus, veritas, vita, vox.

**9** A popina is (**a**) an illegitimate daughter of a pope; (**b**) a small flower found in Rumania, which produces opium; (**c**) an ancient inn or take-away – a place to pop in for a quick snack?

# 13

## Paulus sub aqua
### Paulus under water

In this unit you will learn about
- *Past participles*
- *Perfect passive (past participles with* esse*)*
- *Participle phrases (including the ablative* absolute*)*
- *Irregular verb:* eo, ire *(to go)*
- *And find out more about Latin in 'A winter's night'*

### Past participles

The past participle, like the present participle (see Unit 11), is an adjective formed from a verb. The endings of the past participle are like **sanctus-a-um**:

| | |
|---|---|
| **cibus devoratus** | *the devoured food* |
| **unguenta desiderata** | *the desired perfumes* |
| **libri scripti** | *the written books* |

### Insight
The past participle is an adjective formed from a verb with endings like **sanctus-a-um**: e.g. **cibus devoratus** = *'the devoured food'*, **puella amata** = *'the loved girl'*.

Past participles are mostly passive. So far almost all the verbs you have seen have been active, i.e. the subject 'does it' to the object.

A passive verb switches it around with the subject being 'done to'; in other words it would be the object if the verb were active: e.g. '*the student loves* (active verb) *the girl*' and '*the girl is loved* (passive verb) *by the student*'.

The past participle is passive, whereas the present participle is active. The difference may be significant ...

| | | |
|---|---|---|
| Present participle (active): | **monachus devorans** | *the monk (while) devouring...* |
| Past participle (passive): | **monachus devoratus** | *the monk having been devoured* |

> ### Insight
> Past participles are mostly passive, i.e. the noun they qualify or refer to is being done to and not doing it: e.g. **puella amata** = '*the loved girl*' (she is the one loved, not doing the loving).

### Practice (I)

Are the underlined verbs active or passive?

(a) The bishop <u>was not loved</u>.
(b) We <u>will drink</u> more wine.
(c) All the wine <u>has been drunk</u>.
(d) She <u>would sing</u> all day if she was happy.
(e) That hymn <u>has never been sung</u> before.
(f) His clothes <u>were left</u> on the ground.

### Translating past participles

The past participle usually describes an action which is completed before that of the main verb. As with present participles, there are different ways we can translate them. You will see that the first and most literal translation is the least suitable one:

160

**Danus in monasterio visus in silvam festinavit.**

The Dane seen in the monastery hurried into the wood.

The Dane having been seen in the monastery hurried into the wood.

After the Dane was seen in the monastery he hurried into the wood.

The Dane, who had been seen in the monastery, hurried into the wood.

The Dane was seen in the monastery and hurried into the wood.

And there are other ways too we may express this. You decide according to the general sense and what feels right in English.

### Practice (II)

Translate each sentence and include the English word 'after':

**(a)** Theodorus in ecclesia visus in silvam festinavit.
**(b)** Episcopus abbatissam visam laudavit.
**(c)** Monachi auditi e monasterio festinaverunt.
**(d)** Carmina audita laudavimus.

### The 'principal parts' of a verb

The past participle presents a form of the verb that can be a little different from its other forms, e.g. **scribo, scribere** (*I write, to write*) is **scriptus-a-um** in the past participle. The neuter form (**scriptum**) is the fourth 'principal part' of a verb. The principal parts are the key forms of a verb:

| | |
|---|---|
| **scribo** | *I write* |
| **scribere** | *to write* |
| **scripsi** | *I wrote/have written* |
| **scriptum** | *written* |

## Practice (III)

Complete the table of the four main parts (or 'principal parts') of
a verb. A fifth column is added for English words which are very
similar to the past participle (in many cases you can replace the
final -**um** of the past participle with *-ion* and vice versa).

| Present ('I...') | Infinitive ('to...') | Perfect ('I have...') | Past participle (neuter) | Derivative |
|---|---|---|---|---|
| oro | orare | oravi | oratum | oration |
| narro | narrare | narravi | narratum | narrative |
| aestimo | aestimare | ...... | aestimatum | estimation |
| sto | stare | steti | statum | ...... |
| saluto | salutare | salutavi | ...... | salutation |
| recito | ...... | recitavi | recitatum | recitation |
| vaco | vacare | vacavi | ...... | vacation |
| damno | damnare | damnavi | damnatum | ...... |
| maneo | manere | mansi | mansum | ...... |
| rideo | ...... | risi | risum | (de)rision |
| sedeo | sedere | sedi | ...... | session |
| teneo | tenere | tenui | ...... | (at)tention |
| video | videre | vidi | visum | ...... |
| moneo | ...... | monui | ...... | (ad)monition |
| dico | dicere | dixi | ...... | diction |
| duco | ...... | duxi | ...... | (in)duction |
| relinquo | ...... | reliqui | relictum | (de)reliction |
| scribo | scribere | scripsi | ...... | (de)scription |
| ascendo | ascendere | ascendi | ...... | ascension |
| ago | agere | egi | ...... | action |
| audio | audire | audivi | ...... | audition |
| venio | venire | veni | ...... | (in)vention |
| perficio | perficere | perfeci | ...... | perfection |
| recipio | recipere | recepi | ...... | reception |

## Past participles with *est* or *sunt*

A past participle with the verb 'to be' forms the perfect passive in Latin:

| | |
|---|---|
| **Monachi in silva visi sunt.** | *The monks were seen/have been seen in the wood.* |
| **Sumus non laudati.** | *We were not/have not been praised.* |
| **Ancilla ad oppidum missa est.** | *The maid was/has been sent to the town.* |

## Insight

With a past participle, **est** is translated as '*was*' or '*has been*' (and not '*is*'): e.g. **abbatissa est laudata** = 'the abbess *was praised*'.

### Practice (IV)

Complete each sentence with the past participle in its correct form, and translate:

**(a)** Theodorus in agro (sepelio-ire-ivi, sepultum) est.
**(b)** Peregrini in silva (video-ere, vidi, visum) sunt.
**(c)** Mulus ab umbris (terreo-ere, terrui, territum) est.
**(d)** Virgo a patre (laudo-are-avi, laudatum) est.
**(e)** Unguenta ab abbatissa sunt (desidero-are-avi, desideratum).
**(f)** Vinum a mulo (porto-are-avi, portatum) est.

***Natalis Christi dies*** *Christ's birthday*

🔊 CD2, TR 3

Menses lente transibant. Hiems erat severissima et frigus monasterium invadit. Paulus Luciam videre solam non poterat, quod virgo semper cum matre ambulabat aut in ecclesia orabat. Infelix per longas gelidasque noctes per fenestram stellas spectans in cella iacebat.

Mox natalis Christi dies a monachis celebratus est. Karolus et Egberta et Lucia ad missas audiendas advenerunt et postea domum cum episcopo abbatissaque discesserunt. In monasterio Augustinus ceterique discipuli fabulam agebant: Iosephus et Maria a tabernis reiecti stabulum inveniunt. Omnes monachi ab Augustini fabula sunt exhilarati praeter abbatem qui eam iocosiorem vocabat. Multae vini amphorae exhaustae, multi anseres devorati sunt. Sic paucos dies omnes curae sublatae sunt.

Per multos menses monachi anxii fuerant, populus incertus. Media in hieme plurimi Danos propter frigus atque mare turbulentum non exspectabant; itaque res suas apud se tenebant. Vere tamen veniente res bovesque in monasterium adductae sunt. Primo thesaurus in ecclesia modicus erat quod exiguae pauperibus servisque res. Sed post paucos dies fictilia, fibulae, scuta, lintea et cetera in ecclesiam tradita sunt; thesaurus igitur gradatim crescebat.

QUICK VOCAB

| | |
|---|---|
| adduco-ere-xi-ductum | bring |
| amphora-ae [f] | jug |
| anser-is [m] | goose |
| apud se | at their homes |
| aspicio-ere | look at |
| atque | and |
| aut | or |
| celebro-are-avi-atum | celebrate |
| cella-ae [f] | cell, room |
| Christus-I | Christ |
| cresco-ere | grow |
| discedo-ere-essi | depart |
| domum | homewards |
| eam | her, it |
| exhaurio-ire-ivi, exhaustum | drain, empty |
| exhilaro-are-avi-atum | cheer |
| exiguus-a-um | scant, bare |
| fibula-ae [f] | brooch |
| fictilia-ium [n] | earthenware |
| frigus-oris [n] | chill, cold |
| fuerant | (they) had been |
| gelidus-a-um | cold |

| | |
|---|---|
| **gradatim** | *gradually* |
| **hiems, hiemis** [f] | *winter* |
| **iocosiorem** | *too flippant* |
| **linteum-i** [n] | *linen cloth* |
| **mare-is** [n] | *sea* |
| **medius-a-um** | *mid-, middle of* |
| **mensis-is** [m] | *month* |
| **modicus-a-um** | *modest, small* |
| **natalis** dies [m] | *birthday* |
| **pauper-is** [m] | *pauper* |
| **plurimi** *most* | *people* |
| **postea** | *afterwards* |
| **propter** [+acc.] | *because of* |
| **reicio-ere-eci-ectum** | *reject, refuse* |
| **scutum-i** [n] | *shield* |
| **severissimus-a-um** | *very severe, hard* |
| **stabulum-i** [n] | *stable* |
| **stella-ae** [f] | *star* |
| **sublatae sunt** | *were raised, lifted* |
| **suus-a-um** | *their/his/her own* |
| **taberna-ae** [f] | *inn* |
| **thesaurus-i** [m] | *store* |
| **trado-ere-didi-ditum** | *hand over* |
| **transeo-ire** | *pass, go by* |
| **ver-is** [n] | *spring* |

## Participles within the sentence

A participle agrees with the noun it describes just as an adjective does. That noun may be the subject of the main verb:

| | |
|---|---|
| <u>**Iosephus**</u> a taberna <u>reiectus</u> stabulum invenit. | *Joseph, <u>having-been-rejected</u> by the inn, finds a stable.* |

Or object of the main verb:

| | |
|---|---|
| <u>**Multos**</u> in agris <u>laborantes</u> spectabat. | *He watched <u>many (people) working</u> in the fields.* |

Or in another case (below, the dative):

**Domina <u>coquo</u> <u>laudato</u> pecuniam dedit.**    *The lady gave money <u>to the having-been-praised cook.</u> (The lady praised the cook and gave him money.)*

And don't forget that a present participle can have an object of its own:

**Coquum <u>crusta</u> devorantem spectabam.**    *I was watching the cook devouring <u>the cakes</u>.*

### Practice (V)

Complete each sentence with the past participle in its correct form, and translate:

**(a)** Benedictus cenam ab ancillis (paro-are-avi, paratum) devoravit.

**(b)** Crusta a coquo (devoro-are-avi, devoratum) non invenire poteramus.

**(c)** Domina mihi epistulam (scribo-ere, scripsi, scriptum) dedit.

**(d)** Augustinus monachi (sepelio-ire, sepelivi, sepultum) discipulus erat.

### The 'ablative absolute'

You will find many noun-and-participle phrases in the ablative. These expressions are almost detachable from the core of the sentence. They work as extra clauses, and are neither subject nor object of the main verb:

**Monachi <u>Theodoro sepulto</u> in monasterium revenerunt.**    *The monks, <u>with Theodorus having been buried,</u> came back into the monastery. (The monks, after burying Theodorus, ...)*

| | |
|---|---|
| **Visis mulis aliis mulus Pauli rudere incepit.** | *With other mules having-been-seen, Paul's mule began to bray. (Upon seeing other mules ...)* |
| **Vere veniente monachi in agros redierunt.** | *With spring coming the monks returned to the fields. (At the arrival of spring...)* |

The ablative of the present participle ends **-ente**, not **-enti**, when it is used in an ablative absolute. Otherwise the endings of the present participle are the same as those of **prudens** – see Unit 11.

## Insight

Some noun-and-participle phrases have no grammatical link to the main verb (i.e. are neither subject nor object) and these are in the ablative case: e.g. **cibo devorato coquus culinam reliquit** = '*with the food devoured the cook left the kitchen*' ('*after the cook had devoured the food he left the kitchen*'). This is called the Ablative Absolute.

### Practice (VI)

Choose the correct word and translate (and remember that present participles are active and past participles are passive):

**(a)** Paulus, Augustino Tibulli carmina (**legente/legentia**), regulam monasterii exscribebat.

**(b)** Theodorus alienos in silva (susurranti/susurrantes) vidit.

**(c)** Multo cibo (devoratus/devorato) Benedictus obdormivit.

### Irregular verb: *eo, ire, ii (ivi), itum* To go

No language course would be complete without some space devoted to irregular verbs. They are 'irregular' because they do not conform to the patterns of the main conjugations, adopting their abnormal shape partly from breadth of use (words which are confined to grammarians, lexicographers and crossword buffs may keep their shape for generations, but those which enjoy widespread use can be affected by any number of things); and partly from evolving as a fusion of different roots. Consider for example our verb 'to go' and its different forms: 'go', 'going', 'gone', 'went', 'been'. The French for 'to go' also has radically different forms: the Latin words **ambulo**, **ambulare**, **vado**, **vadere**, and **eo**, **ire** are all roots of *aller* (*je vais, j'irai*).

| **ire** *to go* | Present | Future | Imperfect | Perfect |
|---|---|---|---|---|
| *I* | **eo** | **ibo** | **ibam** | **ii** |
| *you* (s.) | **is** | **ibis** | **ibas** | **isti** |
| *s/he, it* | **it** | **ibit** | **ibat** | **iit** |
| *we* | **imus** | **ibimus** | **ibamus** | **iimus** |
| *you* (pl.) | **itis** | **ibitis** | **ibatis** | **istis** |
| *they* | **eunt** | **ibunt** | **ibant** | **ierunt** |

Compound forms: **abeo-ire** *to depart,* **redeo-ire** *to return,* **adeo-ire** *to approach/go to,* **exeo-ire** *to go out.*

### Practice (VII)

Translate:

**(a)** We depart.
**(b)** They will return.
**(c)** We were approaching.
**(d)** She goes out.
**(e)** They have departed.

### Castellum Comitis Karoli *Count Charles' Castle*

🔊 **CD2, TR 3, 02:21**

Paulus, aestate adveniente, ad oppidum rediit. Die aestuoso sub arbores frondescentes cum mulo per iter insolitum ambulabat; nam Luciae villam spectare volebat. Post tria milia e silvis venerunt et Paulus videre poterat magnum castellum in quo Lucia cum matre Egberta et patre Karolo, viro nobili et ditissimo, habitabat. Comes Karolus regionem totam regebat. Abbas Laurentius et Comes Karolus erant duo in regione potentissimi.

Paulus multos in agris prope castellum laborantes spectabat. Alii herbam metebant, alii faenum in praedium portabant. Subito visis mulis aliis mulus rudere incepit. 'Eheu, tace!' clamavit Paulus habenas quatiens et celeriter mulum in silvam duxit. Prope silvam Paulus visum ad stagnum adiit ubi multam aquam mulus sitiens bibit. Deinde, mulo arbori in silva ligato, Paulus ad stagnum revenit et veste deposita in aquam frigidam se immersit: sub aquam natavit et rediens ad aequor exhalavit. 'Utinam hic maneam per totum diem,' suspiravit Paulus, et otiosus in aequore innavit caelum contemplans. Haud multo post mulum rudentem audivit. 'Quid est tibi, mule? Tace, improba bestia!'

| | |
|---|---|
| **aequor-is** [n] | *surface* |
| **aestas-tatis** [f] | *summer* |
| **aestuosus-a-um** | *hot* |

| | |
|---|---|
| depono-ere-sui-situm | put down |
| ditissimus-a-um | very rich |
| faenum-i [n] | hay |
| frondesco-ere | put forth leaves |
| habena-ae [f] | rein |
| haud multo post | not long afterwards |
| herba-ae [f] | grass |
| improbus-a-um | troublesome |
| inno-are-avi | swim, float |
| insolitus-a-um | unusual, unfamiliar |
| iter-ineris [n] | way, route |
| ligo-are-avi-atum | tie, bind |
| meto-ere | gather, reap, mow |
| nato-are-avi | swim |
| otiosus-a-um | lazy |
| potentissimus-a-um | most powerful |
| praedium-i [n] | store, barn |
| quatio-ere | shake |
| quid est tibi? | what's the matter with you? |
| sitiens | thirsty |
| stagnum-i [n] | pond, lake |
| suspiro-are-avi | sigh |
| tria milia | three miles |
| utinam maneam | if only I might stay |

## Living Latin

◄) CD2, TR 3, 04:28

### A winter's night

**1**  No room in the inn:

**\*Exiit edictum a Caesare Augusto, ut describeretur universus orbis. Haec descriptio prima facta est praeside Syriae Quirino: et ibant omnes ut profiterentur singuli in suam civitatem. Ascendit autem**

et Ioseph a Galilaea de civitate Nazareth, in Iudaeam civitatem
David, quae vocatur Bethleem: eo quod esset de domo et familia
David, ut profiteretur cum Maria desponsata sibi uxore praegnate.
Factum est autem cum essent ibi, impleti sunt dies ut pareret.
Et peperit filium suum primogenitum, et pannis eum involvit: et
reclinavit eum in praesepio, quia non erat eis locus in diversorio.

(St Luke ii, 1–7)

*A formal command was issued by Caesar Augustus that there should be
a census of the whole world. This census first took place when Quirinus
was governor of Syria: each and every person went to his own town
to be registered. And Joseph went up from Galilee, from the town of
Nazareth, into Judaea, to the town of David which is called Bethlehem:
he went there, since he belonged to the house and line of David, to
register with his wife, Mary, who was heavy with child. And during the
time they were there, the day arrived when she gave birth. And she bore
a son, her firstborn, and wrapped him in swaddling clothes, and laid him
in a manger as there was no room for them in the inn.*

**2**  Refusal of entry is a stock convention of ancient comedy and
love poetry. Languishing outside his mistress's house, a lover
may have to contend with the door, doorkeeper, dog, husband
and bad weather.

Nam posita est nostrae custodia saeva puellae,
  clauditur et dura ianua firma sera.
Ianua difficilis domini te verberet imber,
  te Iovis imperio fulmina missa petant.
Ianua, iam pateas uni mihi victa querellis,
  neu furtim verso cardine aperta sones.
Et mala si qua tibi dixit dementia nostra,
  ignoscas; capiti sint precor illa meo.
Te meminisse decet quae plurima voce peregi
  supplice cum posti florida serta darem.
Tu quoque ne timide custodes, Delia, falle.
  Audendum est: fortes adiuvat ipsa Venus.

(Tibullus, Elegies i, 2, 5–16)

*A tight security has been put on my girl, and the thick door is closed with an uncaring bolt. You, door, belong to an unfeeling master, and I pray the rain lash you, I pray Jupiter aim his lightning down upon you. Now look here, door, won't you be won over by my pleas and open up just for me? Quietly turn your hinges and don't make a sound as you open. Forgive me if I ever spoke ill of you – I was unhinged. May my curses rebound on my own head. Better you recall my many moments of suppliant pleading when I laid flowery wreaths about your post. And you too, Delia, be fearless and evade your guards. Be bold: Venus herself looks well on the brave.*

\*post-classical

# TESTING YOURSELF

**1** Translate into Latin and include a present participle in each sentence:

   **(a)** Theodorus, fearing the pilgrims, went out of the wood.

   **(b)** For a long time the cook was watching the maidservants working in the garden.

   **(c)** Father Stephen sat in the church, grieving.

   **(d)** While Paul was swimming in the pond, the pilgrims were approaching the wood.

**2** Translate into Latin and include a past participle in each sentence. Remember that they are passive (e.g. (a) 'The Danes having-been-heard, ...')

   **(a)** Upon hearing the Danes, Lucia returned to the monastery.

   **(b)** The meal was prepared by the maids and devoured by the monks.

   **(c)** The letter was written by the monk and handed over to the count.

   **(d)** After the horse had been tied to a tree, the student swam in the pond.

**3** Complete the table, which includes a column for derivatives similar to the present/infinitive forms:

| Present ('I...') | Infinitive ('to...') | Derivative |
|---|---|---|
| efficio | efficere | efficient |
| relinquo | relinquere | relinquish |
| delinquo | delinquere | ......... |
| rideo | (de)ridere | ......... |
| duco | (pro)ducere | ......... |
| scribo | scribere | ......... |
| recipio | recipere | ......... |

**4** Translate these past participles and identify their present and infinitive forms:

E.g. **amatus** Answer: 'having been loved, **amo, amare**'

(a) dictus (b) missus (c) confirmatus (d) liberatus (e) scriptus
(f) factus (g) ductus (h) inceptus (i) perfectus (j) visus
(k) inflammatus (l) apertus (m) doctus (n) reiectus (o) traditus.

**5** **Caveat emptor** means (a) the space must be sold empty;
(b) there is no food left; (c) the buyer should be cautious?

# 14

---

# Venatrix in silva
## A huntress in the wood

In this unit you will learn about
- *Fourth declension nouns*
- *Fifth declension nouns*
- *Pluperfect tense*
- *And find out more about Ovid's story of Diana and Actaeon in 'A hunting moral'*

### Nouns: fourth declension

These are similar to nouns of the second declension, although the ending **-us** is not limited to the nominative singular: **-us** could also indicate a genitive singular, nominative plural or accusative plural:

|  | **arcus** (m) *bow, arch* | |
|  | Singular | Plural |
| Nom. | arc-us | arc-us |
| Acc. | arc-um | arc-us |
| Gen. | arc-us | arc-uum |
| Dat. | arc-ui | arc-ibus |
| Abl. | arc-u | arc-ibus |

> You have now seen all three kinds or noun which end **-us** in
> the nominative singular: **mulus** (second declension), **tempus**
> (third declension neuter) and **arcus** (fourth declension).

### Practice (I)

**1** Match each noun to its meaning:

**(a)**

| | |
|---|---|
| metus | *spirit* |
| casus | *chance* |
| gradus | *fear*   *verse* |
| spiritus | *step* |
| versus | |

**(b)**

| | |
|---|---|
| gemitus | *hunt*   *hand* |
| vultus | |
| exercitus | *face/expression* |
| manus | *army* |
| venatus | *groan* |

**(c)**

| | |
|---|---|
| domus* | *weeping* |
| fletus | *lake* |
| tumultus | *attack* |
| lacus # | *noise* |
| impetus | *home/house* |

*domus was frequently and widely used, and picked up one or two
endings from the second declension: the genitive could be **domus**
or **domi**, the dative **domui** or **domo** and the ablative was always

**domo.** In the plural all endings were as above (fourth declension) except the accusative plural which was sometimes **domos** instead of **domus.** 'At home' was **domi.**

\# a **stagnum** was a pond or small lake, smaller than a **lacus.**

**2** Translate into Latin:
  **(a)** with a sad expression
  **(b)** by chance
  **(c)** pleasing verses
  **(d)** by hand
  **(e)** of the holy spirit
  **(f)** with a groan
  **(g)** the count's armies
  **(h)** the maiden's bow and arrows
  **(i)** in the lake
  **(j)** at home

## Prepositions with the ablative

The prepositions **in** *in*, **ex** *out of, from*, **ab** *by, from*, and **cum** *with, in the company of* are all used with the ablative. The ablative is also used without a preposition, for example explaining how or with what something is done:

| | |
|---|---|
| **Gemitu dixit.** | *He spoke with a groan.* |
| **Metu pavidus...** | *Quaking with fear...* |

## Pluperfect tense

The pluperfect is another past tense, whose English equivalent uses the auxiliary 'had'. It is a further step into the past:

| | |
|---|---|
| **Numquam abbatem audiveramus.** | *We had never heard the abbot.* |
| **Peregrini nos viderant.** | *The pilgrims had seen us.* |

The stem of the pluperfect is the same as that of the perfect, the endings are those of **esse** in the imperfect:

| | Pluperfect | |
|---|---|---|
| *I had...* | **vid-eram** | **audiv-eram** |
| *you had... (s.)* | **vid-eras** | **audiv-eras** |
| *s/he had...* | **vid-erat** | **audiv-erat** |
| *we had...* | **vid-eramus** | **audiv-eramus** |
| *you had... (pl.)* | **vid-eratis** | **audiv-eratis** |
| *they had...* | **vid-erant** | **audiv-erant** |

## Insight

The pluperfect tense is always represented in English with 'had': e.g. 'she <u>had</u> swum before'.

**Luciae venatus** *Lucia's chase*

◆) CD2, TR 4

> **Shared endings key**
> **-us** mulus: nom.
> tempus: nom. or acc.
> **arcus: nom., gen., nom. pl., acc. pl.**

Interea Lucia venatu, qui fuerat longus et sine praemio, fessa erat. Equus eius quoque erat calidus fessusque. Illa igitur in stagno natare constituerat et nunc per silvam ad stagnum adibat. Gemitu tamen muli audito 'Heus, ecquis hic est?' dicens circumspexit. Nullo ergo respondente, sagitta e pharetra erepta, equum lente ad sonitum duxit. In silva mulum atque relictam Pauli vestem agnoscens, ex equo descendit et arcum sagittamque manu tenens furtim ad stagnum adibat.

Paulus, qui mulum audiverat, adhuc caelum contemplabat. Subito vocem 'Tolle manus tuas!' audivit. 'Qu... qu... qu... quis es?' metu balbus rogavit, 'Quid vis?'

'Tu-ne anas?' inquit Lucia ridens, simul et arcum sagittamque tenens ex arboribus venit.

'Lucia! Ego Paulus. Nonne me agnoscis?'

'Paulus?'

'Ita vero. Salve, salve! Eheu, tumultu perterritus sum! Vis-ne natare? Age, tibi arcum deponere licet.'

'Cur in hoc loco ades?'

'Natare volui. Si tibi placet, arcum deponere licet.'

'Semper arcum teneo,' respondit illa.

'Tu es sagittaria?' rogavit ille.

'Ita certe sum. Pater me tela conicere docuit. Et tu, quo vadis?'

'Ad oppidum. Ignoscas mihi si non licet natare in hoc stagno.'

'Manere tibi licet.'

'Gratias tibi. In quid arcum intendis?'

'In arborem illam,' inquit Lucia arborem in ulteriore ripa demonstrans.

'Numquam illam percuties!' Paulus risit. Luciae tamen telum per auras stridens eundem in arborem adhaesit. Paulus balbus 'Incredibile ... mirabile,' inquit. 'Tu vera es venatrix. Animalia saepe interficis?'

'Non numquam,' inquit Lucia ridens et stagnum ad sagittam recuperandam circumvenit. 'Hodie tamen nihil cepimus.'

'Nisi me!' risit Paulus.

'Nisi te. Sed bestias multo saeviores quam te vidi.'

'Ego bestias omnes amo nec umquam interficio. Sub caelo omnes vivimus, animalia hominesque ...'

'Hssh, taceas, quis est ille?' inquit Lucia.

'Quem dicis?'

'Voces audire possum. Ecce quidam ad stagnum adeunt.'

| | | |
|---|---|---|
| adhaereo-ere-si | *stick* | |
| agnosco-ere | *recognize* | |
| anas-atis [f] | *duck* | |
| animal-is [n] | *animal* | |
| balbus-a-um | *stammering* | |
| calidus-a-um | *warm* | |
| conicio-ere | *throw* | |

| | |
|---|---|
| **constituo-ere-ui** | *decide* |
| **depono-ere** | *put down* |
| **ecquis?** | *who?* |
| **eius** | *her, his* |
| **eripio-ere-ripui-reptum** | *take out, snatch* |
| **eundem** [acc.] | *same* |
| **hues** | *hey!* |
| **illa(m)** | *she, her, that (fem.)* |
| **intendo-ere** | *aim* |
| **interficio-ere** | *kill* |
| **licet** | *it is permitted* |
| **locus-i** [m] | *place* |
| **multo saeviores** | *much more savage* |
| **non numquam** | *sometimes* |
| **nullus** | *not any, no one* |
| **per auras** | *through the air* |
| **percutio-ere** | *strike, hit* |
| **perterritus-a-um** | *thoroughly scared* |
| **pharetra-ae** [f] | *quiver* |
| **praemium-i** [n] | *reward* |
| **quam** | *than* |
| **quem** | *whom* |
| **quidam** [nom.] | *some (men)* |
| **quo** | *where (to)* |
| **quoque** | *also* |
| **recupero-are** | *recover* |
| **ripa-ae** [f] | *bank* |
| **sagittaria-ae** [f] | *archeress* |
| **simul** | *at the same time* |
| **sonitus-us** [m] | *sound, noise* |
| **strideo-ere** | *hum, whistle* |
| **telum-i** [n] | *missile* |
| **tolle!** | *raise, lift!* |
| **ulterior** | *far* |
| **umquam** | *ever* |
| **vado-ere** | *go* |
| **venatrix-icis** [f] | *huntress* |

## Nouns: fifth declension

This is the last of the declensions, and there are not many nouns belonging to this one. They are very similar to the third declension, with the exception of the genitive singular:

| res (f) thing, matter | | |
|---|---|---|
| | Singular | Plural |
| Nom. | res | res |
| Acc. | rem | res |
| Gen. | rei | rerum |
| Dat. | rei | rebus |
| Abl. | re | rebus |

### Practice (II)

Match each noun to its meaning:

| | | |
|---|---|---|
| dies | faith | |
| facies | | day |
| fides | hope | |
| spes | | face |

## Compound verbs

These are verbs such as **venire, facere, capere** with prefixes which add to the essential meaning. See Unit 3 for the changes to the root syllable of compound verbs (e.g. f**a**cere, ref**i**cere), and Unit 6 for English derivatives.

## Practice (III)

Fill the gaps in the following table, adding a prefix from the list below to the left-hand column:

Prefixes: **a(b)**, **ad**, **circum**, **cum**, **de**, **e(x)**, **in**, **per**

| Prefix | Simple verb | | Compound verb | |
|--------|-------------|--------|---------------|---------------|
| **ad** | ire | ......... | **adire** | *go to, approach* |
| ......... | ......... | *go* | ......... | *go out* |
| ......... | esse | *be* | ......... | *be absent* |
| ......... | ......... | ......... | **adesse** | *be present* |
| ......... | mittere | *send* | **amittere** | *send away, lose* |
| **ad** | capere | *take* | ......... | *receive, welcome* |
| ......... | ......... | ......... | **effugere** | *flee away* |
| **circum** | ......... | *come* | **circumvenire** | ......... |
| ......... | ......... | *call* | **convocare** | *call together* |
| ......... | ......... | *send* | **demittere** | *send down, lower* |
| ......... | facere | *make* | **afficere** | *treat, afflict* |
| ......... | putare | *think* | **computare** | *sum up, reckon* |
| ......... | ......... | *take, snatch* | **eripere** | *snatch out* |
| ......... | ruere | *rush* | **irruere** | *rush in* |
| ......... | venire | ......... | **invenire** | *come upon, find* |
| **per** | facere | *make* | ......... | *make thorough, finish* |

### *Peregrini ad stagnum* Strangers at the lake

🔊 **CD2, TR 4, 00:42**

> **Shared endings key**
> **-i** second declension: muli: nom. pl.; muli, vini: gen.
> third declension: dat.
> **fifth declension: gen., dat.**
> first person, perfect (I have ...)

'Qui sunt illi?' rogavit Paulus.

'Nescio. Numquam eos vidi.'

'Ocius, in aquam, ocius!' Lucia celeriter se immersit in aquam
et ambo inter calamos se celaverunt. Mox peregrini ad stagnum
advenerunt.

'... Postero die pecora et aurum rapiemus,' inquit quidam.
'Immo,' inquit alius, 'aurum est non rapiendum.... sola pecora.
Ecclesiae est aurum. Omnes res rapiendae sunt, praeter aurum et
argentum.'

Paulus, voce agnota, attonitus 'Est Pater Ricardus!' exclamavit,
'cellerarius noster qui in nostro monasterio habitat!'

'Ssst!' susurravit Lucia ponens manum ad os eius; quam Paulus
basiavit et virgo removit.

'Quid facit Ricardus in hoc loco?' Paulus in animo volutabat.
'Qui sunt socii eius? Mercatores?' Facies hominum videre non
poterant; multas voces alias audierunt sed non agnoverunt. Equos
virorum quoque bibentes audire poterant. Subito mulus Pauli
in silva rudivit. 'Quid est illud?' clamavit quidam. 'Ne timeas,'
respondit alter, 'ecce muli in agris.' Nec multo post viri abierunt.

'Mulus tuus est loquax!' inquit Lucia ex aqua resurgens.

'Quo abis? Nonne natare vis?'

'Minime! Illae voces erant Danorum.'

'Illi viri erant Dani? Cum Ricardo? Nonne erravisti?'

'Certa sum. Olim Danos hospites in nostro castello accepimus.
Age, illi statim sequendi.'

'Statim? Sed vestes induere debeo.'
'Ergo festina, ne eos amittamus!'

| | |
|---|---|
| **agnosco-ere-ovi-otum** | *recognize* |
| **ambo** | *both* |
| **animus-i** [m] | *mind* |
| **argentum-i** [n] | *silver* |
| **aurum-i** [n] | *gold* |
| **basio-are-avi** | *kiss* |
| **calamus-i** [m] | *reed* |
| **cellerarius-i** [m] | *procurator* |
| **eos** | *them* |
| **erro-are-avi** | *make a mistake* |
| **hospes-itis** [m] | *host, guest* |
| **illi** | *those men* |
| **immo** | *on the contrary* |
| **induo-ere** | *put on* |
| **loquax** | *noisy* |
| **mercator-is** [m] | *trader* |
| **ne amittamus** | *lest we lose* |
| **ne timeas** | *don't be afraid* |
| **nescio-ire** | *do not know* |
| **ocius** | *quick!* |
| **olim** | *once (upon a time)* |
| **os, oris** [n] | *mouth* |
| **pecus-oris** [n] | *herd, flock* |
| **postero die** | *on the next day* |
| **quam** | *which* |
| **resurgo-ere** | *reappear* |
| **se celo-are-avi** | *hide oneself* |
| **sequendus-a-um** | *to be followed* |
| **socius-i** [m] | *colleague, associate* |
| **voluto-are** | *ponder, turn* |

# Living Latin

◀ CD2, TR 4, 02:18

### A hunting moral

In his Metamorphoses Ovid recounts many tales from Greek mythology, each one included by virtue of a 'metamorphosis', a change of form. There are characters who turn into trees, into stone, into animals.

The story of Actaeon and Diana is an example of the kind of divine justice dished out by the ancient gods. It was not so much a set of universal moral values which you might conform to or transgress, but rather a personal affair between worshipper and god. Offend the deity and you were in a spot of bother...

**1** Diana bathes in a forest pool, attended by her nymphs. Meanwhile Actaeon and his hunting friends have decided to rest a while before renewing their sport. He takes a walk through the forest and chances upon the pool.

**Ecce nepos Cadmi dilata parte laborum**
**per nemus ignotum non certis passibus errans**
**pervenit in lucum: sic illum fata ferebant.**
**Qui simul intravit rorantia fontibus antra,**
**sicut erant, nudae viso sua pectora nymphae**
**percussere viro subitisque ululatibus omne**
**implevere nemus circumfusaeque Dianam**
**corporibus texere suis; tamen altior illis**
**ipsa dea est colloque tenus supereminet omnis.**

*Uh oh! Cadmus' grandson, enjoying a break from hunting makes his way through the unfamiliar wood, uncertain of his course, and reaches the grove: thus the fates guided him. As soon as he stepped into the grotto bedewed with fountain spray, the nymphs saw him and just as they were, naked, beat their breasts, and filling the whole wood with* their sudden cries thronged around Diana and obscured her with their bodies; the goddess herself, however, was taller than they, and stood out head and shoulders above them all.

**2** Diana turns the unfortunate intruder into a stag. He escapes, but sees his reflection in some water.

'Me miserum!' dicturus erat: vox nulla secuta est!
Ingemuit: vox illa fuit, lacrimaeque per ora
non sua fluxerunt; mens tantum pristina mansit.
Quid faciat? Repetat-ne domum et regalia tecta
an lateat silvis? Pudor hoc, timor impedit illud.
Dum dubitat, videre canes, primique Melampus
Ichnobatesque sagax latratu signa dedere.

*'I'm done for ...' he tried to say, but no words followed! He groaned –
the limit of his speech – and tears flowed down his strange face;
only his mind remained from before. What should he do? Make his way
back home to the royal palace, or hide in the woods? He is afraid to try
one, and ashamed of the other. While he dithered his hounds caught
sight of him: Melampus and keen-scented Ichnobates were first to give
the signal with their cry.*

**3** Actaeon's hounds surround him, eager to finish him off.

Heu! Famulos fugit ipse suos. Clamare libebat:
'Actaeon ego sum: dominum cognoscite vestrum!'
Verba animo desunt; resonat latratibus aether.

*Oh no! He flees his own retainers. He wanted to shout: 'I am Actaeon:
recognize your own master!' But words fail his will; and the air
resounds with their baying.*

(Metamorphoses iii, 174–82, 201–5, 229–31)

# TESTING YOURSELF

**1** Write out all the endings, singular and plural, in all cases:
   **(a)** gradus, gradus; corpus, corporis; monachus, monachi;
   **(b)** dies, diei; miles, militis; sagitta, sagittae

**2** Translate into Latin:
   **(a)** The maiden had never swum in the pond.
   **(b)** After much food had been devoured (*use an ablative absolute*), the pilgrims left the monastery.
   **(c)** We had found neither food nor water, but we never lost hope.
   **(d)** The students sitting on the steps of the church were listening to the verses of Augustine.
   **(e)** The monks had written all the books by hand.

**3** Check you know the meaning of these nouns:
   amor, animus, annus, arcus, argentum, aura, aurum, casus, cella, dies, exercitus, facies, fama, fides, gemitus, gradus, impetus, lacus, locus, manus, mercator, metus, pecus, praemium, regnum, res, ripa, sagitta, socius, spes, spiritus, stella, tempus, tumultus, verbum, versus, viator, vinclum, vultus.

**4** From the words in 3, list the following with their genitive forms:
   **(a)** all nouns like **silva-ae** (1st declension)
   **(b)** all nouns like **mulus-i** (2nd declension)
   **(c)** all nouns like **vinum-i** (2nd declension neuter)
   **(d)** all 3rd declension nouns like **amor-is**, **opus-eris**, etc.
   **(e)** all 4th declension nouns, like **arcus-us**
   **(f)** all 5th declension nouns like **res, rei**.

**5** What is the difference in meaning between **animus-i** and **anima-ae**?

# 15

## Audire est intellegere
## To hear is to understand

In this unit you will learn about
- Hic, ille, is
- Se, ipse
- *The passive*
- *And find out more about Latin in 'All's fair in philosophy, love and war'*

### Third person pronouns: *ille, hic* and *is*

Latin has several equivalents of the third person pronoun (*he, she, it, they, him, her, them*):

| he | she | it | |
|------|------|-------|-------------------|
| hic | haec | hoc | (this one here) |
| ille | illa | illud | (that one there) |
| is | ea | id | |

In classical Latin, **is** is a less emphatic pronoun than **ille** 'that person' or **hic** 'this person'. This distinction grows weaker in post-classical Latin, when all three pronouns are almost interchangeable. See Reference tables for all pronoun endings.

The equivalent of our 'it' may also be masculine or feminine in Latin, according to the gender of the noun it represents, e.g. **ea** (f) for **silva** *a wood*.

> ### Insight
>
> A pronoun is a word we use in place of a noun (**pro** =
> '*in place of*', '*on behalf of*').

### Practice (I)

**1** Choose a noun to replace a pronoun, and translate:
vinum, ancillarum, Luciae, monachi
   **(a)** Vultus <u>eius</u> tristis erat.
   **(b)** Cibus <u>harum</u> a Benedicto devoratus est.
   **(c)** <u>Illi</u> in monasterio habitant.
   **(d)** <u>id</u> ab abbate desideratum est.

**2** Replace each underlined word with the correct form of the
pronoun in brackets, and translate:
   **(a)** Filia <u>Comitis</u> <u>Karoli</u> in castello habitat. (ille)
   **(b)** Abbatissa in ecclesia cum <u>Lucia</u> orabat. (hic)
   **(c)** Paulus semper cibum <u>mulo</u> dabat. (is)
   **(d)** <u>Peregrini</u> in silva cum <u>monachis</u> visi sunt. (ille/hic)

### *Hic, ille* and *is* as adjectives

Hic, ille and is as described above are pronouns, words used in
place of nouns. If, however, one is used with a noun, not in place
of it, it is an adjective:

> **hic mulus**          *this* mule
> **illa silva**          *that* wood

Hic can also mean 'here':

> **hic vivo, hic moriar**          *here I live, here may I die*

A development in later Latin is the use of **ille** as a definite article
(*the*):

> **bonus ille Thomas**          *the good Thomas*

Ille is the ancestor of the words for both *s/he* and *the* in the Romance languages:

|  | French | Spanish | Italian |
|---|---|---|---|
| *s/he* | **elle, il** | **ella, él** | **lei, lui** |
| *the* (m/f) | **le, la** | **el, la** | **il, la** |

> ## Insight
> Hic, ille and is can be pronouns ('he'/'she', etc.); or adjectives if they are used with nouns (e.g. **hic mulus** = '*this mule*', **illa domina** = '*that lady*').

### Practice (II)

**1** Translate using **hic, haec, hoc**, etc.:
  **(a)** this wood
  **(b)** these perfumes
  **(c)** of these students

**2** Translate using **ille, illa, illud**, etc.:
  **(a)** that mistress
  **(b)** those songs
  **(c)** I see that mule

**3** Translate using **is, ea, id**, etc.:
  **(a)** that letter
  **(b)** with those monks
  **(c)** that is

### *Se* and *ipse: himself, herself, themselves*

One kind of the -*self* pronouns is reflexive, i.e. it refers back to the subject (Latin: **se**):

| | |
|---|---|
| **Lucia se celat.** | *Lucia hides herself.* |
| **Captivi se liberant.** | *The captives free themselves.* |

There are only four cases: **se** (accusative or ablative), **sui** (genitive) and **sibi** (dative). There is no separate plural form as **se** can be either singular or plural (or masculine or feminine) – it depends on the verb's subject.

The other kind of -*self* pronoun is used for emphasis (Latin **ipse**):

| | |
|---|---|
| **Abbas ipse Ricardum vidit.** | *The abbot himself saw Richard.* |
| **Luciam ipsam sed non patrem** | *I love Lucia herself, but not her* |
| **amo.** | *father.* |

Occasionally **ipse** is used similarly to **is, ea, id**, i.e. as an ordinary third person pronoun (*s/he*, *him*, *her*, etc.) – see Reference tables for all the forms.

## Insight

Reflexive and non-reflexive '*self*': **monachus <u>se</u> caedit** = '*the monk strikes himself*'; **monachus episcopum <u>ipsum</u> caedit** = '*the monk strikes the bishop himself*'.

### Practice (III)

Fill each gap with the correct form of **se** or **ipse**:

**(a)** Mulus in stagno ____ vidit et attonitus est.

**(b)** Abbatissa _____
sarcinas portabat.

_**In dumis se celant**_ They hide in the thickets

🔊 **CD2, TR 5**

Peregrini per silvam ad monasterium iter faciebant, sequentibus furtim Lucia et Paulo. Mox peregrini prope monasterium constiterunt, et aliis Ricardus ecclesiam monstravit. Itaque Lucia et Paulus ad eos audiendos se in dumis celaverunt.

'Ecce ecclesia,' vocem Ricardi audire potuerunt, 'Nunc abite quod in hoc loco estis non conspiciendi. Valete.'

'Ille est proditor,' murmuravit Paulus, 'Pater Ricardus est proditor. Malus, turpis, ignavus, saevus, crudelis, scelestus …'

'Sst,' iterum illa ad os eius manum posuit, iterum eam Paulus basiavit.

'Desine! Cave ne peregrini nos audiant.'

'Quid est agendum?' rogavit Paulus.

'Pete fideles amicos quibus omnia referas. Cui monachorum credis?'

'Magistro Stephano, qui est aliquando austerus sed vero benignus.'

'Huic ergo refer; i, in monasterium festina! Eho, siste! Mulus ducendus.' His dictis Lucia in equum ascendit.

'Et tu,' respondit ille, 'Quid in animo habes?'

'Ego Ricardum observabo. Nunc abeundum!' Lucia eum cum mulo ad monasterium lente euntem spectavit; deinde ipsa, equo citato, abiit.

| | |
|---|---|
| **abite** | *depart, go away!* |
| **aliquando** | *sometimes* |
| **audiant** | *(they) may hear* |
| **benignus-a-um** | *kind* |
| **cave ne...** | *be careful lest...* |
| **cito-are-avi-atum** | *rouse/stir* |
| **consisto-ere-stiti** | *stop* |
| **credo-ere** [+dat.] | *believe, trust* |
| **cui** [dat.] | *whom* |
| **dumus-i** [m] | *thicket* |
| **euntem** | *him as he went* |
| **fidelis** | *loyal* |
| **i!** | *go!* |
| **in animo habeo-ere** | *have in mind, intend* |
| **iter facio-ere** | *make one's way* |
| **observo-are** | *watch* |
| **peto-ere** | *seek* |
| **pono-ere-sui-situm** | *place, put* |
| **proditor-is** [m] | *traitor* |
| **quibus** | *to whom* |
| **refer** | *tell, report!* |
| **referas** | *you may report* |
| **scelestus-a-um** | *wicked* |
| **sequens** | *following* |
| **siste** | *stop!* |

## Passive forms

So far almost all the verbs you have met have been <u>active</u>, e.g.:

| | |
|---|---|
| **Mulus silvam spectat.** | *The mule watches the wood.* |
| **Silva mulum spectat.** | *The wood watches the mule.* |

In the passive voice, the verb is not a 'doing' word but 'done-to'.
If you want to make a verb passive and keep the same meaning,
the object of the active verb becomes the subject of the passive one:

| | |
|---|---|
| **Silva a mulo spectatur.** | *The wood is watched by the mule.* |
| **Mulus a silva spectatur.** | *The mule is watched by the wood.* |

The subject of the active verb has become an 'agent' in the ablative, while the previous object is now the subject. When a verb is passive, it is the subject, not the object, which is on the receiving end. If a verb is active, it's in the active 'voice', if passive, then passive voice.

The passive form of the third person, singular or plural, has **-ur** added to the active ending, whether present, future or imperfect.

### Practice (IV)

Fill in the gaps:

| Active | | Passive | |
|---|---|---|---|
| *s/he watches* | **spectat** | **spectatur** | *s/he is watched* |
| *they were watching* | **spectabant** | **spectabantur** | *they were being watched* |
| *s/he will love* | **amabit** | ......... | *s/he will be loved* |
| *they will see* | ......... | **videbuntur** | *they will be seen* |
| *s/he was hearing* | ......... | **audiebatur** | ......... |
| ......... | ......... | **capietur** | *s/he will be captured* |

You have already come across the passive in both gerundives (e.g. **agendus** *to be done*) in Unit 9 and the past participle (e.g. **actus** *having been done*) in Unit 13. You have also met the perfect passive with **esse**:

| | |
|---|---|
| **duxit** | *s/he led (active)* |
| **ductus est** | *he was led (passive)* |
| **amavit** | *s/he loved (active)* |
| **amata est** | *she was loved (passive)* |

## Practice (V)

**1** Fill the gaps with the corresponding active or passive forms:

| Active | | Passive | |
|---|---|---|---|
| *she sent* | **misit** | **missa est** | *she was sent* |
| *they led* | ......... | **ducti sunt** | ......... |
| *he heard* | ......... | ......... | *he was heard* |
| *she captured* | ......... | ......... | *she was captured* |
| *he advised* | ......... | ......... | *he was advised* |

**2** Rewrite each sentence making the verb passive, and translate (and look out for singular subjects being replaced by plural ones, and vice versa):
e.g. **Discipuli librum legunt** (*the students are reading the book*) **Liber a discipulis legitur** (*the book is being read by the students*)

(a) **Pater Ricardus discipulos in schola castigat.**
(b) **Mulus ex oppido omnes sarcinas portabat.**
(c) **Augustinus amicis carmen Catulli recitavit.**
(d) **Paulus virginem matri dicentem vidit.**

**3** Rewrite each sentence making the verb active, and translate:

(a) **Cibus a Benedicto devoratus est.**
(b) **Virgo in silva a Paulo est visa.**
(c) **Historia monasterii a monachis narrabitur.**
(d) **Corpus in horto a Danis sepultum est.**

***Credere est intellegere*** *To believe is to understand*

◀◗ **CD2, TR 5, 01:10**

Discipuli in schola theologiam a Stephano docebantur.
   'O discipuli, non quaero intellegere ut credam, sed credo ut intellegam. Praeterea,' inquit Stephanus, 'philosophiam

per dialecticam scimus sed veritatem ipsam agnoscimus gratia Dei. Scribitis-ne? Nunc est scribendum.'

'Veritatem-ne autem agnoscere possumus per dialecticam?' rogavit Augustinus.

'Minime,' respondit magister. 'Cur tu semper contradicis, Augustine? Maioribus numquam credis?'

'Nonne autem, ut dixit Socrates, homo veritatem per dialecticam agnoscere potest?'

'Cave ne blasphemes,' admonuit Stephanus, 'Graeci quidem sapientes erant, sed nos sapientiores sumus quod Dei sapientiam illorum eruditioni additam habemus. Veritatem iam habemus. Per veritatem opus Dei in terra revelatur. Nunc est scribendum: credere est scire, scire est intellegere, intellegere est credere....'

'Videre est spectare bellissimam!' exclamavit Augustinus.

'Quid dixisti?' rogavit Stephanus.

'Illic est amica Pauli,' exclamavit Augustinus per fenestram spectans.

'O Augustine, nisi tacebis, Pater Ricardus ad vos docendos reveniet.'

'Ibi quoque ipse est Paulus! Ducens mulum in monasterium,' inquit Augustinus.

'Paulus? Num Paulus iam adest?' inquit Stephanus ad fenestram festinans. 'Eheu, ecce coquus est iratus. Paulus nihil emisse videtur.'

Mox Paulus e culina fugiens in scholam irruit et Stephano 'Pater, Pater!' clamavit, 'Pater Stephane ... Pater Ricardus ... Pater Ricardus ...' inquit Paulus balbus.

'Pater Ricardus non adest. Quid tibi cum Patre Ricardo est? Dic mihi.'

| | |
|---|---|
| **addo-ere-idi-itum** | *add* |
| **bellissimus-a-um** | *most beautiful* |
| **contradico-ere** | *contradict* |
| **dialectica-ae** [f] | *discussion, argument* |
| **dic** | *tell, say* |
| **emisse** | *to have bought* |
| **eruditio-nis** [f] | *learning* |
| **gratia-ae** [f] | *favour, grace* |

QUICK VOCAB

| | |
|---|---|
| ibi | *there* |
| intellego-ere | *understand* |
| maiores-um | *betters, ancestors* |
| praeterea | *besides* |
| quaero-ere | *seek* |
| quid tibi ... est | *what is your problem ...* |
| sapientia-ae [f] | *wisdom* |
| sapientiores | *wiser* |
| ut credam | *that I may believe* |
| veritas-tatis [f] | *truth* |
| videtur | *is seen, seems* |

## Living Latin

◀） CD2, TR 5, 02:09

### All's fair in philosophy, love and war

**1** Cicero was inspired by the philosophy of Socrates and other Greeks:

**O vitae philosophia dux, o virtutis indagatrix expultrixque vitiorum!**

(Tusculan Disputations v, 5)

*O Philosophy, guide of life, you bring us to right and rid us of wrongs.*

**2** Propertius' philosophy was guided by hedonism. A good life meant a good time:

**Qualem si cuncti cuperent decurrere vitam**
  **et pressi multo membra iacere mero,**
**non ferrum crudele neque esset bellica navis,**
  **nec nostra Actiacum verteret ossa mare,**
**nec totiens propriis circum oppugnata triumphis**
  **lassa foret crines solvere Roma suos.**

Haec certe merito poterunt laudare minores:
  laeserunt nullos proelia nostra deos.

(Elegies ii, 15, 41–8)

*I wish everyone desired to lead this life and relax their limbs heavy*
*with draughts of wine, then there'd be no cruel steel, no warship, and*
*the bones of our people would not be churned about on the sea of*
*Actium, and Rome would not be overwhelmed with so many victories*
*over her own subjects and be weary of loosening her hair in grief. Truly*
*will this deserve posterity's praise: our skirmishes have not injured*
*any gods.*

**3** Ovid saw common ground between lover and soldier. Both may
suffer from battle-fatigue:

Quis nisi vel miles vel amans et frigora noctis
  et denso mixtas perferet imbre nives?
Mittitur infestos alter speculator in hostes:
  in rivale oculos alter, ut hoste, tenet.
Ille graves urbes, hic durae limen amicae
  obsidet. Hic portas frangit, at ille fores.

(Amores i, 9, 15–20)

*Who but a soldier or lover will endure the chill of night and snow*
*and driving rain? As one is sent to spy on the dangerous enemy, the*
*other keeps an eye on his rival, as he would on an enemy. The soldier*
*camps outside hostile cities, the lover outside the door of an unfeeling*
*girlfriend. The former breaks down gates, the latter the door.*

**4** The heat of battle brings a case of passion-fatigue for Tibullus:

Hic mihi servitium video dominamque paratam:
  iam mihi, libertas illa paterna, vale.
Servitium sed triste datur, teneorque catenis,
  et numquam misero vincla remittit Amor,
et seu quid merui seu nil peccavimus, urit.
  Uror, io, remove saeva puella faces.

(Elegies ii, 4, 1–6)

*Here I see enslavement and mistress ready for me. Now farewell,*
*freedom, which was my family's right, farewell. Bleak slavery lies*
*ahead, and I am held in chains. Love is never one to loosen a wretched*
*prisoner's knots. He burns me whether I've deserved it or done no*
*wrong. I'm on fire! Oh! You cruel girl, take away those brands.*

# TESTING YOURSELF

**1** Identify the past participles of these verbs, add the right endings, and translate:

   **(a)** Multae epistulae Luciae ab Augustino (scribo-ere) sunt.

   **(b)** Monasterium a peregrinis (relinquo-ere) est.

   **(c)** Corpus monachi (sepelio-ire) est.

   **(d)** Libri in bibliotheca (pono-ere) sunt.

**2** Translate into Latin:

   **(a)** Soon the students will free themselves.

   **(b)** Do the monks themselves teach? Are they taught to teach?

   **(c)** Paul and Lucia were seen walking out of the wood (*if there is a 'mixed gender plural' the masculine tends to prevail*).

   **(d)** Paul hid himself in the pond as the pilgrims approached ('*as... approached*': *the present participle of* **adeo-ire** *is irregular:* **adiens**, *then* **adeunt-**).

   **(e)** Many beasts were captured by the maiden herself.

   **(f)** The oxen were being guarded by an army of Danes.

**3** Create Ablative Absolutes: e.g. *after the bishop had been seen...* = **episcopo viso** ...

   **(a)** After the Danes had been freed ...

   **(b)** After the letter had been written ...

   **(c)** After the report had been confirmed ...

   **(d)** After the attack had been made ...

   **(e)** After the noise had been heard ...

   **(f)** After the monk had been buried ...

**4** **Bona fide** means **(a)** Good dog! **(b)** in good faith **(c)** of good character

# 16

## Quis in monasterio conspirat?
Who is plotting in the monastery?

In this unit you will learn about
- *The subjunctive*
- *Wishes and commands*
- *Ut, ne, cum*
- *And find out more about the Roman historian, Tacitus*

### More about verbs: the subjunctive (present)

Verbs can be categorized in several different ways. There's the *tense*, (present, future, etc.), the *person* (who's doing it, 'I', 'you', 'he', etc.), the *voice* (i.e. active or passive), and now finally what linguists call the *mood*.

So far we have been dealing with the indicative mood, that is to say dealing with actual actions, things which happen (or have happened or are about to happen).

The subjunctive mood deals with potential, with hope, with what might happen (or might have happened). There are four tenses, active and passive. The endings are common across all five conjugations with the exception of the present subjunctive:

| amare | monere | mittere |
|---|---|---|
| am-em | mone-am | mitt-am |
| am-es | mone-as | mitt-as |
| am-et | mone-at | mitt-at |
| am-emus | mone-amus | mitt-amus |
| am-etis | mone-atis | mitt-atis |
| am-ent | mone-ant | mitt-ant |

| capere | audire |
|---|---|
| capi-am | audi-am |
| capi-as | audi-as |
| capi-at | audi-at |
| capi-amus | audi-amus |
| capi-atis | audi-atis |
| capi-ant | audi-ant |

The second, third, fourth and fifth columns all have the same endings, but verbs in the first column (-are) have an 'e' in place of the 'a'.

## Insight

A verb ending -et (pl. -ent) could be (i) the present of second conjugation verbs like **monere** (**monet** = 'she/he warns'); (ii) the future of third, fourth and mixed conjugation verbs like **mittere, audire** and **capere** (**audiet** = 'she/he will hear'); or (iii) the present subjunctive of first conjugation verbs like **amare** (**amet** = 'may she/he love').

## Practice (I)

Fill the gaps:

| Present indicative | | Present subjunctive | |
|---|---|---|---|
| *we live* | **vivimus** | **vivamus** | *may we live* |
| *s/he (it) stands* | **stat** | ......... | *may s/he (it) stand* |
| *we love* | ......... | **amemus** | *may we love* |
| ......... | ......... | **ignoscas** | *may you forgive* |
| *s/he is careful* | **cavet** | ......... | *may s/he be careful* |
| *we rejoice* | ......... | **gaudeamus** | ......... |
| ......... | **laudamus** | ......... | ......... |
| ......... | ......... | **bibat** | ......... |
| ......... | **taces** | ......... | *may you be quiet* |

### Orders and encouragement (imperative)

The most direct way to tell someone what to do is to use the imperative:

| To one person | | | | |
|---|---|---|---|---|
| **ama!** | **mone!** | **mitte!** | **audi** | **cape** |

| To more than one | | | | |
|---|---|---|---|---|
| **amate!** | **monete!** | **mittite!** | **audite!** | **capite!** |

**Audite me, o molesti discipuli!**   *Listen to me, you lazy students!*

**Sede!**   *Sit!*

The imperative is the most direct, urgent and potentially offensive form of encouragement. In ancient times no doubt it was the standard idiom for addressing menials, dependants and children, but perhaps unwise for anyone old enough, big enough – and not hampered by the bonds of servitude – to clock you one. The subjunctive was a more polite idiom of encouragement, expressing a wish rather than an order:

| | |
|---|---|
| **Audiatis me, o amici.** | *May you hear me, friends.* |
| **Sedeas.** | *May you be seated.* |

### Practice (II)

Choose the appropriate form:

**(a)** (Festinate/Festinetis), o miseri servi!

**(b)** Si vobis placet, in ecclesiam (festinate/festinetis), o milites.

**(c)** O discipuli, (tacete/
taceatis).

**(d)** O Abbatissa, (tace/
taceas).

*Lucia in trabibus celata* Lucia hidden in the beams

◀) CD2, TR 6

---

**Shared endings key**

**-e(n)t**   present: mone(n)t (second conjugation)
       future: mitte(n)t, audie(n)t, capie(n)t (third, fourth and
         mixed conjugations)
       **present subjunctive: ame(n)t (first conjugation)**

**-a(n)t**   present: ama(n)t (first conjugation)
       imperfect: -ba(n)t (all verbs)
       pluperfect: -era(n)t (all verbs)
       **pres. subj.: monea(n)t, mitta(n)t, audia(n)t, capia(n)t
       (second, third, fourth and mixed conjugations)**

---

Interea Lucia, Ricardum in monasterium euntem observans, in
claustri tectum ascenderat ubi in pueritia saepe se celabat; Comes
Karolus enim eam matremque ad monasterium adducere solebat.

Despiciens igitur Lucia de trabibus Ricardum solum sedentem videre poterat. Tandem aliquis ad Ricardum adiit.

'Ubi sunt nostri hospites?' inquit advena. 'Salvi-ne?'

'Salvi sunt,' respondit alter.

'Omnia-ne parata sunt?'

'Ita vero, Domine Abba.'

Lucia est obstupefacta. Abbas! Omnia verba eorum audire non poterat quod duo monachi susurrabant. 'Tace!' dicebat abbas. 'Advenit aliquis, ergo in ecclesiam abi...' et Ricardus abiit. 'Ah Pater Stephane, salve.'

'Te saluto, Domine Abba,' respondit Stephanus, 'Ignoscas mi, sed tibi nuntios graves refero, mirabiles quidem, sed veros.'

'Quos nuntios dicis? Dic mihi, Stephane.'

'Unus ex discipulis meis, puer sapiens, honestus, fidelis ...'

'Quis ex tuis discipulis?'

'Paulus. Hodie cum ad oppidum ambularet, conspirantes in silva Danos conspexit ex quibus unum agnovit. Pater Ricardus in silva cum Danis!'

'Pater Ricardus in silva? Hodie? Sed Ricardus non est Danus. Ille puer elephantum ex musca facit.'

'Ille autem cum Danis erat.'

'Discipulo erranti credis, Pater?' inquit abbas. 'Nonne autem Paulus erat ille discipulus qui frustra filiam Comitis Karoli amabat? Ignoscas mihi sed puer fervidus amore est,' risit abbas. 'Ille Veneris discipulus non Christi esse videtur – eho Magister? Nos ne fabulas eius audiamus, sed tu eum saepius verberes. *Percute puerum tuum virga,* ut dixit sanctus Benedictus, *et liberabis animam eius a morte.* Regula XXVIII.'

'Ut vis, Domine, ut vis. Rumorem tamen ad te referendum esse putavi.'

'Sane, Pater. Ecce, nunc Ricardus adit: eum ipsum interrogemus ... Pater Ricarde, adsis.'

'Semper tibi pareo libens, o Domine...'

Lucia adhuc in trabibus immota omnia, quae homines infra dicebant, audire non poterat. Mox dicere desierunt et Stephanus Ricardusque abierunt.

| | |
|---|---|
| **abi!** | *go away!* |
| **advena-ae** [m] | *newcomer* |
| **anima-ae** [f] | *soul* |
| **claustrum-i** [n] | *cloister* |
| **conspiro-are** | *conspire, plot* |
| **credo-ere** [+dat.] | *believe, trust* |
| **cum … ambularet** | *when he was walking* |
| **despicio-ere** | *look down* |
| **dic** | *tell* |
| **euntem (iens, euntis)** | *going* |
| **fervidus-a-um** | *burning, impetuous* |
| **frustra** | *in vain, to no avail* |
| **honestus-a-um** | *decent, honourable* |
| **immotus-a-um** | *stationary* |
| **infra** | *below* |
| **libens** | *gladly* |
| **musca-ae** [f] | *fly* |
| **nuntii-orum** [m] | *news* |
| **obstupefactus-a-um** | *stupefied* |
| **pareo-ere** [+dat.] | *be obedient to* |
| **percutio-ere** | *strike, beat* |
| **pueritia-ae** [f] | *childhood* |
| **saepius** | *more often* |
| **salve** | *hello* |
| **salvus-a-um** | *safe* |
| **sane** | *certainly* |
| **trabs-bis** [f] | *beam* |
| **virga-ae** [f] | *rod* |

## *Ut* and *ne*

Ut followed by a verb in the indicative usually means *as*, or *when*.
With the subjunctive **ut** is often used to express a wish or intention
(negative **ne**).

## Practice (III)

Pair the Latin sentences with the corresponding English ones:

| | |
|---|---|
| **Cave ne audiant.** | *May you be quiet!* |
| **Credo ut intellegam.** | *If only you'd be quiet* |
| **Ne silvam timeas.** | *If only he'd believe us!* |
| **Taceas!** | *Do not be afraid of the wood.* |
| **Ut nobis credat!** | *Careful lest they hear.* |
| **Ut taceas!** | *I believe so that I may understand.* |

The words which **ut** and **ne** introduce are often part of a larger sentence. The customary English equivalents are *that*, *so that*, or *in order that*:

| | |
|---|---|
| **Monent eum ut nobis credat.** | *They advise him to believe us (that he should believe us).* |
| **Monent eum ne abbati credat.** | *They advise him not to believe the abbot (that he should not believe the abbot).* |
| **In dumis se celant ne a Danis videantur.** | *They hide themselves in the thickets so that they may not be seen by the Danes.* |

Sometimes **ut** + subjunctive introduces a result or consequence:

| | |
|---|---|
| **Tam celeriter currebant ut ad ecclesiam ante noctem pervenirent.** | *They used to run so fast that they would reach the church before nightfall.* |

### Imperfect and pluperfect subjunctive

The three most used tenses are: the present, the imperfect, and the pluperfect.

The imperfect subjunctive is easy to recognize because the stem is the verb's infinitive. The pluperfect has the ordinary stem of the perfect with **'iss'** as part of the ending:

| Imperfect subjunctive | | |
|---|---|---|
| amare | -m | **amarem** |
| monere | -s | **moneres** |
| mittere | -t | **mitteret** |
| audire | -mus | **audiremus** |
| capere | -tis | **caperetis** |
| esse | -ent | **essent** |

| Pluperfect subjunctive | | |
|---|---|---|
| amav-i | -issem | **amavissem** |
| monu-i | -isses | **monuisses** |
| mis-i | -isset | **misisset** |
| audiv-i | -issemus | **audivissemus** |
| cep-i | -issetis | **cepissetis** |
| fu-i | -issent | **fuissent** |

The imperfect subjunctive is generally used when the main verb in the sentence is in a past tense. The imperfect subjunctive is translated in different ways depending on the sense required, e.g. 'might...', 'should...':

**In dumis se <u>celaverunt</u> ne a Danis <u>viderentur</u>.**

*They <u>hid</u> themselves in the thickets so that they <u>might</u> not <u>be seen</u> by the Danes.*

It helps to be able to recognize a subjunctive; for instance the meaning of **ut** varies according to whether it is used with the indicative or subjunctive:

**...ut credimus**       *as we believe*
**...ut credamus**       *so that we may believe*

For all the forms of the subjunctive, including those of **sum, esse**, see Reference tables.

### Practice (IV)

Choose the correct form and translate:

**(a)** Bibo ut (intellegam/intellego).

**(b)** Lucia in stagnum se immersit ut se (celaret/celabit).

**(c)** Discipuli, ut Stephanus (dicit/dicat), theologiam docentur ut opus Dei (intellegunt/intellegant).

**(d)** Augustinus nos
monuit ut carmina
sua (audiremus/
audiemus).

### Cum

The preposition **cum** *with* is followed by a noun in the ablative.
**Cum** is also used as a conjunction, meaning *when* (sometimes *since*
and occasionally *although*). It is usually followed by a verb in the
subjunctive:

**Paulus, cum in silva <u>ambularet</u>,** *When Paul was walking in the wood*
**monachorum voces audivit.** *he heard the voices of the monks.*
**Lucia, cum abbatem in** *When Lucia had seen the*
**claustro <u>vidisset</u>, attonita erat.** *abbot in the cloister she was*
*astonished.*

*Mulus et plaustrum* *The mule and the cart*

🔊 **CD2, TR 6, 01:32**

Interea Paulus, cum Stephanus ut abbatem quaereret scholam
reliquisset, ipse abiit ut Luciam inveniret. Paulus Augustinum et
ceteros subvenire volentes ut manerent in schola monuit, ne a
Ricardo aut consociis viderentur. Nec multo post Paulus, cum per
monasterium solus ambularet, campanas ad monachos in ecclesiam
convocandos resonantes audivit. Itaque, cum ipse adesse in ecclesia
deberet, furtim e claustro in hortum ibat, ubi mulum plaustro
vinctum vidit. 'Io mule, quo nunc vadis? Quo hoc plaustrum
trahis? Quid hic habemus?' Deinde Paulus cum in plaustro omnes
res quae in ecclesia erant custodiendae conspexisset valde attonitus
erat 'Mehercule! Cur haec in plaustro?' murmuravit.

Prope plaustrum erat magna sarcina. 'Eheu!' gemuit ille, 'Vae! Vae! Miserrimum Stephanum!' corpore magistri caesi in sarcina invento. 'Propter me, o Magister, trucidatus es. Ut in schola remansisses!' flebat iuvenis. 'Statim abbati ut omnia referam ibo,' et gemitu in monasterium effugit.

| | |
|---|---|
| caedo-ere, cecidi, caesum | kill, cut |
| campana-ae [f] | bell |
| consocius-i [m] | associate |
| furtim | secretly |
| miserrimus-a-um | most wretched |
| plaustrum-i [n] | cart, waggon |
| remaneo-ere-si-sum | remain |
| traho-ere | pull, drag |
| trucido-are-avi-atum | slaughter |
| vae | alas, woe |
| valde | very much |

## Living Latin

◀) CD2, TR 6, 02:57

### Friends, Romans ... and family

Of the Roman historians, Tacitus is perhaps the most compelling. His contemporaries tell us he was a lawyer, and a good one (unlike Virgil who could not cope with the forum and retreated to a quieter life of reading and writing). His work is full of rhetorical cleverness, of withering irony interspersed with mischievous asides and occasional blasts of front-on invective.

1 After poisoning his stepbrother, Britannicus, Nero decided it was his mother's turn to die. Agrippina had been instrumental in helping Nero to power, and was almost as ruthless; but she later lost influence over him. First there was a botched job with a collapsing boat, from which she escaped to her villa. Then,

after she sent Agerinus to Nero to tell him she had survived an attempt on her life, Nero confirmed her worst suspicions by sending assassins to finish her off.

**Cubiculo modicum lumen inerat et ancillarum una, magis ac magis anxia Agrippina quod nemo a filio ac ne Agerinus quidem: aliam fore laetae rei faciem; nunc solitudinem ac repentinos strepitus et extremi mali indicia. Abeunte dehinc ancilla 'tu quoque me deseris' prolocuta respicit Anicetum trierarcho Herculeio et Obarito centurione classiario comitatum: ac, si visendum venisset, refotam renuntiaret, sin facinus patraturus, nihil se de filio credere; non imperatum parricidium. Circumsistunt lectum percussores et prior trierarchus fusti caput eius adflixit. Iam in mortem centurioni ferrum destringenti protendens uterum 'ventrem feri' exclamavit multisque vulneribus confecta est.**

(Annals xiv, 8)

*The room was dimly lit with only one maid for company. Agrippina became more and more fretful – no news from her son, no sign even of Agerinus. If all were well things would look otherwise; now there was loneliness and a sudden din, which pointed towards extreme danger. Her maid got up to go and she started to speak 'You're leaving me too…' when she saw Anicetus and the commander Herculeius and warrant officer Obaritus. 'If you have come to visit me,' she said, 'you may report that I am recovering. But if you are here to kill me, I believe my son has nothing to do with it – he would not order his mother's death!' The assassins stood round her couch. First the captain hit her on the head with a staff. Then as the lieutenant drew his sword to finish her off, she pointed to her womb and shouted 'Strike here!' After several blows she died.*

**2** Tacitus' picture of humanity is a desolate grey purpled by the lust of ambition, weakness or cruelty. The story of Octavia is an oasis of human innocence and virtue, and her murder shows to what lengths a cruel tyrant will go. Historians might have given their attention to less melodramatic material, such as the rise or fall in interest rates, achievements of engineering, or

social statistics garnered from different corners of the empire –
but this never occurred to the writers, or their readers.

Octavia was the sister of Britannicus, and the daughter of the
emperor Claudius. She was also Nero's wife. She was murdered in
her twentieth year to make way for Nero's mistress, Poppaea.

**Restringitur vinclis venaeque eius per omnis artus exolvuntur;
et quia pressus pavore sanguis tardius labebatur, praefervidi
balnei vapore enecatur. Additurque atrocior saevitia quod caput
amputatum latumque in urbem Poppaea vidit.**

(Annals xiv, 64)

*She was bound and veins in all her limbs were cut; and then because
the flow of blood was checked by her panic, she was put in a very hot
bath and finished off by its stifling heat. More appalling cruelty was to
follow: her severed head was taken to Rome for Poppaea to see.*

# TESTING YOURSELF

**1** Change the underlined clauses into ablative absolutes without significantly changing the meaning:

e.g. **Augustinus <u>cum virginem conspexisset</u> diu per fenestram spectabat.**

Answer: **Augustinus <u>virgine conspecta</u> diu per fenestram spectabat.**

    **(a)** Mulus <u>cum sarcinas omnes vidisset</u> gemuit.

    **(b)** Paulus <u>cum Ricardum audivisset</u> in monasterium festinavit.

    **(c)** Stephanus <u>cum corpus amici sepelivisset</u> in ecclesiam abiit.

    **(d)** Coquus <u>cum cibum devoravisset</u> in silvam ambulavit.

**2** Translate into Latin:

    **(a)** May they capture all the Danes!

    **(b)** May the abbot not see your book of poems, Augustine!

    **(c)** Drink the wine, friends! May everyone drink the wine!

    **(d)** The abbot advised him to leave the monastery (that he should leave – **ut** + *imperfect subjunctive*).

**3** Write out the:

    **(a)** present tense of **gaudeo-ere**;

    **(b)** future tense of **scribo-ere**;

    **(c)** present subjunctive of **laudo-are**.

**4** Translate into Latin with one word for each answer (use the present subjunctive):

    **(a)** Let us sleep!

    **(b)** Let us live!

    **(c)** Let us pray!

    **(d)** Let us read!

    **(e)** Let us work!

    **(f)** Let us drink!

    **(g)** Let us run!

    **(h)** Let us write!

**(i)** Let us be careful!

**(j)** Let us laugh!

**(k)** Let us believe!

**5** Complete each sentence with a verb with the correct (subjunctive) ending:

**(a)** Bibo ut (that I may live).

**(b)** Libros-ne legis ut (that you may understand)?

**(c)** Fortis sum ut illa me (that she may love me).

**(d)** Illa nos rogat ut (that we be quiet).

# 17

# Peior quam diabolus
## Worse than the devil

In this unit you will learn about
- *More passive forms*
- *Deponent verbs*
- *More and most*
- *And find out more about the philosopher Boethius*

### More passive forms

The third persons of the present, future and imperfect passive
have **-ur** added to the active ending. Other passive forms are in the
Reference tables.

### Practice (I)

Identify the corresponding passive form of the bracketed verb and
translate:

**(a)** Me felicem! a mea domina (laudo).

**(b)** A virgine in trabibus sedente (audimus).

**(c)** O sceleste puer, a magistro (castigabis).

### Deponent verbs: passive verbs with active meanings

There are quite a large number of verbs which have passive endings, but are active in meaning. These are called 'deponent' verbs. In this list of some of the more common deponent verbs, note the three principal parts, not four, as the past participle is part of the perfect form:

| Present | Infinitive | Perfect |
|---------|-----------|---------|
| **sequor** *I follow* | **sequi** *to follow* | **secutus-a sum** *I (have) followed* |
| **loquor** *I speak* | **loqui** *to speak* | **locutus-a sum** *I (have) spoke(n)* |
| **progredior** *I advance* | **progredi** *to advance* | **progressus-a sum** *I (have) advanced* |
| **miror** *I admire, wonder at* | **mirari** *to admire* | **miratus-a sum** *I (have) admired* |

These verbs should be translated like active ones, despite their passive endings.

# Insight

Deponent verbs look like passive ones but have active meanings (e.g. **sequor** = '*I follow*' (not '*I am followed*'), **secutus sum** = '*I followed*' not '*I have been followed*').

### Practice (II)

Identify the correct form of the verb in the tense as directed, and translate:

**(a)** Lucia Ricardum in monasterium (sequor, sequi, secutus sum). (*perfect*)

**(b)** Omnes homines mea carmina (miror, mirari, miratus sum). (*future*)

Their passive form but active meaning extends to past participles:

| | | |
|---|---|---|
| **secutus-a-um** | *having followed* | <u>*not*</u> *having been followed* |
| **miratus-a-um** | *having admired* | <u>*not*</u> *having been admired* |

But gerundives of deponent verbs remain passive, like other verbs:

| | |
|---|---|
| **sequendus-a-um** | *to be followed* |
| **mirandus-a-um** | *to be admired* |

**Gravis in discipulo stupor** *The pupil is out of his mind*

---

**Shared endings key**

**-or**     third declension nominative: *stupor, amor,* etc.
        passive first person ('I ...')

---

Paulus igitur, Lucia in trabibus adhuc celata, in claustrum irruit ut abbatem quaereret, 'Pater, Pater,' exanimatus clamans, 'Pater Abba!' Lucia vocem eius audire poterat et anxia erat.

'Quid est tibi, puer?' rogavit abbas.

'Stephanus est mortuus.'

'Deliras.'

'Sincerus vero loquor!'

'O stulte puer! Cur semper vanis de somniis loqueris? Sed tibi iam pro certo dico: Pater Stephanus nuper abiit et in ecclesiam ingressus est. Patrem Ricardum ceterosque in ecclesiam ad vesperas parandas sequebatur.'

'Ricardum?'

'Ita vero.'

'Pater, si tibi placet, e fenestro specta ut sarcinam videas quae corpus Stephani continet – in pace requiescat.'

'Nullam sarcinam videre possum.'

'Sequere me, Pater, ut eam ipse videas.'

Haud multo post duo homines redierunt Paulo dicente, 'Crede mihi, o Domine, corpus Stephani illa in sarcina fuerat!'

'Iam satis rumorum. Hoc tempore nos in ecclesia, ut vesperas dicamus, adesse debemus. Tu, o puer, amore es captus. Ah, ecce, Pater Ricarde,' inquit abbas adeunte Ricardo. 'Pater Ricarde, gravis in hoc discipulo stupor esse videtur; itaque ad medicum statim est ducendus.'

'Libenter eum ducam, mi Domine,' respondit Ricardus.

'Immo! vera dico,' clamavit Paulus.

'Puer sane est inops animi.'

Subito saeviens, furiosissima, exanimataque, irruit Lucia.

QUICK VOCAB

| | |
|---|---|
| **contineo-ere** | *contain, hold* |
| **deliro-are-avi** | *be silly, insane* |
| **exanimatus-a-um** | *breathless* |
| **haud** | *not* |
| **ingredior-i, ingressus sum** | *enter* |
| **inops animi** | *out of his mind* |
| **libenter** | *gladly* |
| **medicus-i** [m] | *doctor* |
| **nuper** | *recently* |
| **pro certo** | *for certain* |
| **saevio-ire** | *rage* |
| **sequere** | *follow!* |
| **somnium-i** [n] | *dream, fantasy* |
| **stultus-a-um** | *foolish* |
| **stupor-is** [m] | *senselessness* |
| **vanus-a-um** | *empty, false* |

## Comparative adjectives: '*more ...*'

An adjective qualifies a noun. Sometimes an adjective is used to make a comparison between two nouns: 'the dog is <u>bigger</u> than the cat'. This form of an adjective is called the comparative, and the English adjective either ends '-er' (big<u>ger</u>) or is preceded by 'more' – 'Latin is <u>more exciting</u> than space travel'. The Latin equivalent of the comparative form has the syllable '**ior**' in most endings. See **maior** in the Reference tables for all the forms. The Latin for 'than' is **quam**.

### Practice (III)

**(1)** Match legends to pictures and translate:

**(a)** Ancilla furiosior quam monachus est.

**(b)** Discipuli ignaviores quam ancilla sunt.

**(c)** Abbatissa sanctior quam milites est.

**(d)** Equus celerior quam mulus est.

**(2)** With **quam**, the two things compared are always in the same case. Sometimes the ablative is used for the second element, without quam: e.g. **Ancilla furiosior monacho est.** Rewrite (**b**), (**c**) and (**d**) above, using the ablative and without using **quam**.

### Superlative adjectives: 'most …'

The comparative form of Latin adjectives means 'more…' or occasionally 'quite…', 'rather…'. The comparative deals with a comparison between <u>two</u> things: 'My dog is bigger than yours'. The superlative is for three or more: 'My dog is the <u>biggest</u> in the street'. The English adjective either ends '-est', or is preceded by 'most': 'That film was the <u>most exciting</u> I have ever seen.' The Latin equivalent is easily detected, for most superlative forms have the ending **-issimus-a-um** attached to the simple adjective:

|  | Comparative (of two) | Superlative (of three or more) |
|---|---|---|
| **furios-us** *furious* | **furios-ior** *more furious* | **furios-issimus** *most/very furious* |
| **trist-is** *sad* | **trist-ior** *sadder* | **trist-issimus** *saddest* |

### Practice (IV)

**(1)** Identify the correct forms of the superlative of each of the adjectives and translate:

    **(a)** Abbas-ne (sanctus-a-um) ex omnibus monachis est?

    **(b)** Benedicti unguenta (suavis-e) sunt.

    **(c)** Filia Karoli in terra (bellus-a-um) est.

**(2)** Here are some irregular ones. See how many gaps you can fill:

| Meaning | Adjective | Comparative | Superlative | Derivative |
|---|---|---|---|---|
| *good* | ...... | **melior** | **optimus-a-um** | ...... |
| ...... | **malus** | **peior** | ...... | pessimist |
| *great, large* | ...... | **maior** | ...... | maximum |
| *small* | **parvus** | **minor** | ...... | minimum |

**Puer turpissimus!** *The boy is quite scandalous!*

◀) CD2, TR 7, 03:59

---

**Shared endings key**

**-or**   third declension nominative: pudor, amor, etc.

      passive first person ('I.....')

      **Comparative form of an adjective: sanctior**

---

'Domina Lucia? Quid tibi est in hoc loco?' rogavit abbas e solio surgens.

'Ille est peior quam diabolus!' exclamavit illa, gestu in Paulum attonitum furiosissimo.

'Si vis, o virgo, placidior sis,' inquit abbas.

'Semper mihi versus lascivos mittit. Tacere volui sed me pudor vetat.'

'Versus? Cuius versus?'

'Catulli carmina amatoria.'

'Catulli? In hac ecclesia? Quid dicis, puer?'

'Immo, numquam huic virgini versus Catulli misi,' inquit Paulus iam ipse anxius.

'Ecce liber,' inquit virgo, simul et abbati librum quem ex Augustino petiverat tradens. Tum ore Pauli manu percusso, 'Ille,' inquit Lucia, 'est scelestus et turpissimus!'

'Mea carissima, desiste,' inquit abbas, mollire eam conans.

'Ignoscas mi, Pater Abba!' et illa flere incepit.

'Crimina, o puer, audivisti. Quid dices?' Iam plurimi monachi aderant.

'Nescio, Domine, nescio.'

'Tu ergo poenas valde dabis, miserrime!' et Paulo secundum ictum dedit.

'Desiste, Pater Abba!' exclamavit Lucia.

'Rogas ut desistam? Ille tamen castigari debet!'

'Certe poenas dabit, sed Comes Karolus ipse iudicare vult. Reus ad castellum statim in vinclis ducendus.'

'Illum videre volet Comes Karolus?'

'Certe. Ille filiam suam curat.'

'Esto,' inquit abbas, 'Peregrini quidam hodie monasterium relinquent qui vos ad castellum comitentur,' sic locutus librum Augustini in ignem iniecit. Deinde cum monachi reum deduxissent, omnibus praeter se ipsum atque Ricardum digressis, 'Impera ut puerum virginemque trucident,' susurravit abbas.

QUICK VOCAB

| | |
|---|---|
| **castigari** | *to be punished* |
| **comitor-ari** | *accompany* |
| **conor-ari-atus sum** | *try, attempt* |
| **crimen-inis** [n] | *charge, crime* |
| **cuius** | *whose* |

| | |
|---|---|
| **digredior-i, digressus sum** | *depart* |
| **esto** | *so be it* |
| **gestus-us** [m] | *gesture* |
| **ictus-us** [m] | *blow* |
| **ignis-is** [m] | *fire* |
| **impero-are** | *order, instruct* |
| **inicio-ere, inieci, iniectum** | *throw in* |
| **iudico-are** | *try, adjudicate* |
| **lascivus-a-um** | *wanton, licentious* |
| **miserrimus-a-um** | *very wretched* |
| **mollio-ire** | *soften, calm* |
| **placidus-a-um** | *calm* |
| **plurimi** | *several* |
| **pudor-is** [m] | *shame* |
| **quem** | *which* |
| **reus-i** [m] | *defendant* |
| **secundus-a-um** | *second* |
| **solium-i** [n] | *seat* |
| **surgo-ere** | *rise* |
| **suus-a-um** | *his/her/their own* |
| **veto-are** | *forbid* |
| **vinclum-i** [n] | *chain* |

## Living Latin

### The Consolation of Philosophy

Boethius (c.480–524) has been described as the last of the Roman philosophers and the first of the scholastic theologians. In more senses than one his life represents something of a gateway, a passing point between the two worlds of ancient Rome and medieval Europe, between philosophical fatalism and Christian hope, between Roman pluralism and the one God. He was among the last of the Stoics and first of the martyrs.

A statesman and philosopher under Theodoric, ruler of Italy and the most powerful figure in western Europe, Boethius fell from favour, was wrongly condemned and imprisoned in Pavia, where he wrote *The Consolation of Philosophy*.

The central figure of the *Consolation* is the 'Lady Philosophy', a pagan presence in a Christian world. She visits his cell and encourages him to look beyond his immediate suffering and to recognize the manipulations of Fortuna, for whose fair-weather charms she urges caution.

The Stoics shared with Christians an inclination to confront life's hardships without complaint, but viewed the causes of their suffering differently. Fortuna was a hazard of life, who had to be tolerated; she was the most worshipped deity in the ancient world. Christians, on the other hand, were inspired by an omniscient and benign God. Boethius – a born Christian but with the education of a Stoic – wrestles with a dilemma that has been at the heart of Christian thought all through the ages, from Genesis to today: the reconciliation of human suffering and divine goodness. His *Consolation* was one of the most prized and influential books of the Middle Ages, and was translated into English by Alfred the Great, and much later again by Geoffrey Chaucer. Boethius died under torture in prison.

1 Philosophy reaches Boethius' cell to find him writing poetry under the influence of the Muses, whom she immediately dismisses:

**\*Quis has scenicas meretriculas ad hunc aegrum permisit accedere quae dolores eius non modo nullis remediis foverent, verum dulcibus insuper alerent venenis?**

*Who let these thespian tarts visit this sick fellow? They have no treatment for his condition – only sweet poisons to make it worse.*

2 She asks the nature of his complaint:

**\*Si operam medicantis exspectas, oportet vulnus detegas.**

*If you wish to have the attention of a doctor, then you must lay bare your wound.*

**3** Boethius says he has been a good philosopher-politician.

**\*Haecine praemia referimus tibi obsequentes? Atqui tu hanc sententiam Platonis ore sanxisti: beatas fore res publicas, si eas vel studiosi sapientiae regerent vel earum rectores studere sapientiae contigisset. Tu eiusdem viri ore hanc sapientibus capessendae rei publicae necessariam causam esse monuisti, ne improbis flagitiosisque civibus urbium relicta gubernacula pestem bonis ac perniciem ferrent.**

*Are these the rewards we earn for our loyalty to you? After all it was your idea you put into the mouth of Plato: that those political states which were ruled by philosophers – or by kings who had experience of studying philosophy – would be happy. Through the same man you said there was an inevitable case for a republic to be guided by philosophers, to prevent the business of government falling into the hands of unprincipled and wicked characters which would bring ruin and destruction upon good people.*

**4** Boethius cannot understand how evil can succeed.

**\*Non ita sensus nostros maeror hebetavit ut impios scelerata contra virtutem querar molitos, sed quae speraverint effecisse vehementer admiror. Nam deteriora velle nostri fuerit fortasse defectus, posse contra innocentiam, quae sceleratus quisque conceperit inspectante deo, monstri simile est.**

(i, 1–4)

*My grief has not so blunted my senses that I should complain about those no-good sorts who try to topple virtue with their wicked schemes, but that they should have succeeded in their ambitions is frankly a shock. For we all have it in us to be less than perfect, but in full view of God, the wicked overcoming innocence? – it's appalling.*

**5** Philosophy says Boethius has mistakenly courted Fortuna:

**\*Fortunae te regendum dedisti; dominae moribus oportet obtemperes. Tu vero volventis rotae impetum retinere conaris?**

(ii, 1)

*You allowed yourself to be ruled by Fortuna; so your mistress's ways must be accommodated. Are you really going to try to stop the momentum of her turning wheel?*

\*post-classical

# TESTING YOURSELF

**1** Change each underlined verb into the perfect tense, and translate:
   **(a)** Discipuli Danos in silvam <u>sequuntur</u>.
   **(b)** Lucia in ecclesiam <u>progreditur</u>.
   **(c)** In silva <u>loquimur</u>.
   **(d)** Augustinus filiam comitis <u>miratur</u>.

**2** Change each underlined verb into the present tense, and translate:
   **(a)** Lucia peregrinos in monasterium <u>secuta est</u>.
   **(b)** De gravissimis rebus <u>locutus sum</u>.
   **(c)** Peregrini in silva conspirantes <u>visi sunt</u>.
   **(d)** Augustini-ne carmen <u>miratus es</u>?

**3** Translate into Latin:
   **(a)** Are horses lazier than mules?
   **(b)** Is Augustine the best student?
   **(c)** Paul, have you ever seen a holier abbess?
   **(d)** Richard was more cruel than the Danes themselves.

**4** Complete each sentence with the correct adjective:
   **(a)** Me ........ (lucky)!
   **(b)** Coquus, vir ........ (most foolish), cibum ipse totum devoravit.
   **(c)** Domina (very lazy) ........ est illa.
   **(d)** Abbas est ........ (calmer) quam Dani.
   **(e)** Quis ........ (more faithful) quam mulus est?
   **(f)** Quis te rogavit ut illa carmina ........ (licentious) recites?

**5** Does **in camera** mean **(a)** the picture is ready; **(b)** in private; **(c)** having a sculpture made of your head?

# 18

## Versus Catulli combusti sunt!
The verses of Catullus have been incinerated!

In this unit you will learn about
- *'If' clauses*
- *Direct and reported speech*
- *And find out more about the story of Dido and Aeneas*

### 'If' clauses

The Latin for 'if' is **si** ('if...not': **nisi**). For something which could happen (or have happened) as easily as not, the verb is in the indicative:

| | |
|---|---|
| **Si e monasterio effugiemus, ad castellum ibimus.** | *If we escape from the monastery, we will go to the castle.* |
| **Si haec putas, stultus es.** | *If you think this, you are foolish.* |
| **Si haec putavisti, stultus fuisti.** | *If you thought this, you were foolish.* |

For a more remote possibility, or for musing on what-might-have-been, the subjunctive is used:

| | |
|---|---|
| **Stephanus, si viveret, nobis subveniret.** | *If Stephen were alive (now), he would be helping us.* |

| Si in Hispaniam ambules, stultus sis. | *If you were to walk to Spain, you'd be a fool.* |
| Si Benedictum vidisses, risisses. | *If you had seen Benedict, you would have laughed.* |

## Practice (I)

Match pictures to sentences, and translate:

**(a)** Si mulus opulentus esset, plaustra non traheret.
**(b)** Si magister in schola mansisset, nunc viveret.
**(c)** Si effugere conabitur, eum occide!
**(d)** Si bellus esses, te amarem.

**Vale Augustine!** *Farewell, Augustinus!*

◀) CD2, TR 8

Augustinus ad cellam in qua Paulus erat vinctus furtim adiit. 'Psst, Paule,' susurravit amicus, 'adsum ego. Si fortuna tibi favebit mox eris liber!'

'Augustine!'

'St; ne custodes excites. Tandem Lucia librum meum accepit. Me-ne quoque amat? Quid putas? Si antea cognovissem, iam rivalis tuus essem. Donum, quod Luciae dedi, erat solum exemplar Catulli.'

'Eheu, malos tibi nuntios refero,' susurravit Paulus.

'Quid dicis?'

'Liber ille est combustus.'

'Catulli liber?'

'Ita vero.'

'Combustus? A quo? Num Lucia versus Catulli delevit?'

'Abbas librum in ignem iniecit.'

'Non ita.'

'Vero.'

'Vae! Vae! Me miserrimum!' magna voce gemuit Augustinus.

'Taceas, ne custodes veniant.'

'Illi erant soli Catulli versus in bibliotheca, in monasterio, in terra! Quid agam?'

'Si potes omnes versus eius revocare, alium librum exscribas. Nunc mi ignoscas, amice, sed ego maiore in periculo sum quam tu.'

'Quid? Vero. Dico tibi, Paule: tu es fortunatus.'

'Vero? Num felix in vinclis?'

'Ecce, accipe hunc librum.'

'Alium librum?'

'De Philosophiae Consolatione.'

'O Augustine, quid agis? Boethius, cum Consolationem scripsisset, in vinclis trucidatus est. Ego non consolationem sed auxilium desidero!'

'Si librum leges,' respondit Augustinus, 'et consolationem et auxilium invenies. Lucia consilium cepit. Mox te iuvabit in teneris dominae iacere lacertis. Vale Paule,' inquit Augustinus librum, in quo Lucia epistulam scripserat, tradens.

'Vale amice.'

| a quo | by whom |
|---|---|
| antea | beforehand |
| auxilium-i [n] | help |
| cognosco-ere-ovi | discover |
| combustus-a-um | incinerated |

| | |
|---:|:---|
| **consilium-i** [n] | *plan* |
| **consolatio-nis** [f] | *consolation* |
| **deleo-ere-evi-etum** | *destroy* |
| **donum-i** [n] | *gift* |
| **excito-are** | *wake, arouse* |
| **exemplar-is** [n] | *copy* |
| **faveo-ere** [+dat.] | *favour* |
| **felix** | *fortunate, happy* |
| **iuvabit** | *it will please, delight* |
| **lacertus-i** [m] | *arm* |
| **liber-a-um** | *free* |
| **periculum-i** [n] | *danger* |
| **revoco-are** | *recall* |
| **rivalis-is** [m] | *rival, competitor* |
| **tener-a-um** | *tender* |

### Direct and reported speech

An author can use direct speech ("…") to show what his characters say. However, it is far more common in Latin for the words of a character to be expressed indirectly, with the help of a construction called the 'accusative and infinitive'. This gives us not the exact words spoken, but a report of what was said:

| | |
|:---|:---|
| **Dixit Paulum vivere.** | *S/he said Paul to be alive* |
| | *(that Paul was…).* |

The accusative (**Paulum**) is the subject, and the infinitive (**vivere**) the verb, of the original statement: "**Paulus vivit**", what she or he actually said.

The accusative and infinitive is used for reported thoughts as well as spoken words:

| | |
|:---|:---|
| **Paulus credidit Stephanum** | *Paul believed Stephen to be pious* |
| **pium sed abbatem** | *but the abbot wicked* |
| **scelestum esse.** | *(that Stephen was…).* |

---

You will meet this construction all the time in Latin texts. If, however, the reported words are a question rather than statement, then a question word (e.g. **quid, cur**) is used with a verb in the subjunctive:

| | |
|---|---|
| **Virgo rogavit cur in stagno natarem.** | *The maiden asked why I was swimming in the pond.* |
| **Nescio quid sit amor.** | *I do not know what love is.* |

If the reported words are a command or piece of advice, then **ut** is used with the subjunctive (negative **ne**):

| | |
|---|---|
| **Abbas nobis imperavit ne scholam relinqueremus.** | *The abbot ordered us not to leave the school.* |
| **Paulus virginem monuit ut in stagno se celaret.** | *Paul advised the maiden to hide in the pond.* |

### Practice (II)

**1** Write down the actual words or thoughts:
e.g. **Dixit Paulum vivere.**
'Paulus vivit.'
  **(a)** Paulus credidit Stephanum pium esse.
  **(b)** Augustinus dixit abbatem scelestum esse.
  **(c)** Stephanus discipulis imperavit ut in monasterium festinarent.
  **(d)** Virgo rogat ubi peregrini sint.

**2** Complete the sentences reporting what was said:
  **(a)** 'Scelestus puer poenas dare debet.'
  Abbas dixit ____.
  **(b)** 'Corpus magistri in sarcina est.'
  Paulus abbati dicit ____.
  **(c)** Ubi sunt versus Catulli?'
  Augustinus rogat ubi ____.

**In antro** *In the cave*

🔊 **CD2, TR 8, 02:37**

Eodem igitur die ad castellum septem Dani et Lucia et Paulus et
mulus, qui plaustrum trahebat, e monasterio profecti sunt. Mox,
cum omnes obscuram per silvam iter facerent, Paulus vinctus
plaustrum sequens 'Io mule, lente, lente!' susurrare incepit. Unus
Danorum anxius perturbatusque 'Sst, puer!' inquit, arbores
umbrasque circumspiciens. Subito exclamavit Lucia 'Ecce aliquis in
arboribus! Illum-ne vidistis?'

'Ubi?' respondit unus ex Danis.

'Credo alios pravos in animo habere illum liberare,' inquit virgo,
cui alius se videre nihil posse respondit. Tertius socios rogavit ut
festinarent dicens 'Silvam hanc non amo'.

'Vos hic remanete dum illos quaero,' inquit virgo.

'Immo vero! Absit ut nos relinquas.' Omnes Luciam obsecrabant
ut maneret; quae tamen, equo citato, mediam in silvam evanuit.
Ceteris diu moratis, stridens ex arboribus per auras sagitta plaustro
adhaesit. Dani, cum se opprimi vidissent, attoniti paulisper ex equis
descenderunt et se in dumis celaverunt. Deinde illum, qui Paulum
custodiebat, gladio stricto ut captivum trucidaret, alia sagitta per auras
stridens transfixit. Inde Paulus gladio Dani vulnerati rapto se liberavit
et 'Io! Io!' magna voce equos Danorum adeo terruit ut non solum illi
sed etiam mulus ipse quam celerrime densas in arbores effugerint.

'Vae! Plaustrum, plaustrum!' gemuit quidam et e latebra desiluit
ut mulum sisteret; frustra. Mulus iam mediam in silvam abierat
secum plaustrum atque praedam Danorum trahens. 'Et ubi est
noster captivus?' rogavit alius. Dani tamen animis collectis Paulum
nusquam invenire poterant.

Interea Lucia et Paulus mediam per silvam iter faciebant, et
tandem defessa pluviaque madida 'Ohe caballe, ohe caballe!' inquit
Lucia. 'Ecce antrum!'

'Hoc antea numquam vidi,' inquit Paulus ex equo descendens.
In antro Paulus aquam e facie virginis tergens 'Tu es mirabilis,'
susurravit, 'Bellissima Lucia, te amo.'

'Ergo da mi basia.'

'Quidquid imperas, labor est suavis.'

'Impero ut taceas.'

Nec multo post tumultu excitati e spelunca furtim exierunt ut quis adesset cognoscerent. Primo nihil viderunt; deinde conspexerunt Lucia atque Paulus plaustrum et res omnes, quas Dani ex ecclesia rapuerant, et placidum sub arboribus pascentem mulum.

| | |
|---|---|
| **absit ut** [medieval] | *far be it that* |
| **adeo** | *so much, to such an extent* |
| **antea** | *before* |
| **antrum-i** [n] | *cave* |
| **captivus-i** [m] | *prisoner* |
| **colligo-ere-egi-ectum** | *recover* |
| **cui** | *to whom* |
| **desilio-ire-ui** | *leap out* |
| **dum** | *while* |
| **effugerint** [perf. subj.] | *(they) fled* |
| **eodem** [abl.] | *same* |
| **evanesco-ere, evanui** | *disappear* |
| **gladius-i** [m] | *sword* |
| **latebra-ae** [f] | *hiding-place* |
| **madidus-a-um** | *soaked* |
| **moror-ari-atus** | *delay, wait* |
| **nusquam** | *nowhere* |
| **obsecro-are** | *implore* |
| **ohe!** | *whoa!* |
| **opprimi** [passive infin.] | *to be attacked* |
| **pascor-i** | *graze, eat* |
| **paulisper** | *a little while* |
| **pluvia-ae** [f] | *rain* |
| **praeda-ae** [f] | *loot* |
| **pravus-a-um** | *wicked* |
| **proficiscor-i, profectus** | *set out* |
| **quam celerrime** | *as quickly as possible* |
| **quas** [acc.f. pl.] | *which* |
| **quidquid** | *whatever* |

|          |                |
|---------:|----------------|
| **septem** | *seven* |
| **sisto-ere** | *stop* |
| **spelunca-ae [f]** | *cave* |
| **stringo-ere-nxi-ctum** | *draw (sword)* |
| **tergo-ere** | *wipe* |
| **terreo-ere-ui-itum** | *frighten* |
| **tertius-a-um** | *third* |
| **vulnero-are-avi-atum** | *wound* |

---

## Living Latin

🔊 **CD2, TR 8, 06:48**

### Love in the rain

1 The story of Dido and Aeneas is one of the most celebrated in
literature. Aeneas lands in north Africa, a fugitive from Troy,
and is looked after by the queen of Carthage, Dido, who falls in
love with him. During his stay, she and her fellow Carthaginians
entertain Aeneas and his Trojans to a hunt in the forest.

Tandem progreditur magna stipante caterva
Sidoniam picto chlamydem circumdata limbo;
cui pharetra ex auro, crines nodantur in aurum,
aurea purpuream subnectit fibula vestem.
Nec non et Phrygii comites et laetus Iulus
incedunt. Ipse ante alios pulcherrimus omnis
infert se socium Aeneas atque agmina iungit.

*Now at last Dido steps out, a great throng all around her. She wears
a Sidonian habit with a colourful hem, and a quiver of gold and her
hair tied back in a golden pin, and gold is the brooch which fastens her
purple cloak. There too come the Trojans, and cheerful Iulus. Aeneas
himself, the most handsome of all, rides up to her side and brings the
two parties together.*

**2** A thunderstorm brings Dido and Aeneas alone together.

Interea magno misceri murmure caelum
incipit, insequitur commixta grandine nimbus.
Et Tyrii comites passim et Troiana iuventus
Dardaniusque nepos Veneris diversa per agros
tecta metu petiere; ruunt de montibus amnes.
Speluncam Dido dux et Troianus eandem
deveniunt. Prima et Tellus et pronuba Iuno
dant signum; fulsere ignes et conscius aether
conubiis, summoque ulularunt vertice Nymphae.

(Aeneid iv, 136–42, 160–8)

*Before long there was a loud rumbling in the sky, and there followed a downpour of rain with hailstones. The young men of Troy and their Carthaginian friends and he of Dardan's line, grandson of Venus, all scattered helter-skelter across the fields in fright, looking for cover, while torrents of water sweep down from the hill-tops. Dido and Aeneas, the prince of Troy, happen upon the same cave. Mother Earth – she's first – and Juno in nuptial attendance give the signal; lightning flickers, heaven witnesses their coupling, and on peak-tops the Nymphs wail in ecstasy.*

# TESTING YOURSELF

**1** Rewrite these sentences making the underlined words plural, and translate:

    **(a)** Si <u>ille discipulus</u> Danos non timeret, stultus esset.

    **(b)** Stephanus <u>mihi</u> dixit cucullum monachum non facere.

    **(c)** Qui ab <u>amico</u> amatur est felix.

    **(d)** <u>Monachus</u>, si avaritia non movetur, laudandus est.

**2** Translate:

    **(a)** I believe that Augustine is a good friend to Paul.

    **(b)** Stephen, if you find (*use the future*) Richard, ask (*imperative*) him to come (*pres. subj.*) to the cloister.

    **(c)** The students say that Lucia is the most beautiful of all the maidens.

    **(d)** Surely we do not believe that the daughter of the count loves the humble student?

**3** What do these three words mean: **liber-bri, libero-are, liber-a-um**?

**4** Does **in flagrante delicto** mean **(a)** caught in the act; **(b)** a delicious hot meal; **(c)** profiting from a crime?

# Tables

Reference tables

# NOUNS: FIVE DECLENSIONS

| | First declension | | Second declension | | |
|---|---|---|---|---|---|
| | *wood* | *mule* | *master* | *boy* | *wine* |
| | Singular | | Singular | | |
| *Nom.* | silva | mulus | magister | puer | vinum [n] |
| *Acc.* | silvam | mulum | magistrum | puerum | vinum |
| *Gen.* | silvae | muli | magistri | pueri | vini |
| *Dat.* | silvae | mulo | magistro | puero | vino |
| *Abl.* | silva | mulo | magistro | puero | vino |
| | Plural | | Plural | | |
| *Nom.* | silvae | muli | magistri | pueri | vina |
| *Acc.* | silvas | mulos | magistros | pueros | vina |
| *Gen.* | silvarum | mulorum | magistrorum | puerorum | vinorum |
| *Dat.* | silvis | mulis | magistris | pueris | vinis |
| *Abl.* | silvis | mulis | magistris | pueris | vinis |

# NOUNS: FIVE DECLENSIONS – CONTINUED

## Third declension

### Singular

| | father | abbot | maiden | song, poem | time |
|------|--------|-------|--------|------------|------|
| Nom. | pater | abbas | virgo | carmen [n] | tempus [n] |
| Acc. | patrem | abbatem | virginem | carmen | tempus |
| Gen. | patris | abbatis | virginis | carminis | temporis |
| Dat. | patri | abbati | virgini | carmini | tempori |
| Abl. | patre | abate | virgine | carmine | tempore |

### Plural

| | father | abbot | maiden | song, poem | time |
|------|--------|-------|--------|------------|------|
| Nom. | patres | abbates | virgines | carmina | tempora |
| Acc. | patres | abbates | virgines | carmina | tempora |
| Gen. | patrum | abbatum | virginum | carminum | temporum |
| Dat. | patribus | abbatibus | virginibus | carminibus | temporibus |
| Abl. | patribus | abbatibus | virginibus | carminibus | temporibus |

|  | Fourth declension | | Fifth declension |
|  | *bow* | *hand* | *thing* |
| | Singular | Singular | Singular |
| Nom. | arcus | manus | res |
| Acc. | arcum | manum | rem |
| Gen. | arcus | manus | rei |
| Dat. | arcui | manus | rei |
| Abl. | arcu | manu | re |
| | Plural | | Plural |
| Nom. | arcus | manus | res |
| Acc. | arcus | manus | res |
| Gen. | arcuum | manuum | rerum |
| Dat. | arcibus | manibus | rebus |
| Abl. | arcibus | manibus | rebus |

## PRONOUNS

| | *I/me* | *you (s.)* | *we/us* | *you (pl.)* | *himself, herself, themselves* |
|---|---|---|---|---|---|
| *Nom.* | ego | tu | nos | vos | — |
| *Acc.* | me | te | nos | vos | se |
| *Gen.* | mei | tui | nostri/ nostrum | vestri/ vestrum | sui |
| *Dat.* | mihi | tibi | nobis | vobis | sibi |
| *Abl.* | me | te | nobis | vobis | se |

|  | Masculine | Feminine | Neuter | Masculine | Feminine | Neuter |
|---|---|---|---|---|---|---|
|  | *this, he, she, it* | | | *these, they, them* | | |
|  | Singular | | | Plural | | |
| *Nom.* | hic | haec | hoc | hi | hae | haec |
| *Acc.* | hunc | hanc | hoc | hos | has | haec |
| *Gen.* | huius | huius | huius | horum | harum | horum |
| *Dat.* | huic | huic | huic | his | his | his |
| *Abl.* | hoc | hac | hoc | his | his | his |

|  | Masculine | Feminine | Neuter | Masculine | Feminine | Neuter |
|---|---|---|---|---|---|---|
|  | *that, he, she, it* | | | *those, they, them* | | |
| *Nom.* | ille | illa | illud | illi | illae | illa |
| *Acc.* | illum | illam | illud | illos | illas | illa |
| *Gen.* | illius | illius | illius | illorum | illarum | illorum |
| *Dat.* | illi | illi | illi | illis | illis | illis |
| *Abl.* | illo | illa | illo | illis | illis | illis |

# PRONOUNS – CONTINUED

## that, he, she, it / those, they, them

|  | Singular |  |  | Plural |  |  |
|---|---|---|---|---|---|---|
| Nom. | is | ea | id | ei | eae | ea |
| Acc. | eum | eam | id | eos | eas | ea |
| Gen. | eius | eius | eius | eorum | earum | eorum |
| Dat. | ei | ei | ei | eis | eis | eis |
| Abl. | eo | ea | eo | eis | eis | eis |

## who, which

|  | Singular |  |  | Plural |  |  |
|---|---|---|---|---|---|---|
| Nom. | qui | quae | quod | qui | quae | quae |
| Acc. | quem | quam | quod | quos | quas | quae |
| Gen. | cuius | cuius | cuius | quorum | quarum | quorum |
| Dat. | cui | cui | cui | quibus | quibus | quibus |
| Abl. | quo | qua | quo | quibus | quibus | quibus |

## he himself, she herself, itself / they themselves

|  | Singular |  |  | Plural |  |  |
|---|---|---|---|---|---|---|
| Nom. | ipse | ipsa | ipsum | ipsi | ipsae | ipsa |
| Acc. | ipsum | ipsam | ipsum | ipsos | ipsas | ipsa |
| Gen. | ipsius | ipsius | ipsius | ipsorum | ipsarum | ipsorum |
| Dat. | ipsi | ipsi | ipsi | ipsi | ipsi | ipsi |
| Abl | ipso | ipsa | ipso | ipsis | ipsis | ipsis |

**ADJECTIVES**

**sanctus-a-um**: *blessed, saintly*

|  | Singular | | | Plural | | |
|  | Masc. | Fem. | Neut. | Masc. | Fem. | Neut. |
|---|---|---|---|---|---|---|
| *Nom.* | sanctus | sancta | sanctum | sancti | sanctae | sancta |
| *Acc.* | sanctum | sanctam | sanctum | sanctos | sanctas | sancta |
| *Gen.* | sancti | sanctae | sancti | sanctorum | sanctarum | sanctorum |
| *Dat.* | sancto | sanctae | sancto | sanctis | sanctis | sanctis |
| *Abl.* | sancto | sancta | sancto | sanctis | sanctis | sanctis |

## omnis: *all, every* / prudens: *wise* / maior: *greater*

### Singular

| | omnis Masc./Fem. | omnis Neut. | prudens Masc./Fem. | prudens Neut. | maior Masc./Fem. | maior Neut. |
|---|---|---|---|---|---|---|
| Nom. | omnis | omne | prudens | prudens | maior | maius |
| Acc. | omnem | omne | prudentem | prudens | maiorem | maius |
| Gen. | omnis | | prudentis | | maioris | |
| Dat. | omni | | prudenti | | maiori | |
| Abl. | omni | | prudenti | | maiore | |

### Plural

| | omnis Masc./Fem. | omnis Neut. | prudens Masc./Fem. | prudens Neut. | maior Masc./Fem. | maior Neut. |
|---|---|---|---|---|---|---|
| Nom. | omnes | omnia | prudentes | prudentia | maiores | maiora |
| Acc. | omnes | omnia | prudentes | prudentia | maiores | maiora |
| Gen. | omnium | | prudentium | | maiorum | |
| Dat. | omnibus | | prudentibus | | maioribus | |
| Abl. | omnibus | | prudentibus | | maioribus | |

# REGULAR VERBS: INDICATIVE ACTIVE

| amare<br>*to love* | monere<br>*to warn* | mittere<br>*to send* | capere<br>*to capture* | audire<br>*to hear* |
|---|---|---|---|---|
| | | Present | | |
| amo | moneo | mitto | capio | audio |
| amas | mones | mittis | capis | audis |
| amat | monet | mittit | capit | audit |
| amamus | monemus | mittimus | capimus | audimus |
| amatis | monetis | mittitis | capitis | auditis |
| amant | monent | mittunt | capiunt | audiunt |
| | | Future | | |
| amabo | monebo | mittam | capiam | audiam |
| amabis | monebis | mittes | capies | audies |
| amabit | monebit | mittet | capiet | audiet |
| amabimus | monebimus | mittemus | capiemus | audiemus |
| amabitis | monebitis | mittetis | capietis | audietis |
| amabunt | monebunt | mittent | capient | audient |

# REGULAR VERBS: INDICATIVE ACTIVE – CONTINUED

| amare<br>to love | monere<br>to warn | mittere<br>to send | capere<br>to capture | audire<br>to hear |
|---|---|---|---|---|
| | | Imperfect | | |
| amabam | monebam | mittebam | capiebam | audiebam |
| amabas | monebas | mittebas | capiebas | audiebas |
| amabat | monebat | mittebat | capiebat | audiebat |
| amabamus | monebamus | mittebamus | capiebamus | audiebamus |
| amabatis | monebatis | mittebatis | capiebatis | audiebatis |
| amabant | monebant | mittebant | capiebant | audiebant |
| | | Perfect | | |
| amavi | monui | misi | cepi | audivi |
| amavisti | monuisti | misisti | cepisti | audivisti |
| amavit | monuit | misit | cepit | audivit |
| amavimus | monuimus | misimus | cepimus | audivimus |
| amavistis | monuistis | misistis | cepistis | audivistis |
| amaverunt | monuerunt | miserunt | ceperunt | audiverunt |

## Pluperfect

| | | | | |
|---|---|---|---|---|
| amaveram | monueram | miseram | ceperam | audiveram |
| amaveras | monueras | miseras | ceperas | audiveras |
| amaverat | monuerat | miserat | ceperat | audiverat |
| amaveramus | monueramus | miseramus | ceperamus | audiveramus |
| amaveratis | monueratis | miseratis | ceperatis | audiveratis |
| amaverant | monuerant | miserant | ceperant | audiverant |

## REGULAR VERBS: INDICATIVE PASSIVE

### Present

| | | | | |
|---|---|---|---|---|
| amor | moneor | mittor | capior | audior |
| amaris | moneris | mitteris | caperis | audiris |
| amatur | monetur | mittitur | capitur | auditur |
| amamur | monemur | mittimur | capimur | audimur |
| amamini | monemini | mittimini | capimini | audimini |
| amantur | monentur | mittuntur | capiuntur | audiuntur |

### Future

| | | | | |
|---|---|---|---|---|
| amabor | monebor | mittar | capiar | audiar |
| amaberis | moneberis | mitteris | capieris | audieris |
| amabitur | monebitur | mittetur | capietur | audietur |
| amabimur | monebimur | mittemur | capiemur | audiemur |
| amabimini | monebimini | mittemini | capiemini | audiemini |
| amabuntur | monebuntur | mittentur | capientur | audientur |

# REGULAR VERBS: INDICATIVE PASSIVE – CONTINUED

## Imperfect

| | | | |
|---|---|---|---|
| amabar | monebar | mittebar | capiebar | audiebar |
| amabaris | monebaris | mittebaris | capiebaris | audiebaris |
| amabatur | monebatur | mittebatur | capiebatur | audiebatur |
| amabamur | monebamur | mittebamur | capiebamur | audiebamur |
| amabamini | monebamini | mittebamini | capiebamini | audiebamini |
| amabantur | monebantur | mittebantur | capiebantur | audiebantur |

## Perfect

| | | | |
|---|---|---|---|
| amatus sum | monitus sum | missus sum | captus sum | auditus sum |
| amatus es | monitus es | missus es | captus es | auditus es |
| amatus est | monitus est | missus est | captus est | auditus est |
| amati sumus | moniti sumus | missi sumus | capti sumus | auditi sumus |
| amati estis | moniti estis | missi estis | capti estis | auditi estis |
| amati sunt | moniti sunt | missi sunt | capti sunt | auditi sunt |

## Pluperfect

| | | | |
|---|---|---|---|
| amatus eram | monitus eram | missus eram | captus eram | auditus eram |
| amatus eras | monitus eras | missus eras | captus eras | auditus eras |
| amatus erat | monitus erat | missus erat | captus erat | auditus erat |
| amati eramus | moniti eramus | missi eramus | capti eramus | auditi eramus |
| amati eratis | moniti eratis | missi eratis | capti eratis | auditi eratis |
| amati erant | moniti erant | missi erant | capti erant | auditi erant |

# VERBS: SUBJUNCTIVE (ACTIVE)

## Present

| | | | | | |
|---|---|---|---|---|---|
| amem | moneam | mittam | capiam | audiam | sim (esse) |
| ames | moneas | mittas | capias | audias | sis |
| amet | moneat | mittat | capiat | audiat | sit |
| amemus | moneamus | mittamus | capiamus | audiamus | simus |
| ametis | moneatis | mittatis | capiatis | audiatis | sitis |
| ament | moneant | mittant | capiant | audiant | sint |

## Imperfect

| | | | | | |
|---|---|---|---|---|---|
| amarem | monerem | mitterem | caperem | audirem | essem |
| amares | moneres | mitteres | caperes | audires | esses |
| amaret | moneret | mitteret | caperet | audiret | esset |
| amaremus | moneremus | mitteremus | caperemus | audiremus | essemus |
| amaretis | moneretis | mitteretis | caperetis | audiretis | essetis |
| amarent | monerent | mitterent | caperent | audirent | essent |

## Pluperfect

| | | | | | |
|---|---|---|---|---|---|
| amavissem | monuissem | misissem | cepissem | audivissem | fuissem |
| amavisses | monuisses | misisses | cepisses | audivisses | fuisses |
| amavisset | monuisset | misisset | cepisset | audivisset | fuisset |
| amavissemus | monuissemus | misissemus | cepissemus | audivissemus | fuissemus |
| amavissetis | monuissetis | misissetis | cepissetis | audivissetis | fuissetis |
| amavissent | monuissent | misissent | cepissent | audivissent | fuissent |

# IRREGULAR VERBS

| esse | posse | velle | ferre | ire |
|------|-------|-------|-------|-----|
| to be | to be able | to wish | to carry | to go |

**Present**

| esse | posse | velle | ferre | ire |
|------|-------|-------|-------|-----|
| sum | possum | volo | fero | eo |
| es | potes | vis | fers | is |
| est | potest | vult | fert | it |
| sumus | possumus | volumus | ferimus | imus |
| estis | potestis | vultis | fertis | itis |
| sunt | possunt | volunt | ferunt | eunt |

**Future**

| esse | posse | velle | ferre | ire |
|------|-------|-------|-------|-----|
| ero | potero | volam | feram | ibo |
| eris | poteris | voles | feres | ibis |
| erit | poterit | volet | feret | ibit |
| erimus | poterimus | volemus | feremus | ibimus |
| eritis | poteritis | voletis | feretis | ibitis |
| erunt | poterunt | volent | ferent | ibunt |

## Imperfect

| | | | | |
|---|---|---|---|---|
| eram | poteram | volebam | ferebam | ibam |
| eras | poteras | volebas | ferebas | ibas |
| erat | poterat | volebat | ferebat | ibat |
| eramus | poteramus | volebamus | ferebamus | ibamus |
| eratis | poteratis | volebatis | ferebatis | ibatis |
| erant | poterant | volebant | ferebant | ibant |

## Perfect

| | | | | |
|---|---|---|---|---|
| fui | potui | volui | tuli | ii |
| fuisti | potuisti | voluisti | tulisti | isti |
| fuit | potuit | voluit | tulit | iit |
| fuimus | potuimus | voluimus | tulimus | iimus |
| fuistis | potuistis | voluistis | tulistis | istis |
| fuerunt | potuerunt | voluerunt | tulerunt | ierunt |

# IRREGULAR VERBS – CONTINUED

| esse<br>*to be* | posse<br>*to be able* | velle<br>*to wish* | ferre<br>*to carry* | ire<br>*to go* |
|---|---|---|---|---|
| | | **Pluperfect** | | |
| fueram | potueram | volueram | tuleram | ieram |
| fueras | potueras | volueras | tuleras | ieras |
| fuerat | potuerat | voluerat | tulerat | ierat |
| fueramus | potueramus | volueramus | tuleramus | ieramus |
| fueratis | potueratis | volueratis | tuleratis | ieratis |
| fuerant | potuerant | voluerant | tulerant | ierant |

# Key to the exercises

Note: in many answers either 'a' or 'the' may be correct; there are also different ways to translate Latin tenses, e.g. the present: **ambulat** = 'he walks' or 'he is walking'.

## Unit 1

### Practice (i)

1 (a) me, her, he, us (b) silvam, mulus, sarcina, Paulum 2 (a) sarcinam; the mule carries the bag. (b) Paulus; Paul carries the mule. 3 (a) amat; the mule does not like the wood. (b) ambulat; Paul is walking in the wood. (c) spectat; the mule watches the wood (d) portat; not Paul but the mule is carrying the bag.

### Practice (ii)

| | | |
|---|---|---|
| 1 mulus | mulum | mulo |
| Paulus | Paulum | Paulo |
| sarcina | sarcinam | sarcina |
| silva | silvam | silva |

2 (a) nominative, accusative; Benedict longs for some food. (b) accusative; the mule does not like the bag. (c) ablative; Benedict is not in the wood. (d) nominative; Paul is a monk. 3 (a) Paulus cum mulo in silva ambulat; Paul walks with the mule in the wood. (b) in mulo est sarcina; on the mule is a bag.

### Testing yourself

1 silvam, monachum, sarcina, cibo 2 (a) Benedictus in silva non ambulat. (b) Sarcina in mulo est. (c) Mulus non Paulum sed sarcinam portat. (d) Mulus silvam non amat. 3 (examples of

sentences) (a) Paulus mulum non portat. (b) Cibus in sarcina est. (c) Paulus silvam spectat. (d) Paulus cum monacho ambulat.

4 s/he loves/is loving; s/he walks/is walking; food; with; s/he desires/is desiring; s/he/it/there is; and; tired; in/on; slow; monk; mule, not, now; s/he carries/is carrying; bag; but; wood; s/he watches/is watching.

## Unit 2

### Practice (i)

1 equis, equi, mulo; the mule lives in the field with the horses, but the horses do not work with the mule. 2 (a) portat; the mule carries the bag. (b) habitant; the monks live in the monastery. (c) amant; the mules do not like the horses. (d) laborat; the horse does not work in the field.

### Practice (ii)

1 silvas, silvis, umbrae; the mule does not like woods because in the woods are shadows. 2 (a) sunt; the bags are on the mule. (b) amat; the mule does not like the shadows in the wood. (c) portant; the monks do not carry the bags. (d) habitant; the horses do not live in the wood.

### Testing yourself

1 (a) mulum, muli, mulis; discipulus, discipulo, discipulos; umbra, umbram, umbras; (b) equum, equo, equi, equos, equis; silvam, silva, silvae, silvis; sarcina, sarcina, sarcinae, sarcinas, sarcinis. 2 (a) Paulus saepe in agro cum monachis laborat; Paul often works in the field with the monks. (b) Sarcinae in mulo sunt; the bags are on the mule. (c) Discipuli in monasterio habitant; the students live in the monastery. (d) Mulus umbras non amat; the mule does not like shadows. 3 (a) Umbrae in silvis sunt. (b) Monachi sarcinas non portant. (c) Mulus saepe in silvis ambulat. (d) Mulus equos non amat quod cum mulis non laborat.

4 to/towards; friend; student; s/he buys/is buying; horse; s/he lives/ is living; therefore; s/he works/is working; because; often; they/ there are; shadow; wine.

5 amicable, disciple, equine, habitat, labour, umbrella, vine, etc.

## Unit 3

### Practice (i)

1 agrum, agri, agris; unguento, unguentis, presbyterum, presbyteri, presbyteros. 2 (a) presbyteri, discipulis, laborant; the priests do not work with the students. (b) vino, oleo, unguentis, ovis; the bag is heavy with wine, oil, perfumes and eggs. 3 (a) monachi, habitant; the monks live in the monastery. (b) silvas, agros; the mule does not like the woods but the fields. (c) equi, mulis, laborant; the horses work with the mules in neither the woods nor the fields. (d) vina, unguenta; Benedict desires wines and perfumes.

### Practice (ii)

1 (a) viam; the monks walk along the road. (b) agro; the mule is in the field. (c) monachis; the horse, frightened by the monks, comes out of the monastery. (d) equo, terram; the monk falls off the horse on to the ground 2 (a) in, ex, in; in the wood, the monk falls from the horse and lies on the ground. (b) e, in; the eggs fall from the bag on to the ground. (c) per, ad; the mule walks through the wood towards the monastery.

### Testing yourself

1 silva, silva, silvae, silvis; mulus, mulum, muli, mulos, mulis; puerum, pueri, pueros; vinum, vinis, libro, libri; ancillam, ancillas, ancillis. 2 (a) discipulus, ambulat; the student walks into the kitchen. (b) presbyter, desiderat; the priest often desires food and wine. (c) silvam; the mule always comes through the wood. (d) librum; the master longs for a book, the students long for wine. 3 (a) Equi neque in silva neque in agro laborant. (b) Monachus

unguenta in sarcina portat. (c) Presbyter cum discipulis per silvam ad monasterium ambulat (d) Discipuli non presbyteri sunt.

4 from/by; field; they hear/are hearing; s/he shouts/is shouting; kitchen; out of/away from; today; s/he/it lies; book; master/teacher; s/he sends/is sending; monastery; town; egg; through; boy; always; land/earth; where; s/he comes/is coming; road/way; they see/are seeing.

5 agriculture, audience, clamour, culinary, adjacent, library, magisterial, submit, monastery, oval, peruse, puerile, subterranean, advent, viaduct, video, etc.

## Unit 4

### Practice (i)

1 terram, terrae, terras, terrarum; ramum, rami, ramo, rami, ramorum, ramis; folium, folii, folio, folia, foliorum, foliis.
2 (a) monasterii; the women work in the kitchen of the monastery. (b) feminae; the eggs fall on to the woman's tunic. (c) Benedicti; the students drink Benedict's wine. 3 (a) nominative, genitive; the students desire the maids' wine. (b) nominative, genitive; Stephen is the master of the school. (c) genitive, nominative; Paul is Stephen's student. (d) genitive; the mule is fearful of woods.
4 (a) rami, ramorum; (b) agri, agrorum (c) ovi, ovorum (d) umbrae, umbrarum (e) ancillae, ancillarum

### Practice (ii)

1 (a) Sum Paulus. (b) Sumus Stephani discipuli. (c) Est episcopus. (d) Es in silva. 2 (examples) (a) Ubi est mulus? (b) Cur Paulus in bibliotheca laborat? (c) Femina-ne mortua est? (d) Quis est Stephanus? (Quis est magister?)

### Testing yourself

1 (examples) (a) Femina est in silva. (b) Equus umbras non amat. (c) Magister in bibliotheca laborat. (d) Mulus unguenta oleum

vinum ovaque portat. 2 (a) Sumus-ne in silva? (b) Equus feminae audire ventum potest. (c) Mulus sarcinas monachi portat. (d) Num discipuli vinum Benedicti desiderant? 3 ventus, ventum, venti, ventos, ventorum, ventis; tunicam, tunicae, tunicae, tunicarum, tunicis; ovum, ovum, ovi, ovo, ova, ovorum.

4 s/he is present; water; why; s/he runs/is running; god; for a long time; woman; s/he hurries/is hurrying; leaf; yes; no; surely; surely...not; s/he is able; what; who; branch; s/he asks/is asking; I am; however; s/he fears/is fearing; fearful; wind.

5 aqua, currit, femina, folium, ramus, rogat, ventus.

## Unit 5

### Practice (i)

1 umbrae, ovi, pueri, magister, episcopi, Egberta, libri. 2 (a) umbra-ae, sarcina-ae, Lucia-ae, domina-ae, filia-ae, via-ae, etc. (b) episcopus-i, Paulus-i, equus-i, etc. (c) ovum-i, castellum-i, unguentum-i, oppidum-i, monasterium-i, etc.

### Practice (ii)

1 (a) Bestiae furiosae Christianos sanctos fugant. (b) Christianus furiosus bestias sanctas fugat. (c) Christianum furiosum bestiae sanctae fugant. 2 (a) Bestiae furiosae sanctum monachum spectant; the furious beasts watch the saintly monk. (b) Libri magni in bibliotheca sunt; there are great books in the library. (c) Discipuli ignavi mulos furiosos in agris vident; the lazy students see the furious mules in the fields. (d) Monachi somnulenti in bibliotheca non laborant; the sleepy monks do not work in the library.

### Testing yourself

1 lucid; wall; mural; animal; bestial; leaf; foliage; dubious; loquacious; virile; irate 2 (a) Monachi-ne ignavi in agris laborant? Do lazy monks work in the fields? (b) Num discipuli cognati

Luciae sunt? Surely the students are not kinsmen of Lucia?
(c) Paulus magistri libros in bibliotheca spectat; Paul is looking at
the teacher's books in the library. (d) Num Benedictus ancillarum
avunculus est! Surely Benedict is not the maids' uncle!

3

| | Singular | | | | Plural | | |
|------|---------|---------|---------|------|-----------|-----------|----------|
| Case | Masc. | Fem. | Neut. | | Masc. | Fem. | Neut. |
| *Nom.* | sanctus | sancta | sanctum | *Nom.* | sancti | sanctae | sancta |
| *Acc.* | sanctum | sanctam | sanctum | *Acc.* | sanctos | sanctas | sancta |
| *Gen.* | sancti | sanctae | sancti | *Gen.* | sanctorum | sanctarum | sanctoru |
| *Abl.* | sancto | sancta | sancto | *Abl.* | sanctis | sanctis | sanctis |

4 beast; good; mistress/lady; s/he leads/is leading; bishop; tired; s/he
orders/is ordering; slow; great/large; bad; s/he remains/is remaining;
soon; much/many; wall; s/he laughs/smiles; cruel/mean; blessed;
s/he sits/is sitting; indeed.

5 vero.

6 fugat = s/he chases/is chasing; fugit = s/he flees/is fleeing.

7 nocturnal, canine, culinary, decimal, domestic, ecclesiastical,
filial, fraternal, maternal, solar, bovine.

8 (a) Num episcopus gulosus est? (b) Discipuli fessi in agro saepe
sedent. (c) Domina-ne (femina-ne) furiosa est, Stephane? (d) Muli-
ne obscura in silva laborant?

### Unit 6

Practice (i)

(a) possunt; the monks cannot see the abbess (b) debet; vult; the
abbess ought to be working in the kitchen, but wants to watch the
monks in the church.

## Practice (ii)

1 ager, agro, agro, agri, agros, agrorum, agris; coquus, coquum, coqui, coquo, coqui, coquos, coquorum, coquis; culina, culinam, culinae, culina, culinae, culinas, culinis, culinis; oleum, olei, oleo, olea, olea, oleis, oleis 2 (a) ancilla, discipulis; the maid brings food for the students. (b) episcopo, abbatissae; the student gives perfume not to the bishop but to the abbess. 3 (a) Episcopus historiam monasterii presbytero monachoque narrat; the bishop narrates the story of the monastery to the priest and the monk. (b) Discipulus ignavus Luciam spectat; the idle student watches Lucia. (c) Miser mulus sarcinam onerosam semper portat; the poor mule is always carrying a heavy bag. (d) Cur ancilla cum monacho laborare debet? why should the maid work with the monk?

## Testing yourself

1 (a) ab initio; (b) anno Domini; (c) curriculum vitae; (d) et cetera; (e) ad nauseam; (f) ad infinitum. 2 (a) Bestiae-ne Christianos in amphitheatro devorant? Are the beasts devouring the Christians in the amphitheatre? (b) Monachi boni ludos saevos non amant; Good monks do not like the cruel games. (c) Paulus-ne coquis cibum vinumque semper portat? Does Paul always bring food and wine for the cooks? (d) Cur discipulo libros magister dat? Why does the master give books to the student? 3 paganus, paganum, pagani, pagano, pagani, paganos, paganis, paganis; oppidum, oppidum, oppido, oppido, oppida, oppidorum, oppidis, oppidis; bestia, bestiam, bestiae, bestia, bestiae, bestiarum, bestiis, bestiis 4 (a) Paulus multum cibum coquo dat. (b) Discipulus ambulare non cum ancillis sed cum monachis debet. (c) Monachi ludos spectare volunt sed in monasterio laborare debent. (d) Lucia-ne in culina laborare potest?

5 amphitheatre; maidservant; year; s/he gives/is giving; s/he owes/ must/ought; master/lord; also/even; s/he does/makes/is doing/ making; welcome/pleasing; wretched; s/he narrates/is narrating; people; who/which; s/he recites/is reciting; enough; s/he writes/is writing; one; life; s/he wants/is willing.

7 (b) someone out of favour.

## Revision I

1 (a) Abbatissa bestiam sanctam timet. (b) Ova in episcopum ignavum cadunt. (c) Liber Augustini non discipulis furiosis sed ancillae gratus est. (d) Benedictus gulosus unguenta abbatissae odorae desiderat. 2 (a) Monachi muros monasterii videre possunt; the monks can see the walls of the monastery. (b) Miserae ancillae in culinis semper laborant; the wretched maids are always working in the kitchens. (c) Pueri mulis cibum dant; the boys give food to the mules. (d) Cur sunt abbatissae in bibliotheca? why are the abbesses in the library? (e) ludos monachus non spectat; the monk does not watch the games. (f) Episcopus-ne in monasterio habitat? does the bishop live in the monastery? (g) Monachi feminis aquam dant; the monks give water to the women. 4 (a) Discipuli-ne fessi sunt? (b) Malus monachus in monasterio habitare non potest. (c) Magister furiosus libros discipulis miseris dat. (d) Filia dominae laborare in culina non potest. Num ambulare cum discipulis debet? (e) Equi-ne mulum in silva audire possunt? Cibum equorum ad monasterium portat.

5

| | Singular | | | Plural | | |
|---|---|---|---|---|---|---|
| Case | Masc. | Fem. | Neut. | Masc. | Fem. | Neut. |
| Nom. | magnus | magna | magnum | Nom. magni | magnae | magna |
| Acc. | magnum | magnam | magnum | Acc. magnos | magnas | magna |
| Gen. | magni | magnae | magni | Gen. magnorum | magnarum | magnor |
| Dat. | magno | magnae | magno | Dat. magnis | magnis | magnis |
| Abl. | magno | magna | magno | Abl. magnis | magnis | magnis |

7 (a) water, beast, lady/mistress, woman, daughter, wood, land, shadow, road, life. (b) year, god, lord/master, bishop, horse, son, book, master/teacher, monk, mule, wall, people, boy, slave (classical)/servant (medieval), wind. (c) leaf, town, egg, silence, wine.

8 goddess.

9 good, tired, welcome/pleasing, idle/cowardly, angry, slow, great/large, bad, wretched, much/many, dark, cruel/mean, blessed.

10 (a) a wasp.

## Unit 7

### Practice (i)

1 (a) abbatibus; (b) arboribus; (c) virginis; (d) patri; (e) abbate; (f) arborum (g) patre; (h) virginibus; (i) patris; (j) abbatem
3 (a) Reges in monasterio non habitant; kings do not live in the monastery. (b) Monachus boves in silva potest videre; the monk can see oxen in the wood. (c) Virtutem matrum laudant; they praise the courage of the mothers. (d) Amici-ne abbatum grati sunt militibus? are the friends of the abbots pleasing to the soldiers?

### Practice (ii)

2 (a) nomina abbatum; (b) munera matris; (c) multa opera (multi labores); (d) corpora bestiarum; (e) carmina abbatis; (f) gratis carminibus.

### Testing yourself

1 corpus, corporis, corpore, corpora, corporum, corporibus, corporibus; homo, hominis, homini, homine, homines, homines, hominibus, hominibus; potio, potionem, potioni, potione, potiones, potionum, potionibus, potionibus 2 (a) Munera discipuli dominae grata sunt. (b) Num magister in superstitiones credit? (c) Augustinus carmina virginibus recitat. (d) Monachi pacem, milites bellum desiderant. 3 (a) Quis est dea amoris? Est-ne Diana? (b) Abbatissa in silvam cum Patre Benedicto ambulat. (c) Carmina-ne virginis grata abbati sunt? (d) Cur Benedictus carnem panem crustaque semper desiderat?

4 abbot, come!, love, soul, tree, war, well/fine, ox, sky/heaven, poem/song, dinner, body, favour/thanks, man/human, garden,

meanwhile, mother, soldier, gift, for, nothing, name, work, bread, father, peace, king, time, maiden.

5 (a) anima-ae, cena-ae, gratia-ae (b) hortus-i (c) bellum-i, caelum-i (d) carmen-inis, corpus-oris, munus-eris, nomen-inis, opus-eris, tempus-oris (e) abbas-atis, amor-is, arbor-is, bos-vis, homo-inis, mater-tris, miles-itis, panis-is, pater-tris, pax-cis, rex-gis, virgo-inis.

## Unit 8

### Practice (i)

2 (a) exspectant; (b) laudamus; (c) vacat; (d) laboratis; (e) recito; (f) susurrant; (g) equitat; (h) parant; (i) salutat; (j) volitant; (k) praedicat; (l) curat; (m) castigas

### Practice (ii)

2 (a) sedemus; (b) timent; (c) monet; (d) ridetis; (e) manemus; (f) respondent; (g) doces; (h) dolent

### Practice (iii)

1 (a) iacet; (b) cantat/cantabit 2 (a) monebit; (b) amabunt; (c) laudabimus; (d) sedebitis; (e) cantabis; (f) iubebimus; (g) praedicabit; (h) videbis; (i) manebimus

### Testing yourself

1 (a) Equi in caelo volitabunt; horses will fly in the sky. (b) In ecclesia sedebo; I shall sit in the church. (c) Discipulos somnulentos castigabunt; they will punish sleepy students. (d) Lucia mihi in ecclesia susurrabit; Lucia will whisper to me in the church. 2 (a) O Domina, cur doles? mistress, why do you weep? (b) Philosophiam te doceo, o Paule; I am teaching you philosophy, Paul. (c) Labores in agris non toleramus; we do not endure the toils in the fields. (d) Nonne, o virgo, Augustinum amas? surely, maiden, you love Augustinus? 3 munus, munus, muneris, muneri, munera, munerum,

muneribus, muneribus; laborem, labori, labore, labores, labores, laboribus, laboribus; allegoriam, allegoriae, allegoria, allegorias, allegoriarum, allegoriis, allegoriis; dei, deo, deo, deos, deorum, deis, deis 4 (a) Abbatissa magnam cenam parabit. (b) Discipuli-ne in bibliotheca adhuc laborant? (c) Quid, o Lucia, susurras? (d) In ecclesia dolebunt.

5 to value, to walk, friend (female), friend (male), to sing, to shout, to care for, to owe/ought, then/next, to give, to teach, therefore, to grieve, story, false, to have, to lie (position), to order, work, to work, to remain, less, to show, dead, unless/if not, once upon a time, to plead/pray, to prepare, money, full, to reply, to laugh/smile, to keep/save, if, enthusiasm/study, under, to whisper, to hush, to hold, to fear, your, to see.

6 (a) aestimo-are, ambulo-are, canto-are, clamo-are, curo-are, do-dare, laboro-are, monstro-are, oro-are, paro-are, servo-are, susurro-are (b) debeo-ere, doceo-ere, doleo-ere, habeo-ere, iaceo-ere, iubeo-ere, maneo-ere, respondeo-ere, rideo-ere, taceo-ere, teneo-ere, timeo-ere, video-ere.

7 vita = life; via = road/way.

## Unit 9

### Practice (i)

1 (a) omnibus discipulis; (b) breve carmen; (c) difficilia opera; (d) humilium monachorum; (e) turpis superstitio; (f) mollis tunica; (g) fortibus militibus; (h) dulcis amica (domina)

### Practice (ii)

1 a song not to be heard; an abbess to be revered; tasks to be done; a monk to be praised; gifts to be distributed; words to be added; an abbot to be revered; a maid to be admired 2 (a) audiendus; the abbot has to be heard. (b) amandi; the soldiers are not to be loved. (c) perficiendum; the work is to be finished.

## Testing yourself

1 (a) Magnae cenae in culina parandae sunt; large dinners have to be prepared in the kitchen. (b) Dulcis domina semper audienda est; a sweet mistress must always be heard. (c) Turpes discipuli excitandi sunt; the disgraceful students ought to be woken. (d) Humilis servus etiam laudandus est; a humble serf should also be praised. (e) Cur abbas reverendus est? why must an abbot be revered? 2 (a) Carmen fortibus militibus ancillaeque humili dedicabimus. (b) Doleo quod Lucia me amore inflammabit sed non amabit. (c) Nunc puella carmen dulce cantabit et pueri historiam monasterii narrabunt 3 dulcis: see omnis, sanctus in Tables.

4 to drink, short, to sleep, sweet, easy, fate, serious/heavy, terrible/fearful, now/already, grudge/envy, my, wonderful, eye, all/every, to write, sleep, proud/arrogant, at last, sad, disgraceful, truth, to live, voice.

5 brevis, dulcis, facilis, gravis, mirabilis, omnis, tristis, turpis.

6 a bib.

## Unit 10

### Practice (i)

1 (a) mittit; (b) capimus; (c) audiunt; (d) capio; (e) mittunt; (f) auditis; (g) mittimus; (h) audis 3 (a) lego; (b) currunt; (c) scribit; (d) incipimus; (e) sepeliunt; (f) fugiunt; (g) bibitis; (h) venit; (i) audiunt

### Practice (ii)

(a) mittet; (b) capiemus; (c) audient; (d) sedet; (e) audietis; (f) videre poterunt; (g) venire vis; (h) aderimus

### Practice (iii)

(a) fourth; (b) first; (c) mixed; (d) third; (e) first; (f) second; (g) third; (h) fourth; (i) mixed; (j) second; (k) first; (l) third

## Testing yourself

1 (a) ducet; the monk will lead two mules into the wood. (b) perficient; today the students will finish the tasks. (c) relinquemus; shall we leave the monastery? (d) potero; I shall not be able to hear Augustine. 2 (a) credo; I do not believe in superstitions. (b) inflammat; (my) girlfriend inflames me with love. (c) audis; do you hear Augustine's poems? (d) legunt; three students read from the Vulgate. 3 (a) Ancillae carmina Augustini semper audire volunt! (b) Lucia iam legere et cantare et in agris laborare potest. (c) Animas humilium servorum et regum magnorum curabimus. (d) Cur monachi viginti e silva (ef)fugiunt? 4 See Tables of nouns: opus: third declension; nox: third; fabula: first; sepulcrum: second; annus: second. 5. Mille. 6. Ten.

7 to do/drive/perform, to open, to fall, to take/capture, to believe, to say, to lead, to buy, to make/do, to weep, brother, to flee, to begin, again, tear, to read, light, pitiable, death, night, to finish, everlasting, next/nearest, region, kingdom, to rule, blood, to know, to feel, to bury, sun, fear, word, victory.

8 (a) ago-ere, cado-ere, credo-ere, dico-ere, duco-ere, emo-ere, lego-ere, rego-ere. (b) aperio-ire, scio-ire, sentio-ire, sepelio-ire. (c) capio-ere, facio-ere, fugio-ere, incipio-ere, perficio-ere.

## Unit 11

### Practice (i)

1 (a) amabat; (b) audiebant; (c) mittebamus; (d) eras; (e) poteram; (f) monebat; (g) erant 2 (a) pluebat; it was raining. (b) iacebat; the pitiable body lay on (in) the ground. (c) legebamus; we were reading the poems of Catullus. (d) sepeliebant; they were burying the monk near the church. (e) flebat; the maiden was weeping.

### Practice (ii)

1 (a) praedicantem; (b) dormientes 2 (a) ovum ... cadens; Egberta sees the egg falling from the bag. (b) monachum ... cantantem;

Lucia was listening to the monk singing in the church. (c) discipulis stertentibus; Paul was sitting with the snoring students. (d) monacho dormienti; the abbess will not give food to the sleeping monk. (e) ancillas ... susurrantes; Benedict was listening to the maids whispering in the kitchen. (f) feminae ... poterant; the women could see Theodorus running in the wood.

## Testing yourself

1 (examples) (a) Coquum cibum devorantem in culina videre poteram. (b) Monachos in silva ululantes audiebamus. (c) Abbatissa discipulum vinum bibentem spectat. (d) Nunc abbas audiendus est. 2 (a) Augustinus duodecim horas dormiebat. (b) Sapientes/prudentes magistri cum discipulis semper bibebant. (c) Mulum-ne, o Lucia, in agro bibentem audire poteras? (d) Discipuli abbatem ex ecclesia pompam ducentem spectabant. 3 laboratis, mittere, mittam, come, venire, scribere, scribunt, scribebant, capere, capiet, capiebat, fear, times, timebas, dare, dabit, dabat, aperire, aperiam, aperiebam, see, videre, videbunt, videbant, praise, laudare, laudabimus, laudabamus, facit, faciet, docere, docebitis, docebatis.

4 farmer, altar, dear, husband/wife, church, letter, to order, to free, nothing, now, wrongdoer, pilgrim, after/behind, except, first, who, clothing.

5 conjugal, ecclesiastical, primary, etc.

## Unit 12

### Practice (i)

1 (a) ambulavit; (b) viderunt; (c) venimus; (d) cepi; (e) monuisti; (f) audivit; (g) misimus; (h) monuit 2 (a) dixit; the monk (has) spoke(n) to the serf. (b) laudavimus; we (have) praised the maids in the kitchen. (c) ceperunt; have the Danes captured all the monasteries? (d) scripsisti; have you written a letter to the bishop?

## Practice (ii)

(a) nos, vestram; (b) meum, vobis; (c) mea, tibi; (d) tibi

## Testing yourself

1 ambulabit, ambulabat, veniemus, veniebamus, praise, laudare, laudatis, laudabatis, docere, docebo, docebam, say, dicere, dicebas, dixisti, write, scribere, scribunt, scribent, scripserunt, capere, capimus, capiebamus, cepimus, see, vident, videbant, viderunt, esse, est, erat 2 (a) dulcia carmina tua; Augustine, will you read to me your sweet poems? (b) discipulis; poor Stephen was always working with the students in the library. (c) peregrinum; did Lucia hear the stranger/pilgrim in the wood? (d) ancillae ... monuerunt; the maids have warned us. 3 (a) Theodorus-ne vobiscum in silva ambulavit, o discipuli? (b) Abbatem-ne praedicantem audivisti, o Augustine? (c) Abbatissam coquo susurrantem vidi. (d) Epistulam-ne Luciae scripsisti, o Paule?

4 still, however, well/fine, certainly, then/next, for, therefore, both ... and, even/also, perhaps, therefore, for, neither ... nor, indeed, since, again, often, always, thus, without, suddenly, however, at last, or.

## Revision II

1 (a) cantabit; (b) dormiunt, devoraverunt; (c) vidi; (d) scribit
2 (a) recitabit, recitabat, recitavit (b) ridebunt, ridebant, riserunt (c) audietis, audiebatis, audivistis (d) scribam, scribebam, scripsi
3 (a) docendi; (b) sepeliendum; (c) laudandi; (d) scribenda 4 (a) fugiens; (b) ducentem; (c) sedentes; (d) cantantes 5 See Table of nouns: annus-i: second declension; vita-ae: first; oppidum-i: second; potio-nis: third; clamor-is: third; tempus-oris: third. 6 (a) Virginis-ne carmen audivisti, o Pater Stephane? (b) Episcopus omnibus monachis praedicabat. (c) Mox corpus miserabile monachi sepeliemus. (d) Coquus vinum cum tristi discipulo per totam noctem bibebat.

| 7 | hospes, hospitis | host, hospital, hostel, hotel, hospice |
|---|---|---|
| | caput, capitis | capital, cattle, chattel, chapter |
| | discus-i | dish, discus, disk, disco |
| | dignitas, dignitatis | dainty, dignity |
| | phantasia-ae | fancy, fantasy |
| | praedico-are | predicate, preach |
| | blasphemo-are | blame, blaspheme |
| | securus-a-um | sure, secure |
| | computo-are | count, computer |

8 love, amoris; art, artis; kiss, basii; ox, bovis; head, capitis; song/poem, carminis; spouse, coniugis; care, curae; brother, fratris; cold/chill, frigoris; man/human, hominis; work, laboris; light, lucis; mother, matris; soldier, militis; wall, muri; name, nominis; night, noctis; bread, panis; peace, pacis; roof, tecti; time, temporis; fear, timoris; wind, venti; truth, veritatis; life, vitae; voice, vocis.

9 (c) an ancient inn or take-away

## Unit 13

**Practice (i)**

(a) passive; (b) active; (c) passive; (d) active; (e) passive; (f) passive.

**Practice (ii)**

(a) After Theodorus was (had been) seen in the church he hurried into the wood. (b) After the abbess had been seen the bishop praised her (After the bishop saw/had seen the abbess he praised her). (c) After the monks had been heard they hurried out of the monastery. (d) After the songs/poems had been heard we praised them (After we had heard the songs/poems we praised them).

## Practice (iii)

aestimavi, station, salutatum, recitare, vacatum, damnation, mansion, ridere, sessum, tentum, vision, monere, monitum, dictum, ducere, ductum, relinquere, scriptum, ascensum, actum, auditum, ventum, perfectum, receptum.

## Practice (iv)

(a) sepultus; Theodorus was/has been buried in a field. (b) visi; the pilgrims were/have been seen in the wood. (c) territus; the mule was/has been terrified by the shadows. (d) laudata; the maiden was/has been praised by her father. (e) desiderata; the perfumes were/have been desired by the abbess. (f) portatum; the wine was/has been carried by the mule.

## Practice (v)

(a) paratam; Benedictus devoured the dinner which had been prepared by the maids (after the maids had prepared the dinner, Benedictus devoured it). (b) devorata; we were unable to find the cakes, which (after/because they) had been devoured by Benedictus. (c) scriptam; the lady gave me the letter which she had written (after the lady had written the letter, she gave it to me). (d) sepulti, Augustinus was a student of the monk who had been buried.

## Practice (vi)

(a) legente; while Augustine was reading the poems of Tibullus, Paul was copying out the rule of the monastery. (b) susurrantes; Theodorus saw strangers whispering in the wood. (c) devorato; after much food had been devoured (after devouring much food) Benedict fell asleep.

## Practice (vii)

(a) abimus; (b) redibunt; (c) adibamus; (d) abierunt; (e) exit; (f) exeunt

# Testing yourself

1 (a) Theodorus, peregrinos timens, e silva exiit. (b) Coquus ancillas in horto laborantes diu spectabat. (c) Pater Stephanus dolens in ecclesia sedebat. (d) Paulo in stagno natante, peregrini silvam adibant. 2 (a) Lucia, Danis auditis, ad monasterium rediit. (b) Cena ab ancillis parata, a monachis devorata est. (c) Epistula a monacho scripta, comiti tradita est. (d) Discipulus, equo arbori ligato, in stagno natavit (natabat). 3 delinquent; ridere; ducere; scribe, scribble; recipient 4 Past participle of desidero-are, neuter plural: the desired things.

4 (a) having been said, dico, dicere (b) … sent, mitto, mittere (c) … confirmed, confirmo, confirmare (d) … freed, libero, liberare (e) … written, scribo, scribere (f) … made/done, facio, facere (g) … led, duco, ducere (h) … begun, incipio, incipere (i) … finished, perficio, perficere (j) … seen, video, videre (k) … inflamed, inflammo, inflammare (l) … opened, aperio, aperire (m) … taught, doceo, docere (n) … rejected, reicio, reicere (o) … handed over, trado, tradere.

5 (c) the buyer should be cautious.

## Unit 14

### Practice (i)

2 (a) vultu tristi; (b) casu; (c) grati versus; (d) manu; (e) spiritus sancti; (f) gemitu; (g) exercitus comitis; (h) virginis arcus sagittaeque; (i) in stagno/lacu; (j) domi.

### Practice (iii)

| Prefix | Simple verb | | Compound | |
|--------|-------------|------|----------|-----------------|
| ad | ire | *go* | adire | *go to, approach* |
| ex | ire | *go* | exire | *go out* |
| ab | esse | *be* | abesse | *be absent* |
| ad | esse | *be* | adesse | *be present* |
| ab | mittere | *send* | amittere | *send away, lose* |

| ad | capere | *take* | accipere | *receive, welcome* |
|---|---|---|---|---|
| circum | venire | *come* | circumvenire | *surround, come around* |
| ex | fugere | *flee* | effugere | *flee away* |
| cum | vocare | *call* | convocare | *call together* |
| de | mittere | *send* | demittere | *send down, lower* |
| ad | facere | *make* | afficere | *treat, afflict* |
| cum | putare | *think* | computare | *sum up, reckon* |
| e | rapere | *take, snatch* | eripere | *snatch out* |
| in | ruere | *rush* | irruere | *rush in* |
| in | venire | *come* | invenire | *come upon, find* |
| per | facere | *make* | perficere | *make thorough, finish* |

## Testing yourself

1 See Tables: (a) gradus: fourth declension; corpus: third; monachus: second (b) dies: fifth; miles: third; sagitta: first 2 (a) Virgo numquam in stagno nataverat. (b) Peregrini, cibo multo devorato, monasterium reliquerunt. (c) Neque cibum neque aquam inveneramus sed numquam spem amisimus. (d) Discipuli, in gradibus ecclesiae sedentes, versus Augustini audiebant. (e) Monachi omnes libros manu scripserant.

3 love, spirit, year, bow, silver, breeze/air, gold, chance, room/cell, day, army, face/appearance, story/report, faith, groan, step, attack, lake, place, hand, merchant, fear, flock/herd, reward, kingdom, thing, bank, arrow, companion/ally, hope, spirit/breath, star, time, noise, word, verse, traveller, chain, face/expression.

4 (a) aura/aurae; cella/cellae; fama/famae; ripa/ripae; sagitta/sagittae; stella/stellae; (b) animus/animi; annus/anni; locus/loci; socius/socii; (c) argentum/argenti; aurum/auri; praemium/praemii; regnum/regni; verbum/verbi; vinclum/vincli; (d) amor/amoris; mercator/mercatoris;

pecus/pecoris; tempus/temporis; viator/viatoris; (e) arcus/arcus; casus/casus; exercitus/exercitus; gemitus/gemitus; gradus/gradus; impetus/impetus; lacus/lacus; manus/manus; metus/metus; spiritus/spiritus; tumultus/tumultus; versus/versus; vultus/vultus (f) dies/diei; facies/faciei; fides/fidei; res/rei; spes/spei.

5 animus = spirit/courage/mind/will; anima = soul/breath.

## Unit 15

### Practice (i)

1 (a) Luciae; Lucia's face was sad. (b) ancillarum; the maids' food was devoured by Benedict. (c) Monachi; the monks live in the monastery. d) vinum; wine was desired by the abbot. 2 (a) illius; his daughter lives in the castle. (b) hac; the abbess was praying in the church with her. (c) ei; Paul always gave food to him/it. (Note: even an inanimate 'it' may be masculine or feminine, depending on the gender of the noun which the pronoun represents). (d) illi, his; those men were seen in the wood with these men.

### Practice (ii)

1 (a) haec silva; (b) haec unguenta; (c) horum discipulorum
2 (a) illa domina; (b) illa carmina; (c) illum mulum video
3 (a) ea epistula; (b) cum eis monachis; (c) id est

### Practice (iii)

(a) se; (b) ipsa

### Practice (iv)

amabitur, videbunt, audiebat, *s/he was being heard*, *s/he will capture*, capiet

## Practice (v)

1 duxerunt, *they were led*, audivit, auditus est, cepit, capta est, monuit, monitus est

2 (a) Discipuli in schola a Patre Ricardo castigantur; the students are punished in the school by Father Richard. (b) Omnes sarcinae ex oppido a mulo portabantur; all the bags were being carried out of the town by the mule. (c) Carmen Catulli ab Augustino amicis recitatum est; the poem of Catullus was read by Augustine to his friends. (d) Virgo matri dicens a Paulo visa est; the maiden, while speaking to her mother, was seen by Paul. 3 (a) Benedictus cibum devoravit; Benedict devoured the food. (b) Paulus virginem in silva vidit; Paul saw the maiden in the wood. (c) Monachi historiam monasterii narrabunt; the monks will relate the history of the monastery. (d) Dani corpus in horto sepeliverunt; the Danes buried the body in the garden.

## Testing yourself

1 (a) scriptae; many letters were written by Augustine to Lucia. (b) relictum; the monastery was left (abandoned) by the pilgrims. (c) sepultum; the body of the monk was buried. (d) positi; the books were placed in the library. 2 (a) Mox discipuli se liberabunt. (b) Monachi-ne ipsi docent? docere-ne docentur? (c) Paulus Luciaque e silva ambulantes visi sunt. (d) Paulus, peregrinis adeuntibus, in stagno se celavit. (e) Multae bestiae a virgine ipsa captae sunt. (f) Boves a Danorum exercitu custodiebantur.

3 (a) Danis liberatis (b) epistula scripta (c) fama confirmata (d) impetu facto (e) tumultu audito (f) monacho sepulto.
4 (b) in good faith.

## UNIT 16

Practice (i)

| Present indicative | | Present subjunctive | |
|---|---|---|---|
| *we live* | vivimus | vivamus | *may we live* |
| *s/he (it) stands* | stat | stet | *may s/he (it) stand* |
| *we love* | amamus | amemus | *may we love* |
| *you forgive* | ignoscis | ignoscas | *may you forgive* |
| *s/he is careful* | cavet | caveat | *may s/he be careful* |
| *we rejoice* | gaudemus | gaudeamus | *may we rejoice* |
| *we praise* | laudamus | laudemus | *may we praise* |
| *s/he drinks* | bibit | bibat | *may s/he drink* |
| *you are quiet* | taces | taceas | *may you be quiet* |

**Practice (ii)**

(a) festinate; (b) festinetis; (c) tacete; (d) taceas

**Practice (iii)**

May you be quiet! Taceas! If only you'd be quiet! Ut taceas! If only he'd believe us! Ut nobis credat! Do not be afraid of the wood. Ne silvam timeas. Careful lest they hear. Cave ne audiant. I believe so that I may understand. Credo ut intellegam.

**Practice (iv)**

(a) intellegam; I drink so that I may understand. (b) celaret; Lucia plunged herself into the pond that she might hide/in order to hide herself. (c) dicit, intellegant; Students, as Stephen says, are taught theology that they may understand the work of God. (d) audiremus; Augustine advised us to listen/that we should listen to his songs/poems.

## Testing yourself

1 (a) Mulus, sarcinis omnibus visis, gemuit. (b) Paulus, Ricardo audito, in monasterium festinavit. (c) Stephanus, corpore amici sepulto, in ecclesiam abiit. (d) Coquus, cibo devorato, in silvam ambulavit. 2 (a) Danos omnes capiant! (b) Ne abbas librum carminum tuum videat, o Augustine! (c) Vinum bibite, o amici! omnes vinum bibant! (d) Abbas eum monuit ut monasterium relinqueret 3 See Tables. (a) gaudeo-ere: second conjugation; scribo-ere: third; laudo-are: first.

4 (a) dormiamus (b) vivamus (c) oremus (d) legamus (e) laboremus (f) bibamus (g) curramus (h) scribamus (i) caveamus (j) rideamus (k) credamus.

5 (a) vivam (b) intellegas (c) amet (d) taceamus.

## Unit 17

### Practice (i)

(a) laudor; What good fortune! I am praised by my mistress.
(b) audimur; we are being heard by the maiden sitting in the rafters.
(c) castigaberis; o wicked boy, you will be punished by the master.

### Practice (ii)

(a) secuta est; Lucia followed Richard into the monastery.
(b) mirabuntur; all men will admire my songs/poems.

### Practice (iii)

1 (a) The maid is more furious than the monk. (b) The students are lazier than the maid. (c) The abbess is holier than the soldiers. (d) The horse is faster than the mule. 2 (b) Discipuli ignaviores ancilla sunt. (c) Abbatissa sanctior militibus est. (d) Equus celerior mulo est.

## Practice (iv)

1 (a) sanctissimus; is the abbot the holiest of all the monks?
(b) suavissima; Benedict's perfumes are the most delightful.
(c) bellissima; Charles' daughter is the most beautiful in the land.

2

| Meaning | Adjective | Comparative | Superlative | Derivative |
|---------|-----------|-------------|-------------|-----------|
| *good* | bonus | melior | optimus-a-um | *optimist* |
| *bad* | malus | peior | pessimus-a-um | *pessimist* |
| *great, large* | magnus | maior | maximus-a-um | *maximum* |
| *small* | parvus | minor | minimus-a-um | *minimum* |

## Testing yourself

1 (a) secuti sunt; the students followed the Danes into the
wood. (b) progressa est; Lucia went forward into the church.
(c) locuti/ae sumus; we spoke in the wood. (d) miratus est;
Augustine admired the daughter of the count. 2 (a) sequitur;
Lucia follows the pilgrims into the monastery. (b) loquor; I speak
about most serious matters. (c) videntur; the pilgrims are seen
conspiring in the wood. (d) miraris; do you admire the song/
poem of Augustine? 3 (a) Equi-ne ignaviores <u>quam muli/mulis</u>
sunt? (b) Augustinus-ne optimus discipulus est? (c) Abbatissam-ne
sanctiorem umquam vidisti, o Paule? (d) Ricardus <u>quam Dani ipsi /
Danis ipsis</u> saevior erat.

4 (a) felicem (b) stultissimus (c) ignavissima (d) placidior
(e) fidelior (f) lasciva.

5 (b) in private.

## Unit 18

### Practice (i)

(a) If the mule were wealthy, he would not be pulling carts. (b) If he tries to escape, kill him! (c) If the master had remained in the school, he would be alive now. (d) If you were beautiful, I would love you.

### Practice (ii)

1 (a) Stephanus pius est. (b) Abbas scelestus est. (c) O discipuli, in monasterium festinate! (d) Ubi sunt peregrini? 2 (a) Abbas dixit puerum scelestum poenas dare debere. (b) Paulus abbati dicit corpus magistri in sarcina esse. (c) Augustinus rogat ubi versus Catulli sint.

### Testing yourself

1 (a) Si illi discipuli Danos non timerent, stulti essent; if those students were not afraid of the Danes, they would be foolish. (b) Stephanus nobis dixit cucullum monachum non facere; Stephen told us that a hood does not make a monk. (c) Qui ab amicis amatur est felix; he who is loved by his friends is fortunate. (d) Monachi, si avaritia non moventur, laudandi sunt; if the monks are not moved by greed, they should be praised. 2 (a) Credo Augustinum Paulo amicum bonum esse. (b) Si Ricardum invenies, o Stephane, eum roga ut in claustrum veniat. (c) Discipuli Luciam <u>ex omnibus virginibus/omnium virginum</u> esse bellissimam dicunt. (d) Num comitis filiam discipulum humilem amare credimus.

3 book, to free/deliver, free.

4 (a) caught in the act.

# Latin–English vocabulary

a(b)  *by, from*
abbas-atis [m]  *abbot*
abbatissa-ae [f]  *abbess*
abeo-ire-ii-itum  *go away*
absum-esse  *be away, absent*
accipio-ere-cepi-ceptum
  *receive*
ad  *to, towards*
addo-ere-idi-itum  *add*
adduco-ere-xi-ductum  *bring*
adeo  *so much*
adeo-ire-ii-itum  *go to,*
  *approach*
adhaereo-ere-si  *stick*
adhuc  *still*
adiuvo-are  *help*
adsum-esse  *be here, present*
adultero-are  *be adulterous*
advena-ae [m]  *newcomer*
aedifico-are-avi-atum  *build*
aequor-is [n]  *water, surface*
aestas-tatis [f]  *summer*
aestimo-are-avi-atum  *value*
aestuosus-a-um  *hot*
ager, agri [m]  *field*
agnosco-ere-ovi-otum  *recognize*
ago-ere, egi, actum  *do, drive,*
  *perform*
agricola-ae [m]  *farmer*
alienus-i [m]  *stranger*
aliquando  *sometimes*
aliquis  *someone*
alius-a-um  *some, other*

allegoria-ae [f]  *allegory*
alter-a-um  *another*
ambo  *both*
ambulo-are-avi-atum  *walk*
amicus-i [m], amica-ae [f]
  *friend*
amitto-ere  *lose*
amo-are-avi-atum  *like, love*
amor-is [m]  *love*
amphitheatrum-i [n]
  *amphitheatre*
amphora-ae [f]  *jug*
an  *or*
anas-atis [f]  *duck*
ancilla-ae [f]  *maid*
angelus-i [m]  *angel*
anima-ae [f]  *soul*
animal-is [n]  *animal*
animus-i [m]  *mind*
annus-i [m]  *year*
anser-is [m]  *goose*
ante(a)  *before(hand)*
antrum-i [n]  *cave*
anxius-a-um  *concerned*
aperio-ire-ui-itum  *open*
appareo-ere-ui  *appear*
apud  *at, in the presence of*
aqua-ae [f]  *water*
ara-ae [f]  *altar*
arbor-is [f]  *tree*
arcus-us [m]  *bow*
argentum-i [n]  *silver*
ars-tis [f]  *art, skill*

**ascendo-ere-endi-ensum** climb

**aspicio-ere** look at

**at** but, yet

**atque** and

**attonitus-a-um** astonished

**audio-ire-ivi-itum** hear

**aura-ae** [f] air

**aurora-ae** [f] dawn

**aurum-i** [n] gold

**austerus-a-um** severe, gloomy

**aut** or

**autem** however

**auxilium-i** [n] help

**avunculus-i** [m] uncle

**balbus-a-um** stammering

**basio-are-avi** kiss

**basium-i** [n] kiss

**bellum-i** [n] war

**bellus-a-um** beautiful

**bene** fine

**benignus-a-um** kind

**bestia-ae** [f] beast

**bibliotheca-ae** [f] library

**bibo-ere-bibi** drink

**blasphemo-are** blaspheme, swear

**bonus-a-um** good

**bos-vis** [m/f] ox

**brevis-e** short

**caballus-i** [m] horse

**cado-ere, cecidi, casum** fall

**caedo-ere, cecidi, caesum** kill, cut

**caelum-i** [n] heaven, sky

**calamus-i** [m] reed

**calidus-a-um** warm

**campana-ae** [f] bell

**candela-ae** [f] candle

**canto-are-avi-atum** sing

**capio-ere, cepi, captum** take, capture

**captivus-i** [m] prisoner

**caput, capitis** [n] head, capital

**carmen-inis** [n] song, poem

**caro, carnis** [f] flesh, meat

**carus-a-um** dear, special

**castellum-i** [n] castle

**castigo-are-avi-atum** punish

**castitas-tatis** [f] chastity

**casus-us** [m] chance

**Catullus-i** Catullus

**caveo-ere** be careful

**celebro-are-avi-atum** celebrate

**celeriter** quickly

**cella-ae** [f] cell, room

**cellerarius-i** [m] procurator

**celo-are-avi-atum** hide

**cena-ae** [f] dinner

**centum** hundred

**certe** certainly, yes, at least

**certus-a-um** sure, unerring

**ceterus-a-um** other

**chorus-i** [m] choir

**Christianus-i** [m] Christian

**Christus-i** Christ

**cibus-i** [m] food

**circum** around

**circumspicio-ere-exi-ectum** look around

**cito-are-avi-atum** stir up, rouse

**clamo-are-avi** shout

**clamor-is** [m] shout, cry

**clarus-a-um** bright

**claudo-ere** lock

**claustrum-i** [n] cloister

**cogito-are** think

**cognatus-i** [m] *kinsman*

**cognosco-ere-ovi** *discover, learn*

**colligo-ere-egi-ectum** *recover*

**combustus-a-um** *incinerated*

**comes-itis** [m] *count*

**comitor-ari** *accompany*

**commemoror-ari** *remember, relate*

**computo-are** *sum up*

**confirmatus-a-um** *confirmed*

**conicio-ere** *throw*

**coniunx-gis** [m/f] *husband/wife*

**conor-ari, conatus** *try, attempt*

**consilium-i** [n] *plan*

**consisto-ere-stiti** *stop*

**consocius-i** [m] *associate*

**consolatio-nis** [f] *consolation*

**conspicio-ere-spexi-spectum** *catch sight of*

**conspiro-are** *conspire*

**constituo-ere-ui-utum** *decide*

**contentio-nis** [f] *dispute, competition*

**contineo-ere** *contain, hold*

**contradico-ere** *contradict*

**convalesco-ere** *recover*

**convocatio-nis** [f] *conference*

**convoco-are-avi-atum** *call together, assemble*

**coquus-i** [m] *cook*

**cor-dis** [n] *heart*

**Corinthi-orum** [m] *Corinthians*

**corpus-oris** [n] *body*

**cras** *tomorrow*

**creator-is** [m] *creator*

**credo-ere** [+dat.] *believe, trust*

**crepito-are** *rustle*

**cresco-ere** *grow*

**crimen-inis** [n] *charge, crime*

**crudelis-e** *cruel*

**crustum-i** [n] *pastry, cake*

**cucullus-i** [m] *hood*

**cui, cuius** [f] *to whom, whose*

**culina-ae** [f] *kitchen*

**cum 1** *with, in the company of*

**cum 2** *when, since*

**Cupido-inis** [m] *Cupid*

**cur** *why*

**cura-ae** [f] *anxiety, stress*

**curo-are** [+acc.] *care for*

**curro-ere** *run*

**custodio-ire** *guard, watch over*

**custos-dis** [m/f] *guardian*

**damno-are** *condemn*

**Danus-i** [m] *Dane, Viking*

**de** [+abl.] *from, about*

**dea-ae** [f] *goddess*

**debeo-ere-ui-itum** *owe, have to*

**declino-are** *swerve*

**dedico-are** *dedicate*

**defessus-a-um** *exhausted*

**deinde** *then, next*

**deleo-ere-evi-etum** *destroy*

**deliro-are-avi** *be silly, insane*

**demitto-ere** *lower*

**densus-a-um** *thick*

**depono-ere-sui-situm** *put down*

**desidero-are-avi-atum** *long for, desire*

**desilio-ire-ui** *leap out*

**desino-ere, desii** *stop, abandon*

**desisto-ere** *stop*

**despicio-ere**  *look down*
**deus-i** [m]  *god*
**devoro-are-avi-atum**  *devour, eat*
**diabolus-i** [m]  *devil*
**dialectica-ae** [f]  *discussion, argument*
**dico-ere-ixi-ictum**  *tell, say*
**dies-iei** [m]  *day*
**difficilis-e**  *difficult*
**dignitas, dignitatis** [f]  *distinction*
**digredior-i, digressus**  *depart*
**diligentia-ae** [f]  *attentiveness*
**diligo-ere**  *love*
**discedo-ere-essi**  *depart*
**discipulus-i** [m]  *student*
**discus-i** [m]  *disc*
**disputo-are**  *argue, examine*
**diu**  *for a long time*
**divido-ere**  *divide*
**divitiae-arum** [pl.]  *riches*
**divus-i** [m]  *god*
**do-are, dedi, datum**  *give*
**doceo-ere-ui, doctum**  *teach*
**doctus-i** [m]  *learned man*
**doleo-ere**  *grieve*
**dolus-i** [m]  *deceit*
**domina-ae** [f]  *lady, mistress*
**dominus-i** [m]  *lord, sir*
**domum**  *homewards*
**domus-us (-i)** [f]  *house, home*
**donum-i** [n]  *gift*
**dormio-ire-ivi-itum**  *sleep*
**duco-ere-uxi-uctum**  *lead*
**dulcis-e**  *sweet*
**dum**  *while, as long as*
**dumus-i** [m]  *thicket*

**duo**  *two*
**e(x)**  *from, out of*
**ecce**  *look*
**ecclesia-ae** [f]  *church*
**ecquis**  *is there any one who*
**effugio-ere, effugi**  *flee away*
**Egberta-ae** [f]  *Egberta*
**eho**  *eh*
**elephantus-i** [m]  *elephant*
**emo-ere**  *buy*
**enim**  *for, you see*
**eo, ire, ii, itum**  *go*
**episcopus-i** [m]  *bishop*
**epistula-ae** [f]  *letter*
**equidem**  *indeed, to be sure*
**equito-are-avi**  *ride*
**equus-i** [m]  *horse*
**ergo**  *so, therefore*
**eripio-ere-ripui-reptum**  *take out, snatch*
**erro-are-avi**  *make a mistake*
**eruditio-nis** [f]  *learning*
**et**  *and*
**et ... et**  *both ... and*
**etiam**  *also*
**evanesco-ere, evanui**  *disappear*
**exanimatus-a-um**  *breathless*
**excito-are**  *wake, arouse*
**exemplar-is** [n]  *copy*
**exemplum-i** [n]  *example, precedent*
**exerceo-ere-ui-itum**  *occupy, practise, train*
**exercitus-us** [m]  *army*
**exhalo-are-avi-atum**  *breathe out*
**exhaurio-ire-ivi, exhaustum**  *drain, empty*

**exhilaro-are-avi-atum**  *cheer*

**exiguus-a-um**  *slender, scant*

**existimo-are**  *think*

**explico-are-avi-atum**  *explain, undo*

**exscribo-ere-ipsi-iptum**  *write out*

**exsequiae-arum** [f]  *funeral*

**exspecto-are-avi-atum**  *wait for*

**fabula-ae** [f]  *story*

**facies-iei** [f]  *face, appearance*

**facilis-e**  *easy*

**facio-ere, feci, factum**  *do, make*

**faenum-i** [n]  *hay*

**falsus-a-um**  *false*

**fama-ae** [f]  *story, report*

**familia-ae** [f]  *family*

**famulus-i** [m]  *attendant*

**fas**  *not blasphemous*

**fatum-i** [n]  *fate*

**faveo-ere** [+dat.]  *favour*

**felix**  *fortunate, happy*

**femina-ae** [f]  *woman*

**fenestra-ae** [f]  *window*

**fervidus-a-um**  *burning, impetuous*

**fessus-a-um**  *tired*

**festino-are-avi**  *hurry*

**fibula-ae** [f]  *brooch*

**fictilia-ium** [n]  *earthenware*

**fidelis-e**  *loyal*

**fides-ei** [f]  *faith, loyalty*

**figura-ae** [f]  *shape*

**filia-ae** [f]  *daughter*

**flecto-ere**  *bend*

**fleo-ere**  *weep*

**folium-i** [n]  *leaf*

**fortasse**  *perhaps*

**fortis-e**  *brave*

**fortuitus-a-um**  *accidental*

**fortunatus-a-um**  *happy, lucky*

**fragrantia-ae** [f]  *odour*

**frater-tris** [m]  *brother*

**frigidus-a-um**  *cool, cold*

**frigus-oris** [n]  *chill, cold*

**frondesco-ere**  *put forth leaves*

**frustra**  *in vain, to no avail*

**frux-gis** [f]  *fruit*

**fugio-ere, fugi**  *flee*

**fugo-are**  *chase*

**fundo-ere**  *pour*

**furiosus-a-um**  *furious*

**furtim**  *secretly*

**furtum-i** [n]  *theft*

**garrulus-a-um**  *talkative*

**gaudeo-ere**  *rejoice*

**gelidus-a-um**  *cold*

**gemitus-us** [m]  *groan, sigh*

**gemo-ere-ui**  *groan*

**genae-arum** [f]  *cheeks*

**gero-ere**  *conduct, manage*

**gestus-us** [m]  *gesture*

**gladius-i** [m]  *sword*

**gracilis-e**  *elegant, slender*

**gradatim**  *gradually*

**gradus-us** [m]  *step*

**Graecus-i** [m]  *Greek*

**gratia-ae** [f]  *favour, grace*

**gratias tibi**  *thank you*

**gratus-a-um**  *pleasing*

**gravis-e**  *serious*

**gulosus-a-um**  *greedy*

**habena-ae** [f]  *rein*

**habeo-ere-ui**  *have*

**habito-are-avi**  *live*

**haud**  *not, not at all*
**herba-ae** [f]  *grass*
**heus**  *hey!*
**hic**  *here, this*
**hiems, hiemis** [f]  *winter*
**historia-ae** [f]  *story*
**hodie**  *today*
**homo-inis** [m]  *man*
**honestus-a-um**  *decent,*
  *honourable*
**honoro-are**  *honour*
**hora-ae** [f]  *hour*
**horrendus-a-um**  *fearful,*
  *to be feared*
**hortus-i** [m]  *garden*
**hospes-itis** [m]  *host, guest*
**humilis-e**  *humble, meek*
**iaceo-ere-ui**  *lie*
**iam**  *now, already*
**ibi**  *there*
**ictus-us** [m]  *blow*
**igitur**  *and so*
**ignavus-a-um**  *lazy*
**ignis-is** [m]  *fire*
**ignosco-ere** [+dat.]  *forgive*
**ille** [m] **illa** [f]  *he/she, that*
**illic**  *over there*
**immergo-ere-si-sum**  *plunge*
**immo**  *no, on the contrary*
**immotus-a-um**  *stationary*
**impero-are** [+dat.]  *order,*
  *instruct*
**impetus-us** [m]  *attack*
**improbus-a-um**  *troublesome*
**in**  *in, on*
**incensum-i** [n]  *incense*
**incipio-ere-cepi-ceptum**  *begin*
**inde**  *after that, next*

**induo-ere**  *put on*
**ineptus-a-um**  *foolish*
**infirmus-a-um**  *sick*
**inflammo-are-avi**  *inflame*
**infra**  *below*
**ingredior-i, ingressus**  *enter*
**inicio-ere, inieci, iniectum**
  *throw in*
**inimicus-i** [m]  *enemy*
**iniuria-ae** [f]  *harm*
**inno-are-avi**  *swim, float*
**inquit**  *(s/he) says, said*
**insolitus-a-um**  *unusual,*
  *unfamiliar*
**intellego-ere**  *understand*
**intendo-ere**  *aim*
**inter**  *among*
**interea**  *meanwhile*
**interficio-ere**  *kill*
**intro-are-avi**  *enter*
**invado-ere**  *go, come into*
**invenio-ire-veni-ventum**  *find*
**invidia-ae** [f]  *grudge, jealousy*
**io!**  *heyup!*
**iocosus-a-um**  *full of jokes,*
  *humorous*
**ipse**  *s/he her/himself*
**iratus-a-um**  *angry*
**irruo-ere-ui**  *rush in*
**ita**  *thus, so*
**itaque**  *and so, therefore*
**iter-ineris** [n]  *way, route*
**iterum**  *again*
**iubeo-ere, iussi**  *order, tell*
**iudicium-i** [n]  *trial, judgment*
**iudico-are**  *try, adjudicate*
**Iuppiter, Iovis** [m]  *Jupiter*
**iuvenis-is** [m]  *youth, young man*

**iuvo-are** *help, please*
**iuxta** *next to*
**Karolus-i** [m] *Charles*
**labor-is** [m] *work*
**laboro-are-avi** *work*
**lacertus-i** [m] *arm*
**lacrima-ae** [f] *tear*
**lacus-us** [m] *lake*
**laetus-a-um** *happy, cheerful*
**lapis-idis** [m] *stone*
**lascive** *wantonly*
**lascivus-a-um** *wanton, licentious*
**latebra-ae** [f] *hiding-place*
**laudo-are-avi-atum** *praise*
**lego-ere, legi, lectum** *read*
**lente** *slowly*
**lentus-a-um** *slow*
**levis-e** *light*
**libellus-i** [m] *(little) book*
**libens** *glad*
**libenter** *gladly*
**liber-bri** [m] *book*
**liber-a-um** *free*
**Liber-i** [m] *Liber, god of wine*
**libero-are-avi-atum** *free, deliver*
**licet** *it is permitted*
**ligo-are-avi-atum** *tie, bind*
**lilium-i** [n] *lily*
**linteum-i** [n] *linen cloth*
**locus-i** [m] *place*
**longe** *far, distant*
**loquax** *noisy*
**loquor, loqui, locutus** *speak*
**Lucia-ae** [f] *Lucia*
**lucidus-a-um** *clear, bright*
**ludus-i** [m] *game, show*

**lux-cis** [f] *light, life*
**madidus-a-um** *soaked*
**magister-tri** [m] *master, teacher*
**magnus-a-um** *great, large*
**maiores-um** *betters, ancestors*
**maledico-ere** *slander*
**malus-a-um** *troublesome, bad*
**maneo-ere-nsi-nsum** *remain, stay*
**manus-us** [f] *hand*
**mare-is** [n] *sea*
**Martialis-is** [m] *Martial*
**mater-tris** [f] *mother*
**medicus-i** [m] *doctor*
**medius-a-um** *mid-, middle of*
**mehercule** *well I be Hercules*
**mens, tis** [f] *mind*
**mensis-is** [m] *month*
**mercator-is** [m] *trader*
**meridies** [m] *midday*
**meto-ere** *gather, reap, mow*
**metus-us** [m] *fear*
**meus-a-um** *my*
**miles-itis** [m] *soldier*
**mille** *thousand*
**minime** *no, certainly not*
**minus** *less*
**mirabilis-e** *wonderful, marvellous*
**miror-ari-atus** *wonder at*
**miserabilis-e** *pitiable*
**miser-a-um** *wretched*
**misericordia-ae** [f] *pity*
**missa-ae** [f] *mass*
**mitto-ere-isi-issum** *send*
**modicus-a-um** *modest, small*

**modo ... modo**  *one minute ... the next*

**molestus-a-um**  *troublesome*

**mollio-ire**  *soften, calm*

**mollis-e**  *soft*

**monachus-i** [m]  *monk*

**monasterium-i** [n]  *monastery*

**moneo-ere**  *warn, advise*

**monstro-are**  *show, point out*

**moror-ari-atus**  *delay, wait*

**mors, mortis** [f]  *death*

**mortuus-a-um**  *dead*

**mox**  *soon, presently*

**multus-a-um**  *much, many*

**mulus-i** [m]  *mule*

**munimentum-i** [n]  *protection*

**munus-eris** [n]  *gift, show*

**murmuro-are**  *murmur*

**murus-i** [m]  *wall*

**musca-ae** [f]  *fly*

**mutilo-are-avi**  *mutilate*

**nam**  *for*

**narro-are-avi-atum**  *relate, tell*

**natalis dies** [m]  *birthday*

**nato-are-avi**  *swim*

**nec**  *and ... not*

**nec multo post**  *not long afterwards*

**neque ... neque**  *neither ... nor*

**nescio-ire**  *do not know*

**nil (nihil)**  *nothing*

**nisi**  *except*

**nobilis-e**  *noble*

**nomen-inis** [n]  *name*

**non**  *not*

**non ita**  *no, not so*

**non numquam**  *sometimes*

**non solum ... sed etiam**  *not only ... but also*

**nonne**  *surely*

**nos**  *we, us*

**nox, noctis** [f]  *night*

**nugae-arum** [f]  *trifles, nonsense*

**nullus-a-um**  *not any, no one*

**num**  *surely ... not*

**numquam**  *never*

**nunc**  *now*

**nuntii-orum** [m]  *news*

**nuper**  *recently*

**nusquam**  *nowhere*

**obdormio-ire**  *fall asleep*

**oboedientia-ae** [f]  *duty*

**obscurus-a-um**  *dark*

**obsecro-are**  *implore*

**observo-are-avi-atum**  *observe*

**obstupefactus-a-um**  *stupefied*

**occido-ere-cidi**  *fall*

**occido-ere-cidi-cisum**  *kill*

**oculus-i** [m]  *eye*

**odorus-a-um**  *scented, sweet-smelling*

**ohe**  *whoa*

**oleum-i** [n]  *oil*

**olim**  *once (upon a time)*

**omnis-e**  *all, every*

**onerosus-a-um**  *heavy*

**oppidum-i** [n]  *town*

**opprimo-ere**  *attack*

**opto-are**  *choose*

**opulentia-ae** [f]  *wealth*

**opulentus-a-um**  *wealthy*

**opus-eris** [n]  *task, work*

**origo-inis** [f]  *origin*

**oro-are** *pray, beg*
**os, oris** [n] *mouth*
**ostento-are** *show (off)*
**otiosus-a-um** *lazy*
**ovis-is** [f] *sheep*
**ovum-i** [n] *egg*
**paganus-i** [m] *pagan*
**pagina-ae** [f] *page*
**palma-ae** [f] *palm*
**panis-is** [m] *bread*
**par** *equal*
**pareo-ere** [+dat.] *obey*
**paro-are-avi-atum** *prepare*
**pascor-i** *graze, eat*
**pater-tris** [m] *father*
**paucus-a-um** *few*
**paulisper** *a little while*
**Paulus-i** [m] *Paul*
**pauper-is** [m] *pauper*
**pavidus-a-um** *fearful*
**pax, pacis** [f] *peace*
**peccator-is** [m] *sinner*
**pecunia-ae** [f] *money*
**pecus-oris** [n] *herd, flock*
**per** *through, across, along*
**percutio-ere** *strike, beat*
**peregrinus-i** [m] *foreigner, pilgrim*
**perficio-ere-feci-fectum** *finish*
**periculum-i** [n] *danger*
**perpetuus-a-um** *unending*
**perterritus-a-um** *thoroughly scared*
**perturbo-are-avi-atum** *confuse, disturb*
**pervigilo-are** *lie awake all night*
**peto-ere** *seek*
**phantasia-ae** [f] *fancy, notion*

**pharetra-ae** [f] *quiver*
**philosophia-ae** [f] *philosophy*
**philosophus-i** [m] *philosopher*
**pius-a-um** *pious, dutiful*
**placeo-ere** [+dat.] *please*
**placet** *it pleases*
**placidus-a-um** *calm*
**plaustrum-i** [n] *cart, wagon*
**plenus-a-um** [+abl.] *filled (with)*
**pluit** *it is raining*
**plurimi** *most people*
**pluvia-ae** [f] *rain*
**poena-ae** [f] *penalty*
**poeta-ae** [m] *poet*
**pompa-ae** [f] *procession*
**pomum-i** [n] *fruit*
**pono-ere-sui-situm** *place, put*
**populus-i** [m] *people*
**porta-ae** [f] *gate*
**porto-are-avi-atum** *carry*
**possideo-ere** *occupy*
**possum, posse** *be able*
**post** *after*
**postea** *afterwards*
**potens** *powerful, capable*
**potio-nis** [f] *drink*
**praebeo-ere** *give, offer*
**praeda-ae** [f] *loot*
**praedico-are-avi** *preach*
**praedium-i** [n] *store, barn*
**praemium-i** [n] *reward*
**praepono-ere** *prefer*
**praeter** *except, besides*
**praeterea** *besides*
**pravus-a-um** *wicked*
**presbyter-teri** [m] *priest*
**primus-a-um** *first*
**pro** *on behalf of*

**pro certo**   *for certain*
**procedo-ere**   *go forward*
**proditor-is** [m]   *traitor*
**profero-ferre**   *put forward*
**proficiscor-i, profectus**   *set out*
**progredior-i, progressus**
  *advance, go forward*
**prope**   *near*
**Propertius-i** [m]   *Propertius*
**propter**   *because of*
**protego-ere**   *cover*
**proximus-a-um**   *nearest,*
  *previous*
**prudens**   *wise*
**pudor-is** [m]   *shame*
**puer-i** [m]   *boy*
**pueritia-ae** [f]   *childhood*
**purpureus-a-um**   *purple*
**puto-are-avi**   *think*
**quaero-ere**   *seek*
**quam**   *than, which*
**quam celerrime**   *as quickly as*
  *possible*
**quando**   *when*
**quatio-ere**   *shake*
**qui, quae, quod**   *who, which*
**quia**   *that, because*
**quidam**   *somebody, a certain*
**quidem**   *in fact, indeed*
**quintus-a-um**   *fifth*
**quis, quid**   *who, what?*
**quo**   *where (to)*
**quod**   *because, which*
**quomodo**   *how*
**quoniam**   *since*
**quoque**   *also*
**raeda-ae** [f]   *carriage*
**ramus-i** [m]   *branch*

**recipio-ere-cepi-ceptum**
  *welcome, take back*
**recito-are**   *recite, read aloud*
**recupero-are**   *recover*
**redeo-ire**   *return*
**refero, referre**   *report*
**regio-nis** [f]   *region*
**regnum-i** [n]   *kingdom*
**rego-ere, rexi, rectum**   *rule*
**regula-ae** [f]   *rule*
**reicio-ere-eci-ectum**   *reject,*
  *refuse*
**relinquo-ere-liqui-lictum**   *leave,*
  *abandon*
**remaneo-ere-si-sum**   *remain*
**requiesco-ere**   *rest*
**res, rei** [f]   *thing, possession*
**resono-are**   *resound*
**respondeo-ere, respondi**   *reply*
**resurgo-ere**   *reappear*
**reus-i** [m]   *defendant*
**revelo-are-avi-atum**   *reveal*
**revenio-ire**   *return*
**revereor-eri**   *hold in awe*
**revoco-are**   *recall*
**rex, regis** [m]   *king*
**rideo-ere, risi**   *laugh, smile*
**ripa-ae** [f]   *bank*
**rivalis-is** [m]   *rival, competitor*
**rogo-are-avi**   *ask*
**Romanus-i** [m]   *a Roman*
**rosa-ae** [f]   *rose*
**rudo-ere**   *bray*
**rumor-is** [m]   *rumour, gossip*
**rursum (rursus)**   *again*
**saepe**   *often*
**saevio-ire**   *rage*
**saevitia-ae** [f]   *cruelty*

**saevus-a-um**  *cruel, mean*
**sagitta-ae** [f]  *arrow*
**sagittaria-ae** [f]  *archeress*
**saltem**  *at least*
**salutem dicere**  *greet*
**saluto-are**  *greet*
**salve**  *hello*
**salvus-a-um**  *safe*
**sanctus-a-um**  *holy, blessed*
**sane**  *certainly*
**sanguis-inis** [m]  *blood*
**sapiens**  *wise*
**sapientia-ae** [f]  *wisdom*
**sarcina-ae** [f]  *bag*
**satio-are**  *fill, satisfy*
**satis**  *enough*
**saucius-a-um**  *wounded,
  smitten*
**scelestus-a-um**  *wicked*
**schola-ae** [f]  *school*
**scientia-ae** [f]  *knowledge*
**scilicet!**  *my foot!*
**scio-ire**  *know*
**scissus-a-um**  *torn*
**scribo-ere-ipsi-iptum**  *write*
**scutum-i** [n]  *shield*
**se**  *her(him/them)self*
**secundus-a-um**  *second*
**securitas-tatis** [f]  *peace of
  mind*
**securus-a-um**  *sure, secure*
**sed**  *but*
**sedeo-ere**  *sit*
**semel**  *once*
**semper**  *always*
**sentio-ire**  *notice, feel*
**sepelio-ire-ivi, sepultum**  *bury*
**septem**  *seven*

**sepulcrum-i** [n]  *grave*
**sequor-i**  *follow*
**servo-are**  *save*
**servus-i** [m]  *serf, slave*
**severus-a-um**  *severe*
**si**  *if*
**sic**  *thus*
**sicut**  *just as, as if*
**silentium-i** [n]  *silence*
**silva-ae** [f]  *wood*
**simul**  *at the same time*
**sincerus-a-um**  *sound, genuine*
**sine**  *without*
**sino-ere**  *allow*
**sisto-ere**  *stop*
**sitiens**  *thirsty*
**socius-i** [m]  *colleague,
  associate*
**sol-is** [m]  *sun, day*
**solium-i** [n]  *seat*
**solus-a-um**  *only, alone*
**somnium-i** [n]  *dream,
  fantasy*
**somnulentus-a-um**  *sleepy*
**somnus-i** [m]  *sleep*
**sonitus-us** [m]  *sound, noise*
**specto-are-avi-atum**  *watch*
**spelunca-ae** [f]  *cave*
**spes-ei** [f]  *hope*
**spiritus-us** [m]  *spirit, breath*
**splendeo-ere**  *be bright,
  resplendent*
**st!**  *ssh!*
**stabulum-i** [n]  *stable*
**stagnum-i** [n]  *pond, lake*
**statim**  *immediately*
**stella-ae** [f]  *star*
**sterto-ere**  *snore*

**stimulus-i** [m]   *sting*
**sto-are, steti, statum**   *stand*
**strenuus-a-um**   *energetic*
**strideo-ere**   *hum, whistle*
**stringo-ere-inxi-ictum**   *draw (sword)*
**studiosus-a-um**   *hard-working*
**studium-i** [n]   *study*
**stultus-a-um**   *foolish*
**stupor-is** [m]   *senselessness*
**sub**   *beneath*
**subito**   *suddenly*
**subsellium-i** [n]   *pew, bench*
**subvenio-ire** [+dat.]   *help*
**suffragium-i** [n]   *vote*
**superbus-a-um**   *proud*
**supero-are**   *surpass*
**superstitio-nis** [f]   *superstition*
**surgo-ere**   *rise*
**suspiro-are-avi**   *sigh*
**susurro-are-avi**   *whisper*
**suus-a-um**   *his/her/their own*
**taberna-ae** [f]   *inn*
**taceo-ere-ui**   *be quiet*
**tacitus-a-um**   *silent, quiet*
**tam cito**   *so quickly*
**tamen**   *however*
**tandem**   *at last*
**tectum-i** [n]   *ceiling*
**telum-i** [n]   *missile*
**temperantia-ae** [f]   *restraint*
**tempus-oris** [n]   *time*
**tendo-ere**   *stretch*
**teneo-ere-ui, tentum**   *hold*
**tener-era-erum**   *tender*
**tentatio-nis** [f]   *temptation*
**tergo-ere**   *wipe*
**terra-ae** [f]   *ground*

**terreo-ere-ui-itum**   *frighten*
**terribilis-e**   *terrible*
**territus-a-um**   *scared*
**tertius-a-um**   *third*
**testimonium-i** [n]   *evidence, proof*
**theologia-ae** [f]   *theology*
**theologus-i** [m]   *theologian*
**thesaurus-i** [m]   *store*
**timeo-ere**   *fear*
**timidus**   *fearful*
**timor-is** [m]   *fear*
**tolero-are**   *endure, support*
**tollo-ere**   *lift, raise*
**tot**   *so many*
**totus-a-um**   *whole*
**trabs-bis** [f]   *beam*
**trado-ere-didi-ditum**   *hand over*
**traho-ere**   *pull, drag*
**trans**   *across*
**transeo-ire**   *pass, go by*
**trepidus-a-um**   *nervous*
**tres, tria**   *three*
**tristis-e**   *sad*
**trucido-are-avi-atum**   *slaughter*
**tumultus-us** [m]   *din*
**tunica-ae** [f]   *tunic, dress*
**turbulentus-a-um**   *disturbed, confused*
**turpis-e**   *disgraceful*
**turpitudo-inis** [f]   *disgraceful behaviour*
**tutus-a-um**   *safe*
**tuus-a-um**   *your*
**ubi**   *when, where*
**ulterior**   *farther*
**ululo-are**   *howl*

**umbra-ae** [f]   *shadow*
**umbrosus-a-um**   *full of shadows*
**umquam**   *ever*
**unde**   *from where*
**unguentum-i** [n]   *scent, perfume*
**unus-a-um**   *one*
**usque**   *and on to*
**ut**   *as, so that, that*
**ut, utinam**   *if only*
**utilis-e**   *useful*
**vaco-are-avi-atum**   *be idle, empty*
**vacuus-a-um**   *empty*
**vado-ere**   *go*
**vae**   *alas, woe*
**valde**   *very much*
**vale dicere**   *say goodbye*
**valeo-ere**   *be well*
**vanus-a-um**   *empty, false*
**vel**   *or*
**venatio-nis** [f]   *hunt*
**venatrix-icis** [f]   *huntress*
**venatus-us** [m]   *hunt*
**venio-ire-i, ventum**   *come*
**ventus-i** [m]   *wind*
**verbero-are**   *beat*
**verbum-i** [n]   *word*
**ver-is** [n]   *spring*
**veritas-tatis** [f]   *truth*
**vero**   *indeed*
**versus-us** [m]   *verse*
**vester-tra-trum**   *your*
**vestio-ire**   *clothe*

**vestis-is** [f]   *clothing*
**veto-are**   *forbid*
**via-ae** [f]   *road*
**viator-is** [m]   *traveller*
**vicesimus-a-um**   *twentieth*
**victima-ae** [f]   *victim*
**victoria-ae** [f]   *victory*
**video-ere, vidi, visum**   *see*
**vigilo-are**   *be awake, watchful*
**viginti**   *twenty*
**vincio-ire, vinxi, vinctum**
   *bind, tie*
**vinclum-i** [n]   *chain*
**vinco-ere, vici, victum**   *conquer,*
   *defeat*
**vinolentus-a-um**   *fond of booze*
**vinum-i** [n]   *wine*
**virga-ae** [f]   *rod*
**virgo-inis** [f]   *maiden*
**vir-i** [m]   *man*
**virtus-tutis** [f]   *courage, virtue*
**vita-ae** [f]   *life*
**vitium-i** [n]   *vice*
**vivo-ere**   *live*
**volito-are**   *fly*
**volo, velle**   *want*
**voluto-are**   *ponder, turn*
**vos**   *you*
**vox, vocis** [f]   *voice*
**Vulgatum-i** [n]   *the Vulgate*
**vulnero-are-avi-atum**   *wound*
**vultus-us** [m]   *face, expression*

# English–Latin vocabulary

abbess **abbatissa-ae** *[f]*
abbot **abbas-atis** *[m]*
about **de** *[+ abl.]*
advise **moneo-ere-ui-itum**
all, every **omnis-e**
already **iam**
always **semper**
also **etiam, quoque**
amphitheatre **amphitheatrum-i** *[n]*
and **et, atque**
angry **iratus-a-um**
animal **bestia-ae** *[f]*, **animal-is** *[n]*
approach **adeo-ire-ii-itum**
army **exercitus-us** *[m]*
arrow **sagitta-ae** *[f]*
ask **rogo-are-avi**
astonished **attonitus-a-um**
bad **malus-a-um**
bag **sarcina-ae** *[f]*
be able **possum, posse**
be away, absent **absum-esse**
be here, present **adsum-esse**
be quiet **taceo-ere**
beast **bestia-ae** *[f]*
beautiful **bellus-a-um**
because **quod**
believe, trust **credo-ere** *[+dat.]*
bishop **episcopus-i** *[m]*
book **liber-bri** *[m]*
both **ambo**
both ... and **et ... et**
bow **arcus-us** *[m]*
boy **puer-i** *[m]*

branch **ramus-i** *[m]*
brave **fortis-e**
bray **rudo-ere**
bread **panis-is** *[m]*
brother **frater-tris** *[m]*
build **aedifico-are-avi-atum**
bury **sepelio-ire-ivi, sepultum**
but **sed**
buy **emo-ere**
by **a(b)**
cake **crustum-i** *[n]*
capture **capio-ere, cepi, captum**
care for **curo-are** *[+acc.]*
carriage **raeda-ae** *[f]*
carry **porto-are-avi-atum**
cart **plaustrum-i** *[n]*
castle **castellum-i** *[n]*
chase **fugo-are**
cheerful **laetus-a-um**
church **ecclesia-ae** *[f]*
cloister **claustrum-i** *[n]*
clothing **vestis-is** *[f]*
come **venio-ire-i, ventum**
condemn **damno-are**
conspire **conspiro-are**
cook **coquus-i** *[m]*
copy **exscribo-ere-ipsi-iptum**
count **comes-itis** *[m]*
cruel **saevus-a-um, crudelis-e**
Dane **Danus-i** *[m]*
danger **periculum-i** *[n]*
dark **obscurus-a-um**
daughter **filia-ae** *[f]*

*day* **dies-iei** *[m]*
*dead* **mortuus-a-um**
*death* **mors, mortis** *[f]*
*devour* **devoro-are-avi-atum**
*difficult* **difficilis-e**
*dinner* **cena-ae** *[f]*
*disgraceful* **turpis-e**
*do* **facio-ere, feci, factum**
*dress* **tunica-ae** *[f]*
*drink* **bibo-ere-bibi**
*drink* **potio-nis** *[f]*
*duty* **oboedientia-ae** *[f]*
*easy* **facilis-e**
*eat* **devoro-are-avi-atum**
*egg* **ovum-i** *[n]*
*elegant* **gracilis-e**
*elephant* **elephantus-i** *[m]*
*endure* **tolero-are**
*enough* **satis**
*enter* **intro-are-avi**
*ever* **umquam**
*eye* **oculus-i** *[m]*
*face* **vultus-us** *[m]*
*fall* **cado-ere, cecidi, casum**
*fall asleep* **obdormio-ire**
*farmer* **agricola-ae** *[m]*
*father* **pater-tris** *[m]*
*fear* **timeo-ere**
*fear* **timor-is** *[m]*, **metus-us** *[m]*
*few* **paucus-a-um**
*field* **ager, agri** *[m]*
*filled (with)* **plenus-a-um** *[+abl.]*
*find* **invenio-ire-veni-ventum**
*finish* **perficio-ere-feci-fectum**
*fire* **ignis-is** *[m]*
*first* **primus-a-um**
*flee* **fugio-ere, fugi**
*food* **cibus-i** *[m]*

*foolish* **stultus-a-um**
*foreigner* **peregrinus-i** *[m]*
*forgive* **ignosco-ere** *[+dat.]*
*free* **liber-a-um**
*free* **libero-are-avi-atum**
*friend* **amicus-i** *[m]*, **amica-ae** *[f]*
*frighten* **terreo-ere-ui-itum**
*furious* **furiosus-a-um**
*garden* **hortus-i** *[m]*
*gift* **donum-i** *[n]*, **munus-eris** *[n]*
*give* **do-are, dedi, datum**
*go* **eo, ire, ii**
*go away* **abeo-ire-ii-itum**
*god* **deus-i** *[m]*
*goddess* **dea-ae** *[f]*
*gold* **aurum-i** *[n]*
*good* **bonus-a-um**
*great* **magnus-a-um**
*greedy* **gulosus-a-um**
*grieve* **doleo-ere**
*groan* **gemo-ere-ui**
*groan* **gemitus-us** *[m]*
*ground* **terra-ae-us** *[f]*
*hand* **manus-us** *[f]*
*hand over* **trado-ere-didi-ditum**
*happy* **laetus-a-um**
*have* **habeo-ere**
*hear* **audio-ire-ivi-itum**
*heavy* **onerosus-a-um**
*here* **hic**
*hide* **celo-are-avi-atum**
*history* **historia-ae** *[f]*
*hold* **teneo-ere-ui, tentum**
*holy* **sanctus-a-um**
*home* **domus-us (-i)** *[f]*
*hope* **spes-ei** *[f]*
*horse* **equus-i** *[m]*, **caballus-i** *[m]*
*hour* **hora-ae** *[f]*

house **domus-us (-i)** *[f]*
however **tamen, autem**
humble **humilis-e**
hundred **centum**
hurry **festino-are-avi**
if **si**
if only **ut, utinam**
immediately **statim**
inflame **inflammo-are-avi**
kill **interficio-ere**
kitchen **culina-ae** *[f]*
know **scio-ire**
lady **domina-ae** *[f]*
lake **lacus-us** *[m]*, **stagnum-i** *[n]*
large **magnus-a-um**
laugh **rideo-ere, risi**
lazy **ignavus-a-um**
lead **duco-ere-uxi-uctum**
leaf **folium-i** *[n]*
leave **relinquo-ere-liqui-lictum**
letter **epistula-ae** *[f]*
library **bibliotheca-ae** *[f]*
lie **iaceo-ere**
life **vita-ae** *[f]*
listen to **audio-ire-ivi-itum**
live **habito-are-avi, vivo-ere**
long for **desidero-are-avi-atum**
lose **amitto-ere**
love **amo-are-avi-atum**
love **amor-is** *[m]*
maid **ancilla-ae** *[f]*
maiden **virgo-inis** *[f]*
make **facio-ere, feci, factum**
man **vir-i** *[m]*, **homo-inis** *[m]*
meat **caro, carnis** *[f]*
mind **animus-i** *[m]*
monk **monachus-i** *[m]*
monastery **monasterium-i** *[n]*

money **pecunia-ae** *[f]*
mother **mater-tris** *[f]*
much, many **multus-a-um**
mule **mulus-i** *[m]*
my **meus-a-um**
name **nomen-inis** *[n]*
near **prope** *[+acc.]*
neither ... nor **neque ... neque**
never **numquam**
night **nox, noctis** *[f]*
noble **nobilis-e**
not **non**
nothing **nil (nihil)**
now **nunc, iam**
obey **pareo-ere** *[+dat.]*
often **saepe**
one **unus-a-um**
order **impero-are** *[+dat.]*
order, tell **iubeo-ere, iussi**
other **ceterus-a-um**
owe, ought **debeo-ere-ui-itum**
ox **bos-vis** *[m/f]*
peace **pax, pacis** *[f]*
people **populus-i** *[m]*
perfume **unguentum-i** *[n]*
philosophy **philosophia-ae** *[f]*
pilgrim **peregrinus-i** *[m]*
pitiable **miserabilis-e**
plan **consilium-i** *[n]*
pleasing **gratus-a-um**
poem **carmen-inis** *[n]*
poet **poeta-ae** *[m]*
pond **stagnum-i** *[n]*
powerful **potens**
praise **laudo-are-avi-atum**
pray **oro-are**
preach **praedico-are-avi**
prepare **paro-are-avi-atum**

priest **presbyter-teri** [m]

prisoner **captivus-i** [m]

procession **pompa-ae** [f]

punish **castigo-are-avi-atum**

read **lego-ere, legi, lectum**

recite, read aloud **recito-are**

rejoice **gaudeo-ere**

relate **narro-are-avi-atum**

remain **remaneo-ere-si-sum**

return **redeo-ire, revenio-ire**

ride **equito-are-avi**

road **via-ae** [f]

rule **regula-ae** [f]

run **curro-ere**

sad **tristis-e**

say **dico-ere-ixi-ictum**

scared **territus-a-um**

school **schola-ae** [f]

see **video-ere, vidi, visum**

seek **peto-ere, quaero-ere**

send **mitto-ere-isi-issum**

serf **servus-i** [m]

serious **gravis-e**

shadow **umbra-ae** [f]

shout **clamo-are-avi-atum**

shout, cry **clamor-is** [m]

sing **canto-are-avi-atum**

sit **sedeo-ere**

slaughter **trucido-are-avi-atum**

slave **servus-i** [m]

sleep **dormio-ire-ivi-itum**

slow **lentus-a-um**

slowly **lente**

snore **sterto-ere**

soldier **miles-itis** [m]

song **carmen-inis** [n]

soul **anima-ae** [f]

spirit **spiritus-us** [m]

spring **ver-is** [n]

stay **maneo-ere-nsi-nsum**

step **gradus-us** [m]

still **adhuc**

story **fabula-ae** [f]

student **discipulus-i** [m]

surely ... (not) **nonne ... (num)**

sweet **dulcis-e**

sweet-smelling **odorus-a-um**

swim **nato-are-avi**

teach **doceo-ere-ui, doctum**

teacher **magister-tri** [m]

than **quam**

there **ibi**

thick **densus-a-um**

thing **res, rei** [f]

think **puto-are-avi**

thousand **mille**

three **tres, tria**

through **per** [+acc.]

tie **ligo-are-avi-atum**

time **tempus-oris** [n]

tired **fessus-a-um**

town **oppidum-i** [n]

trust **credo-ere** [+dat.]

twenty **viginti**

two **duo**

understand **intellego-ere**

value **aestimo-are-avi-atum**

verse **versus-us** [m]

voice **vox, vocis** [f]

walk **ambulo-are-avi-atum**

wall **murus-i** [m]

want **volo, velle**

wanton **lascivus-a-um**

war **bellum-i** [n]

warn **moneo-ere-ui-itum**

watch **specto-are-avi-atum**

*watch* over **custodio-ire**
*water* **aqua-ae** [f]
*way, route* **iter-ineris** [n]
*weep* **fleo-ere**
*whisper* **susurro-are-avi**
*who? what?* **quis? quid?**
*why* **cur**
*wicked* **scelestus-a-um**
*wind* **ventus-i** [m]
*window* **fenestra-ae** [f]
*wine* **vinum-i** [n]
*wise* **prudens, sapiens**

*with* **cum** [+abl.]
*without* **sine** [+abl.]
*woman* **femina-ae** [f]
*wood* **silva-ae** [f]
*word* **verbum-i** [n]
*work* **opus-eris** [n], **labor-is** [m]
*work* **laboro-are-avi**
*wound* **vulnero-are-avi-atum**
*wretched* **miser-a-um**
*write* **scribo-ere-ipsi-iptum**
*year* **annus-i** [m]

# Index of grammar support

Numbers in references are to units; 'I' refers to the Introduction.
Please also see the Reference Tables.

ablative, *1, 3, 3, 14, 15, 17*
ablative absolute, *13*
accusative, *1, 2, 6, 10, 18*
active, *13, 15*
adjective, *5, 11, 17*

case, *1*
comparative, *17*
compound, *3, 6, 10, 14*
conditionals, *18*
conjugation, *8, 10*

dative, *6*
declension, *5*
deponent, *17*

future, *8, 10*

gender, *3*
genitive, *4, 5*
gerundive, *9*

imperative, *16*
imperfect, *11, 12*
indicative, *16*
infinitive, *6*
inflexion, *1*
interrogative, *4*
irregular verbs, *10, 13*

mood, *16*

nominative, *1, 5*
nouns *I;* neuter *3, 7*

object, *1, 13, 15*

participle, *11, 13*
passive, *9, 13, 15*
perfect, *12, 13*
pluperfect, *14*
plural, *2*
possession, *4, 6, 12*
prefix, *3, 6, 14*
preposition, *3, 14*
present, *I, 8*
principal parts, *13*
pronoun, *2, 12, 15*

questions, *4*

reflexive pronoun, *15*

singular, *2*
subject, *1, 13, 15*
subjunctive, *16*
superlative, *17*

tense, *8*

verbs *I*
vocative, *16*
voice, *16*